EVERY HOME A FORTRESS

A VOLUME IN THE SERIES
Culture in Politics in the Cold War and Beyond
EDITED BY
Edwin A. Martini and Scott Laderman

EVERY HOME A FORTRESS

Cold War Fatherhood and
the Family Fallout Shelter

THOMAS BISHOP

University of Massachusetts Press
Amherst and Boston

Copyright © 2020 by University of Massachusetts Press
All rights reserved

ISBN 978-1-62534-483-0 (paper); 482-3 (hardcover)
Designed by Jen Jackowitz
Set in AlternateGothic and Minion Pro

Cover design by Frank Gutbrod
Cover photo by Al Hixenbaugh, *E. R. Fultz talked on a citizens' short-wave band radio from his fallout shelter on S. Paul's Church Rd. The shelter was made from a 6,000-gallon gasoline tank. Fultz built shelters for others as well.* July 18, 1962. Courtesy of the *Courier-Journal*.

Library of Congress Cataloging-in-Publication Data
Names: Bishop, Thomas E. (Editor of Imagining the end), author.
Title: Every home a fortress : Cold War fatherhood and the family fallout shelter / Thomas Bishop.
Other titles: Cold War fatherhood and the family fallout shelter
Description: Amherst : University of Massachusetts Press, [2020] | Series: Culture in Politics in the Cold War and Beyond | Includes bibliographical references and index.
Identifiers: LCCN 2019042716 | ISBN 9781625344823 (hardcover) | ISBN 9781625344830 (paperback) | ISBN 9781613767283 (ebook) | ISBN 9781613767290 (ebook)
Subjects: LCSH: Civil defense—United States—History—20th century. | Cold War—Social aspects—United States. | Fallout shelters—Social aspects—United States. | Political culture—United States—History—20th century. | Fatherhood—United States—Psychological aspects. | Masculinity—United States—Psychological aspects.
Classification: LCC UA927 .B57 2020 | DDC 363.350973/09045—dc23
LC record available at https://lccn.loc.gov/2019042716

British Library Cataloguing-in-Publication Data
A catalog record for this book is available from the British Library

A portion of chapter 4 was previously published in an earlier form as "'The Struggle to Sell Survival': Family Fallout Shelters and the Limits of Consumer Citizenship," in the *Journal of Modern American History* 2, no. 2 (July 2019): 117-38.

For my parents

Dad didn't like the concept of mutual assured destruction. The idea that no matter who sent over the nukes first, the Soviets or the Americans, both sides would be obliterated. He just wanted his wife and two kids and two incompatible cats to survive.

—Lisa Kadane, "Bunker Mentality"

CONTENTS

ACKNOWLEDGMENTS xi

INTRODUCTION
Fatherhood and the Family Fallout Shelter 1

CHAPTER ONE
The Log Cabin of the Nuclear Age 20

CHAPTER TWO
The Fallout Shelter Father on the New Frontier 48

CHAPTER THREE
Fatherhood in the Target Zone 79

CHAPTER FOUR
The Struggle to Sell Survival 105

CHAPTER FIVE
Survival and Violence at the Shelter Door 131

CONCLUSION
Take to the Hills 159

NOTES 167
INDEX 215

ACKNOWLEDGMENTS

Before I seal myself away in my poorly constructed fallout shelter I wish to make a number of acknowledgments. It is almost a cliché of academic writing for authors to begin their acknowledgments by listing the personal and professional debts accumulated while turning a manuscript into a book. Yet as I come to the end of my first monograph I am all too aware of those who have made its completion possible. This book would not have been possible without the generous support of my degree supervisors, Bevan Sewell and Tony Hutchison. Their advice, pints of beer, patience, humor, and vigilant attention to my typos are greatly appreciated. They have undoubtedly shaped my work as a historian, and for that I will always be grateful.

Thanks must also go out to the amazing editorial team at the University of Massachusetts Press, from the early encouragement of the series editors Edwin A. Martini and Scott Laderman, to the constant support and advice of Matt Becker, to the feedback of my readers, to the editorial help from Rachael DeShano and the truly excellent copyediting support from Dawn Potter. For a first-time author tentatively entering the world of academic publishing, the experience of writing for this press has been a high point. These colleagues have helped me not only produce a better study but also become a better historian.

I would not have been able to start, let alone finish, this book without the financial assistance of a doctoral award from the Arts and Humanities Research Council. Likewise, I am grateful for travel awards from the British Association for American Studies; the

European Association for American Studies; the Historians of the Twentieth Century United States; the University of Nottingham's School of Cultures, Languages, and Area Studies; and the University of Nottingham's Graduate School. Each of these organizations reserves a portion of its funding for research trips, and thus they have been critical in helping me put this book together.

The best part of research is spending time in the archives. I thank Wendy Chmielewski at the Swarthmore College Peace Collection and the archivists at the John F. Kennedy Library for helping a new bewildered researcher battle his way through index cards, finding aids, and request slips. Additionally, I thank the numerous staff members who good-naturedly guided me and answered my questions during visits to the manuscript divisions of the New York Public Library, the Library of Congress, and the British Library. Thanks also go to the brilliant librarians at the Harvard University Design Library and to the staff at the National Archives in College Park, Maryland, who remained enthusiastic even after bringing me box after box of material.

During the past few years I have benefited from meeting some truly great historians. The week I spent in 2015 testing out my ideas and listening to inspiring projects at the Heidelberg Spring Academy remains my most fulfilling intellectual experience. At Nottingham, I have benefited from the support of the Department of American and Canadian Studies. The weekly works-in-progress sessions have been a joy to attend and have, on occasion, provided new insight into my research. In addition, I thank a number of academics who have been generous enough to listen to my ideas over the years: in particular, Andrew Preston and Graham Thompson, who examined my thesis and told me it might make a good book; and Michael Foley, Jon Bell, and Nick Withman, who generously listened to my ideas and offered encouragement. Thanks as well to Sarah T. Phillip and Brooke L. Blower, editors of the *Journal of Modern American History*, which published my first article about fallout shelter salesmen.

I owe a debt of gratitude to people who went out of their way to help with the final stages of writing. James Brookes, Steven Gallo, Daniel King, and Mark Eastwood all provided a welcome respite from the slogs of teaching and writing, and all have read the story of Art Carlson too many times to count. This book would not have been possible without them. I am also grateful for the steady friendship of Richard and Sara and for my brilliant colleagues and friends Alex Bryne, Lorenzo Costaguta, and Michelle Green. This book is as much yours as it is mine.

Finally, I thank my family: my father, who introduced me to the wonders of reading, history, and music; and Irena, who remains a tireless supporter even during my moments of doubt. In closing, I express my deepest gratitude to my mother—for her love and caring, no matter what. This book is dedicated to you all.

EVERY HOME A FORTRESS

INTRODUCTION

Fatherhood and the Family Fallout Shelter

> This is real mobilization. Suddenly thermonuclear war is made to seem familiar, almost cozy. All you need is a shelter, a well-stocked pantry, some Geiger counters.
>
> —I. F. Stone, "Answering *Life*'s '97 Out of 100 People Can Be Saved,'" *I. F. Stone Weekly*, September 25, 1961

In September 1961, as the United States and the Soviet Union tiptoed toward nuclear confrontation, Art Carlson, a thirty-four-year-old plumbing contractor, spent a weekend with his son Claude, age thirteen, converting the basement of their suburban New York home into a room capable of protecting the entire family from a nuclear war. After hearing President John F. Kennedy discuss on July television the "possibility of nuclear war in the missile age" and reading August newspaper headlines about the Soviet Union's resumption of atmospheric testing, Art decided that the time had come to take his family's survival into his own hands.[1] In accordance with official White House guidelines, he purchased a Kelsey Hayes "all-purpose family fallout shelter."[2] Designed for the "typical suburban home," the shelter consisted of seventy-three prefabricated steel sections packaged as a do-it-yourself construction kit and delivered straight to the door for $700.[3] Building the family shelter proved to be quite straightforward. Art and his son worked efficiently together, slotting the steel panels into place using just a screwdriver and a wrench before filling the hollow spaces between each section with sand to add "strength and shielding" to their basement bunker.⁴ With his shelter now built, Art Carlson, responsible homeowner, Cold Warrior, and father, posed confidently, spade in hand and family by his side, as Dmitri Kessel, a photojournalist for *Life*, captured the quintessential image of an all-American family prepared for life underground (see figure 1).

The story of Art Carlson, his family, and his fallout shelter appears in one of the most remarkable issues of *Life*. Published on September 15, 1961, three weeks after the construction of the Berlin Wall, the issue is a stark reminder of the way in which the specter of nuclear war haunted everyday life during the era. On the front cover, a man dressed in a glowing silver radiation suit raises a protective hand against a potential nuclear blast, alongside the headline "How You Can Survive Fallout! 97 out of 100 People Can Be Saved."⁵ Inside,

FIGURE 1. Art Carlson and Claude Carlson raise the roof on the family shelter. Do-it-yourself shelter kits were designed to ease the burden of building a family fallout shelter from scratch. Source: "A $700 Prefabricated Job to Put Up in Four Hours," *Life*, September 15, 1961, 105. Photo by Dmitri Kessel/the LIFE Picture Collection via Getty Images.

readers "can find detailed plans for building shelters and a letter from President Kennedy!"[6] That letter, written under the guidance of Kennedy's chief speechwriter, Theodore Sorensen, and his secretary of defense, Robert McNamara, offers official presidential endorsement for the construction of private family shelters: "There is much you can do to protect yourself and in doing so strengthen your nation. I urge you to seriously consider the content of this issue."[7] The advice printed in *Life* is straightforward, declaring that, with a basic understanding of home improvement, individual effort, an investment of capital, and a patriotic spirit, fathers across the nation can prepare themselves and their families for a new type of war. Ordinary citizens can become "pioneers of self-protection."[8] Suburban homes can be converted into "modern stockades."[9] Every family can become just like the Carlsons.

How did fathers across the United States react to the prospect of nuclear warfare with the Soviet Union? The answer is far more complicated than *Life*'s depiction of domestic and national unity suggests. In August 1961, a month before the Carlson family feature appeared in that magazine, *Time* published an alternative take on how men were preparing for the apocalypse. Under the provocative byline "Gun-Thy-Neighbor," *Time* printed a series of interviews with various white male suburban shelter owners, offering readers a different take on how private citizens were preparing for the end. One Chicago suburbanite, Charles Davis, said that it was his duty as a U.S. citizen and father to "defend his shelter and family at any cost" from "unprepared neighbors" who might try to rush into his private fortress during a nuclear crisis.[10] Davis had stocked his family shelter not only with canned goods but also rifles, handguns, and teargas grenades.[11] He was not the only male shelter owner to embrace this survivalist ethos. Writing for the *Saturday Review*, Norman Cousins, an antinuclear activist and a co-founder of the National Committee for a Sane Nuclear Policy (SANE), described a town hall meeting in Hartford, Connecticut, that descended into chaos when a shelter owner threatened to shoot his neighbor and her baby if they attempted to get into his private shelter in the event of an attack. Justifying his actions, the man told the assembly, "I have my family to look after."[12] Far from acting like Art Carlson, fathers across the United States appeared to be, in the words of *Newsweek*, "behaving like cavemen already."[13]

In this work of Cold War scholarship, I consider the personal histories of fathers challenged with building shelters and the families whom they hoped to protect. Focusing on the turbulent nuclear crisis years of 1957–63, the book examines the intellectual, political, and cultural trends that emerged around discussions of nuclear survival and masculinity and details the remarkable political, cultural, and social story behind one of the most iconic and recognizable figures of the nuclear age: the fallout shelter father. By putting policy documents and presidential addresses into conversation with letters, diaries, local media coverage, and anti-nuclear ephemera, I break down the traditional divide between political histories of the nuclear state and social histories of Cold War masculinity.

The politics of civil defense profoundly shaped private debates over what it meant to be a father in the nuclear age. At the apex of the Cold War's geopolitical tensions, policymakers grounded the rhetoric of home survival in a pervasive discourse of gender, self-reliance, domestic unity, and family preparation. Yet as this state-directed model of nuclear fatherhood trickled down from the federal level into the living rooms of anxious homeowners, a gap began to emerge between the political expectations of the state and the performances of ordinary fathers who were trying to convert their homes into personal fortresses. During these five nuclear crisis years, shelter fatherhood steadily embedded itself into the national imagination as do-it-yourself survival, and federal authority over the political message of home survival rapidly weakened as the idealized notion collided with the fraught dailiness of trying to build a shelter and raise a family in the shadow of nuclear war. By 1963 the backyard shelter and the father building it had become symbols of national disunity and suburban paranoia, while the discourse of patriarchal action and agency, inherent in the era's political language of civil defense, appeared to both the media and the public as militant, survivalist, and deeply troubling.

This book expands on the existing body of nuclear scholarship in two important ways. First, it offers a history of the political and cultural contexts in which a new ideal of the American father as the nuclear safeguard of the suburban family emerged during the Cold War. Second, by focusing on male reaction to the prospect of constructing family shelters, it highlights several overlapping and sometimes competing cultural narratives of Cold War masculinity that emerged around the family fallout shelter. Ideas of what it meant to be a shelter father were neither static nor stable. Indeed, the family fallout shelters inspired three interlinking narratives of Cold War fatherhood: the *domestic,* predicated on building a shelter for his family out of familial responsibility; the *militarized,* premised on turning his suburban home into a psychological and physical fortress; and the *survivalist,* which involved rejecting his community and embracing an ethos of violence, isolation, and individualism. Central to these narratives of fatherhood was the private fallout shelter itself, a malleable Cold War space that inspired a new national discourse around notions of nationhood, domestic duty and collective assumptions of what it meant to be a father in the nuclear age.

I

Since the publication of Paul Boyer's seminal book *By the Bomb's Early Light,* scholars have been pondering how the advent of nuclear science acted as an "agent of social transformation" in society.[14] Those writing on nuclear history, especially in the U.S. context, have produced impressive theoretical frameworks aimed at understanding the nuclear age, through themes such as public anxiety, government policy, civil defense, nukespeak, diplomacy, strategic culture, nuclear subjectivity, individual experience, protest and resistance, gender, decolonization, and civil rights.[15] Yet despite the innovative nature of the field, little attention has been paid to how tropes of masculinity influenced the political and public discourses of national survival and citizenship at the peak of the Cold War. By engaging with content generated by citizens—notably letters, diaries, and oral histories—this book addresses that gap in the scholarship.

In a recent survey of the historiography of Cold War nuclear policy during the Kennedy administration, Phillip Nash notes that scholars who consider the nuclear-related actions of U.S. policymakers must take into account historian Robert Dean's argument that the Cold War foreign policy establishment was defined by an "ideology of masculinity."[16] Nash correctly highlights a limitation in the current literature. While there have been exhaustive studies of the conduct of Cold War nuclear policy, few historians have looked specifically at how the public received the masculinized language in which policymakers discussed the possibility of nuclear survival. It is true that many have, with Dean, reinforced the relevance of gender discourses to 1960s U.S. foreign policy.[17] However, this field of scholarship has limitations, some of which can be attributed to the innovative nature of Dean's and others' arguments; by necessity they adopt a broad historiographical overview that often brushes over the complex internal dynamics between policymakers and the public. While gender historians have long talked about the cultural anxieties arising from the crisis of white suburban masculinity during the Cold War, few have considered how the political elite's "obsessive urge ... to reinstate the man as the head of the house" was experienced by ordinary civilians.[18]

Interestingly, studies of manhood and of Cold War political culture appear to be on a parallel trajectory, with academics on both tracks seeking to understand how the ideas of policymakers affected individuals' lived experiences. During the past thirty years histories of the nuclear age have been moving steadily away from studies dedicated to the "official development of the nuclear state, and its small group of predominantly male decision makers."[19] Of course, early historiographical focus on the decision-making class has made visible the often secretive world of nuclear policymaking. But studies into smaller academic and political circles have bloomed in both scope and complexity as scholars actively set out to incorporate more voices and more identities, on both a local and a global level. To paraphrase Sarah Alisabeth Fox, the duty of the nuclear historian is to give ordinary encounters with the nuclear world the credibility they deserve.[20] In other words, to understand the atomic age we must consider what I have come to understand as the "nuclear everyday."

With the rise of the family fallout shelter, the politics of nuclear war entered directly into the homes of millions of Americans, solidifying the geopolitical realities of life in the nuclear age. Yet studies of social practice and of personal experiences around building and maintaining a shelter site remain on the periphery of our understanding of the local Cold War. Kenneth D. Rose's cultural history of the family fallout shelter, *One Nation Underground*, remains the most detailed appraisal of the role that shelters played in the Cold War imaginary.[21] It provides the groundwork for future histories but lacks an in-depth understanding of local and public reaction that original, multi-archival research can reveal.[22] My book offers a new option for addressing these limitations. At its forefront are stories of American fathers engaging with questions of domestic security during the era. It considers a diverse body of previously unused evidence, including stories of men trying and failing to build shelters, pleas for federal loans, tales of unscrupulous businessmen selling faulty shelters to anxious homeowners, town hall gatherings descending into chaos as neighbors threaten each other over access to private shelter space, narratives of parents protesting at school events, children bringing home shelter construction booklets, survivalists running into the hills to build secret shelters, and government officials trying to manage public perceptions of nuclear war as diplomatic tensions increase. Together these accounts sketch a vast and complex picture of life in the nuclear age, one that historians have yet to fully unearth, study, and delineate. By examining such material, this book begins to shed light on that reality and provide a fuller account of life in the nuclear age.

II

When U.S. citizens talked about the prospect of nuclear survival in the 1960s they did so by referring to government guidelines on civil defense. Within the politics and policies of civil defense the narrative of the American father as his family's nuclear safeguard took shape. During the nuclear crisis years of 1957–63, the federal government used a discourse of masculine fatherhood to make its Cold War foreign policy agenda (based around the proliferation of nuclear weapons) more palatable to the American public. As Dean writes, during an era in which the "ideals of an elite masculinity" influenced the language of U.S. foreign policymakers, the idea of standing up to the Soviet nuclear threat by building a shelter became a clear test of American manhood.[23] Both politicians and popular culture placed a premium on masculine toughness at home as a way to combat Communist aggression overseas, and the notion of building a family shelter to fend off a potential nuclear disaster carried considerable cultural significance. In the pages of *Life,* the family shelter was presented as a space for men to reinforce their domestic identity and fulfill their civic duty by participating in the wider Cold War conflict. Art Carlson in his private shelter was a defender of the free world as well as an effective husband, father, and breadwinner. The ideal of the father as the nuclear safeguard of the family emerged from both a political rhetoric that defined concepts of national defense in terms of domestic readiness and from a reinforced conception of American manhood.[24]

Here, it is worth going into detail about the processes of family militarization during the Cold War as a way to show how the gender dimensions underpinning shelter fatherhood worked in practice. In *Imaginary War* Guy Oakes argues that one of the most important domestic prerequisites for waging the Cold War was the maintenance of a public "resolve for fighting a nuclear war."[25] Civil defense was central to national security planning, acting as both an antidote to "ease public nuclear anxiety" and as the State Department's primary "instrument chosen to convince the American people" that if the bomb dropped they might be able to survive the fallout. According to Oakes, civil defense was a "tool" that gave foreign-policy elites the scope and flexibility to use strategies of containment and deterrence in the conduct of diplomacy.[26] Oakes's thesis can be taken further.

Thanks to newly uncovered internal correspondence and memoranda produced by federal agencies tasked with civil defense, our understanding can be extended away from the specificities of federal policy on nuclear survival toward the values and ideals on which the program was founded. Critically, historians must recognize that at the heart of civil defense policy were two discussions. One focused on technical distinctions of blast radius, fallout, and survivability; the other on conceptions of morality, civic values, family, and fatherhood.

In *Civil Defense Begins at Home*, Laura McEnaney extends Oakes's study by detailing how civil defense policymakers framed policy and practice through a "language of domesticity."[27] She charts the evolution of the Federal Civil Defense Administration (FCDA), the agency in charge of the nation's nuclear protection, and its attempts to encourage U.S. citizens to "imagine a new type of warfare in which they were both combatants and targets."[28] According to McEnaney, a lack of congressional funding, coupled with rapid advances in nuclear technology, hindered FCDA efforts to offer a coherent framework for nationwide survival capable of protecting the entire population. Instead of investing in community shelters, which were deemed too expensive and potentially inefficient, or preparing urban centers for mass public evacuation, the agency instead focused on propaganda, setting out to "educate the public" about their duty to protect themselves as private citizens. It filled its promotional materials with messages of do-it-yourself survival. Throughout the 1950s and into the 1960s the FCDA (later renamed the Office of Civil and Defense Mobilization [OCDM]) produced booklets, pamphlets, radio shows, films, public speeches, and traveling exhibitions to create, in the words of Andrew Grossman, "one of the most extensive federal education programs in U.S. history."[29] During the 1950s alone it produced and freely distributed an estimated 476 million pieces of civil defense literature aimed at embedding a doctrine of self-help at both community and national levels. FCDA literature, as I will discuss, "trumpeted the simplicity of survival."[30] According to the agency, the solution resided not in the actions of the state but in the behavior of the family. "Families, both real and imagined," writes McEnaney, "were the twin pillars of privatized preparedness."[31] The cost of surviving a nuclear war would not be borne by the state but by the citizen, and by families across the United States.

During the 1950s, the civil defense family, with its breadwinner father, homemaker mother, and two children, was presented to the public as the archetypal unit of Cold War survival. Fathers were told to build shelters, mothers to turn kitchens into "Grandma's Pantry," and children to retreat to the family shelter at a moment's notice.[32] As Elaine Tyler May writes in her groundbreaking book *Homeward Bound*, "in virtually all civil defense publicity, safety was represented in the form of the family."[33] Here, she hits on the crux of the argument: the domestication of nuclear war was designed to both reassure and engage the public while remaining relatively cheap.[34] The image in figure 2, circulated to regional FCDA departments in 1953, highlights how civil defense planners envisioned their policy. Nuclear-age defense is shown as a series of concentric circles, running from a federal government charged to "furnish aid and supplies if needed" to

FIGURE 2. "The National Pattern of Civil Defense." Source: U.S. Civil Defense Administration, *Civil Defense and You* (Washington, DC: Government Printing Office, 1953). Courtesy of the National Archives and Records Administration, College Park, Maryland.

the family as "the base of organized survival."[35] The emphasis is first on the family and then shifts to the men—"the individual, calm, and well trained."[36] Men are depicted both as fathers and as individuals positioned at the center of national survival.

As Michael Sherry notes, the family-centric nature of civil defense always "ran the risk of looking ridiculous."[37] By offering an anxious public what was, in effect, a series of household solutions to the national questions of nuclear survival, this vision of a do-it-yourself civil defense program frequently challenged the orders and rationales usually associated with homeland security. Yet to maintain popular public support for the use of nuclear weapons, FCDA policymakers believed that they had to sell a doctrine of self-help to the public. They promoted an erroneous discourse in which citizens willingly accepted the premise that homes were targets and believed that by participating in domestic civil defense practices they would have the personal agency to ensure their own safety. In this way, Oakes argues, civil defense policymakers constructed an "imaginary war," softening the reality of nuclear conflict with a message of domestic resilience.[38] The message was clear: an organized, well-prepared family had a better chance of surviving a nuclear war.

Framing civil defense around the actions of a "strong organized family" was problematic but provided a clear metaphor of civic engagement that dominated FCDA/OCDM propaganda for more than a decade.[39] By 1961 the federal doctrine of do-it-yourself survival was not just the purview of policymakers but also a critical part of the American home-front experience. The story of Art Carlson in *Life* reflects just how widespread discussions of family shelters had become. According to I. F. Stone, a radical journalist and a long-time opponent of civil defense, the family shelter as it appeared in *Life* was "real mobilization," with policymakers using print media to "make thermonuclear war seem familiar, almost cozy."[40] In his response to Carlson's story, Stone highlighted an important aspect of the politics of nuclear survival. The domestication of civil defense was designed to normalize, as much as possible, the presence of nuclear weapons in U.S. diplomacy. Yet as we will see, one of the most fascinating aspects of civil defense history is that this normalization of warfare never truly succeeded.

The patrilineal discourse of national civil defense did have distinct advantages for policymakers. First, it allowed the FCDA to fashion a civil defense policy around one of the most powerful postwar images: the nuclear family. Second, familial survival offered a private solution to a political problem. Critically, however, the language of nuclear war and national security bureaucracy was not exclusively a conversation among agency policymakers, scientists, and intellectuals but also the source of a startling mode of social interaction.

While scholars have been adept at labeling civil defense as the protection of the middle class, they have been less keen to explain what the policy of familial survival actually looked like in practice. To truly understand the nuclear age, we need to put the personal histories of those challenged with building shelters, and the families they hoped to protect, at the forefront of our historical understanding of Cold War America. Indeed, while it is important to note that the creation of a civil defense program necessitated what McEnaney terms "an American-style militarization" in which families were in effect "deputized" as partners in the nation's defense, the public did not simply accept this duty.[41] Civil defense in the United States was as much a patchwork of personal family histories as it was a political story. How did fathers actually go about trying to build a do-it-yourself shelter? What was it like to apply for a loan to build a shelter from the Federal Housing Administration, which was notorious for its refusal to finance African American families? And how did parents talk to their children about the function of this new family room? These questions, obscured in our telling of America's domestic Cold War, are vital windows into the way in which citizens debated, accepted, and protested the roles thrust upon them by the national security state.

As this book will show, there was tension over the politics of parenthood in the nuclear age. McEnaney argues that the definition of civil defense as "home protection" gave activists working with the FCDA the platform they needed to "carve out a space of political action" for women and led to the creation of a number of networks among women within federal bureaucracy who collaborated with government planners to "spread the gospel of home protection, anticommunism and 'women's power.'"[42] Yet while McEnaney's study of women and civil defense is invaluable to our understanding of the domestic Cold War, it does not address the vibrant and often varied public reactions that surrounded discussions of fatherhood in civil defense. In part this is due to the chronological scope of her work, which ends in 1958, prior to the bomb-shelter craze of 1961–63, when newspapers abounded with stories of violent shelter owners, often framed as survivalist fathers, and tales of unscrupulous shelter businesses selling faulty products to neurotic men. Yet questions about fatherhood and the family shelter are important, for they lead us to consider men's often faltering civic engagement with the process of home survival. How did fathers respond to the prospect of building shelters in their homes? How prevalent was the desire to build shelters, and what obstacles did men face? Did the masculinized, individualistic ethos of do-it-yourself shelter construction clash with the complexity of gender formations in 1960s America? What did it mean to be a father in the nuclear age?

To answer these questions this book picks up where McEnaney's left off, in 1958, shortly after the launch of *Sputnik,* when the Eisenhower administration abandoned discussions about urban evacuation and collective shelters in favor of a new policy focused almost entirely on home shelters, one that DC insiders colloquially called "Every Home a Fortress." As we will see, in the public reaction to this development, the image of the fallout shelter father protecting his family from total destruction became one of the most contentious figures of the nuclear age.

III

Throughout the nuclear crisis years, civil defense policymakers set out to persuade citizens that they had the capability and resources to protect themselves and their families in the event of nuclear war. Male household heads were instructed time and again to erect shelters in their domestic spaces to protect their families and, by proxy, ensure the continued survival of the United States. By equating the survival of the self and the family with the survival of the nation, policymakers developed a powerful political discourse that turned the private arrangement of domestic spaces into a matter of public concern and national security. During this moment of intense nuclear anxiety, state actors presented U.S. citizens with a vision of American masculinity that emphasized every man's ability to defend his home through the physical act of constructing a family shelter. To a contemporary observer, policymakers' lack of interest in single men, childless couples, and families who did not own property is striking, and it speaks to the remarkable hold of paternalism and family values in civil defense discourse. In their quest to simplify survival, policymakers overlooked complex questions of class, race, and sexuality to streamline the doctrine of do-it-yourself survival and market the family shelter to a white, middle-class, suburban audience. Such simplification was, as I will discuss, linked to a host of political concerns about the feasibility and cost of sheltering the entire nation, and it privileged propaganda, slogans, and public relations buzzwords over practical solutions. Within this rhetoric of do-it-yourself survival, paternalism functioned as a vehicle that shifted the state discourse of civil defense from the federal government into the family living room. The strategy was designed to normalize preparation for nuclear war by politicizing households and families around the wider imperatives of the nuclear state and encouraging men to view themselves as the nuclear safeguards of the American family.

In addition to filling a gap in the literature, this book may be useful to those who are interested in understanding the reciprocal relationship between the political ideal of civil defense and its performance in the suburban home.[43] As the gender historian Graham Dawson notes, "masculinities are lived out in the flesh, but fashioned in the imagination."[44] This observation is useful when we consider the various cultural and political narratives that emerged during the Cold War around the family fallout shelter. We see, for instance, how a federal agency tasked with protecting the U.S. population from the worst imaginable manmade disaster invested a substantial amount of political capital to promote a vision of national survival that placed the burden of that survival firmly on the shoulders of white male homeowners. In other words, the message was built around a narrow heteronormative vision of American manhood that represented only a slim portion of the population. This book is primarily concerned with the experiences of home-owning fathers, explicitly middle class and implicitly white, precisely because they were the target audience of the family fallout shelter initiative, and their experiences repeatedly highlight the limited educational capital of civil defense during the nuclear crisis years. The book explores the contrast between the politics of civil defense and the lived reality of life in the nuclear age as a way to think critically about how the target audience of the era's civil defense doctrine reacted to the state-constructed message of survival.

During the Cold War, shelter fatherhood became a powerful propagandist device in the nuclear state.[45] Its emergence, however, was not only rooted in the political culture of the time but also entrenched in changing perceptions of fatherhood that characterized 1950s America. In the aftermath of World War II, millions of men who had enlisted in the armed forces returned home to embrace what Ralph LaRossa and others have identified as a "new pivotal role in the emerging domestic culture of the Cold War."[46] As Robert Griswold has observed, male enlistment during World War II and the Korean War created a strong political bond between ideals of fatherhood and conceptions of civic service.[47] "The WWII years not only restored men's breadwinning abilities," he writes, "but reaffirmed the critical role fathers played in the health of the republic."[48] Extending Griswold's thesis, we can consider the political ideal of shelter fatherhood as it appeared in civil defense guidelines in a similar light. The personal became political as the actions of men within the domestic sphere took on an important symbolic role in the survival of both families and the state.

According to James Gilbert's *Men in the Middle: Searching for Masculinity in the 1950s*, scholars writing on gender and masculinity in a Cold War context need to consider the spectrum of masculine identities that existed in postwar America. Studies of masculinity during the era have tended to divide manhood into two dominant cultural narratives: the hypermasculine tough guy that Dean and K. A. Cuordileone argue influenced U.S. foreign policy versus the domesticated male represented as a source of tension in, for example, William Whyte's 1956 social study *The Organization Man* and Sloan Wilson's 1955 novel *The Man in the Grey Flannel Suit*. Whether domestic or tough, masculinity exists on a spectrum of types, as scholars are quick to point out.[49] Such observations are useful when considering the family fallout shelter as a space that linked hypermasculine with domestic forms of postwar fatherhood. Although scholars have been keen to emphasize how narratives of masculinity evolve in political discourse, it is also important to think about what happens when a specific narrative of masculinity constructed at a federal level meets resistance at the grassroots level and starts to break down. In the latter case, understanding how and why perceptions of shelter fatherhood shifted from "responsible citizen" to "neighborhood crackpot" highlights an underexplored aspect of Cold War masculinity: the relationship between the federal message and local performance and the selling of this distinctive vision of civil defense manhood.

When analyzing how the family fallout shelter affected social practices of postwar fatherhood, we do not find a uniform political message in which male household heads acted in service of the state but a series of interlinking cultural narratives that often challenged perceptions of the civil defense ideal. As I have mentioned, one of the key themes of this book is the manner in which discussions of shelter fatherhood inspired three narratives of Cold War fatherhood that emerged in print culture, letters, and oral histories: the domestic, the militarized, and the survivalist. These narratives allow us to track the subtleties around depictions and self-perceptions of fallout shelter fathers and highlight distinct shifts in how fallout shelters were publicly perceived and received. Together, they invite us to reappraise the objectives, behaviors, and actions of civil defense policymakers as well as the emergence of violence around shelters in response to the state's militaristic language.

Domesticated, militarized, survivalist: each term has been used to describe the fallout shelter father during the early Cold War. The militarized narrative of shelter fatherhood is the clearest indication of how family fallout shelters politicized the Cold War household. It is important to note that civil defense educational programs set out to redefine both fathers and Cold War families as paramilitary units. As McEnaney writes, the FCDA/OCDM created a national program that "infused military outlooks and values into post-war family ideology."[50] Yet while she discusses the contradictions and problems involved in household militarization, she pays little attention to how the militarization of the suburban family influenced discussions of fatherhood. There are two reasons to probe this relationship. First, militarization framed fathers as captains of the nuclear family. By linking the experience and agency of the returning G.I. to the new Cold War conflict, civil defense policymakers tasked fathers with training their families in the language and practice of nuclear survival, instructing their dependents to retreat to the fallout shelter at a moment's notice. Second, themes of militarization were frequently discussed in the public letters and popular culture that emerged around shelters. McEnaney may argue that "the increasing family orientation of civil defense pushed paternal rhetoric to the background as it accentuated women's maternal role," but in fact discussions of the militarized father are central to how families reacted to the prospect of nuclear war during the 1950s.[51]

It is important to recognize that shelter fatherhood was also influenced by the consumer culture of postwar America. One of the most striking aspects of the federal policy of privatized do-it-yourself shelter construction was the way in which family protection was framed as consumer choice. Shelter fatherhood was defined by a willingness among ordinary citizens not just to obey the state but also to purchase, construct, and maintain their own family fallout shelter.[52] Consumer, father, and citizen: at a time when the postwar cultural climate was defined by consumption, leisure, and suburbanization, the family shelter offered men a patriotic home-improvement exercise.[53] This is clear in the story of Art Carlson, where the domestic nature of fatherhood becomes a core aspect of the politics of the nuclear state. Undoubtedly, civil defense tapped into this cultural ideal of domestic fatherhood, offering a space of symbolic stability for suburban fathers, who, while in their shelters, could be both active fathers in the home and heroic defenders of the free world. By considering shelter fatherhood in the context of Cold War domesticity and consumerism, this book sheds new light on how ordinary fathers negotiated the idea of personally furnishing their families' safety.

The domestic and militarized aspects of shelter fatherhood are clearly identifiable in the political and cultural records of the era; however, public reaction to the idea of shelters reveals a third story, one involving violence, individualism, and the birth of a new survivalist mentality as neighbors and friends openly discussed the possibility of fighting each other for survival.[54] A study of editorials, the records of the OCDM Public Affairs Office, popular culture, public correspondence, and oral testimonies reveals how discussion of survivalism altered the dialogue over national security and civil defense. During these five nuclear crisis years, the gun-thy-neighbor debate highlighted a growing acceptance of white male violence, filtered through the idea of the survivalist male whose paternal duty was defined by his willingness to embrace radical, aggressive self-interest to ensure the survival of himself and his family.[55] Exploring how and why shelter owners became widely perceived as violent offers insight into how citizens interpreted, discussed, and responded to the ethos of individual male responsibility inherent in the rhetoric of civil defense.[56] Together, the domestic, militarized, and survivalist aspects of shelter fatherhood illustrate the complexity of public reaction to the prospect of nuclear survival.

The next chapters open with a discussion of the civil defense policy of the Eisenhower presidency, treating it as a way to understand why the actions of white suburban fathers became a cornerstone of federal civil defense efforts in the late 1950s and how fallouts shelters became the "log cabins" of the nuclear age. From there we follow the evolution of shelter policy through the Kennedy years—especially, the rise of home-shelter loans—and explore the intersections between suburban credit culture, national security, and male self-determination. While the fallout shelter father may have been the product of a political class looking to manage public fears, his existence also highlighted just how inadequate the national security state was at protecting its citizens. Subsequent chapters look at local and personal histories of shelter fatherhood through a study of the experiences of fathers in Colorado (one of the crucibles of the nuclear age) and of the fallout shelter salesmen who traveled door to door selling survival to anxious homeowners. The book ends by considering the rise of shelter violence and masculinity, focusing on how and why shelter owners became symbolic of a deeply unsettlingly form of antisocial Cold War citizenship.

CHAPTER ONE

The Log Cabin of the Nuclear Age

> A nuclear war will be a sudden war with little warning. In past emergencies, we had time to prepare even after the war had broken out. There can be no question that we shall not have such an opportunity next time. We must prepare now to make ourselves so invulnerable the enemy will be deterred from attacking!
>
> —Franklin B. Ellis, director of the Office of Civil Defense, November 1961

> Do you have a shelter Mr. President? Can we share it?
>
> —Charles J. Smith, age twelve, letter to John F. Kennedy, November 25, 1961

Edward Hazel was worried about the end of the world. A veteran who had served his nation in Korea, he was now a father of two living a quiet life in rural midwestern Ohio and facing the troubling prospect that the war had followed him home. In October 1961, news from Berlin dominated the airwaves, and Hazel decided it was high time to write a letter to the Office of Civil and Defense Mobilization (OCDM) asking, as any concerned parent might, for help and advice on how best to "educate and protect his family from the threat of nuclear war."[1] Like Art Carlson, he had decided to follow the advice of his president and build his own private fallout shelter. His letter to the OCDM does not record details about how much his chosen shelter cost, how difficult it was to assemble, or what other survival tools he purchased.[2] Rather, he wrote about his children—specifically, his worry that they did not seem to take the threat of nuclear war as seriously as he did. "They must learn because it is necessary, but I must tell you it's not easy. I want to teach them but it's tricky. I guess this is something you can't force." He continued: "We live in an age of war. . . . [I]n a world created by these weapons, anything I can do to protect my family must be done. I believe in shelters. My kids do not." For Hazel, building a fallout shelter was not just "a service to his nation" but also his duty as a parent. Closing his letter with a request for more educational material, he asked the OCDM to "please advise a troubled citizen and a worried father."[3]

Edward Hazel's letter, buried for many years in the regional records of the OCDM, hints at the complex interplay between cultures of Cold War paternalism and the domestic practice of shelter construction. In this case, the obligation to be a responsible father entwined with the defense of the nation. While Hazel's letter does not fully represent the experiences of millions of families across the United States as they confronted the prospect of a nuclear war, it does provide a glimpse into some of the personal dilemmas that confronted fathers who were prepping their families for the last war. The family fallout shelter was a powerful symbol for men such as Hazel, who were fraught with anxiety about a world that seemed to be spiraling toward nuclear disaster. It became a site of both action and impotence, a domestic arena in which to perform a politicized model of Cold War fatherhood, a constant reminder that every citizen was a soldier, every family a target, every home minutes away from being obliterated. Hazel's letter demonstrates that the boundaries enclosing shelters and fatherhood were neither static nor stable. As he and other fathers struggled to implement state-sanctioned, do-it-yourself survival, they often found themselves questioning the accepted construct that a nuclear war was conventionally winnable. In other words, when facing the prospect of building a family fallout shelter, such fathers came face to face with the potential limitations of their paternal power.

To understand Hazel's experiences, we must first consider the political history of the fallout shelter father. Building a shelter, protecting the family, believing that home defense might be a viable solution: these were constructed narratives of masculinity created by the political imperatives of the national security state. Since the detonation of the Soviet atomic bomb Joe 1 in 1949, American national security advisors had been fearing that, at any moment, the Cold War might turn hot. But how, in this age of total war, were ordinary citizens to be protected? The unenviable task of answering this impossible question fell to the Federal Civil Defense Administration (FCDA, which later became the OCDM). Equal parts hopeful and cynical, its policymakers spent much of the 1950s informing the public that the solution to survival rested in their own hands and in the actions of their families. By 1961, when Hazel wrote his worried letter, public education campaigns had been telling him for more than a decade that it was his duty to cooperate with the policies of home survival.

AMERICA'S MISSING SHIELD

On October 4, 1957, a few years before Hazel wrote his letter, President Dwight D. Eisenhower received a message that sent shockwaves through the National Security Council (NSC). After arriving in Gettysburg, Pennsylvania, for a relaxing weekend of golf, he was informed via telephone that the Soviet Union had fired an R-7 intercontinental ballistic missile (ICBM) from a silo in the Kazakhstan desert, successfully launching into orbit a small aluminum sphere, twenty-two inches in diameter and weighing 184 pounds.[4] Known as *Sputnik*, the diminutive missile's impact on U.S. national security was enormous. As George Reedy, an assistant to Senate majority leader Lyndon B. Johnson, declared, "Like a brick through a plate-glass window, it shattered into tiny slivers the American illusion of technical superiority over the Soviet Union."[5] *Sputnik*'s successful launch seemingly confirmed two things: first, that at the tail end of 1957 the Soviet Union had achieved dominance over the United States in rocket technology; and, second, that it could theoretically launch a preemptive strike against mainland America.

Speaking later that week on the television news program *Face the Nation*, Edward Teller, a theoretical physicist and ardent militarist known as the father of the hydrogen bomb, told his audience that "this week the U.S. has lost a battle more important and greater than Pearl Harbor."[6] Teller's melodramatic warning may have exaggerated the technological significance of *Sputnik*, but it heralded a shift in strategic language and presented a conception of U.S. vulnerability that would shortly become a running debate in the halls of the Pentagon. Soon, Senator Johnson warned, the Soviets "will be dropping bombs on us from space like kids dropping rocks onto cars from the freeway." He concluded, simply, that "something has to be done."[7] With *Sputnik* in orbit around the earth, the reality of nuclear war came crashing into living rooms across America.

How should U.S. defense planners respond to the challenges posed by *Sputnik*? Was the time right for a national program of government-funded community shelters? Should local authorities ensure that the key metropolitan target zones had plans for mass urban evacuation? Should even more destructive nuclear weapons be developed to ensure that the United States could maintain its overwhelming superiority in destructive power? As C. D. Jackson, government propagandist and senior executive at Time Inc., said, "the impact of *Sputnik*" on the national psyche was "overwhelming. . . . I repeat overwhelming."[8]

Facing what the historian Michael S. Sherry has described as an "intense demand for an active homefront defense," Eisenhower surprised his critics.[9] The Gaither committee, a group of civilian strategists tasked with advising the administration on how best to prepare the nation for a nuclear strike, had recommended a new $40 billion system of national community shelters, but the president opposed it. Instead, he devised a new strategy of atomic survival, one shifting civic duties onto the shoulders of ordinary families. Billing the idea as a program of do-it-yourself survival, the administration declared that the best chance of surviving a preemptive Soviet nuclear strike lay in the behavior of individuals, the fortification of suburban homes, and the preparation of families. Fathers were instructed to build shelters, mothers to stock kitchens with canned goods, and children to watch out for a bright flash of light on the horizon. Every home should become a fortress.[10]

News of *Sputnik*'s launch was not all doom and gloom. As questions circulated in the national press about the administration's ability to defend its citizens, Leo Hoegh, soon to become head of the OCDM, was presented with what he saw as a "unique opportunity" to "reverse the fortunes of civil defense."[11] Removed from the portfolio of the National Security Resource Board in 1950, the civil defense brief had since become political driftwood in Washington.[12] Persistently underfunded by Congress, unpopular with experts at the Atomic Energy Commission (AEC), and routinely ridiculed by cynical sections of the national press, policymakers had repeatedly watched their ambitious nationwide programs be pushed to the sidelines or left off the planning agenda.[13] "When you mention that you work for civil defense in those tiresome parties on Capitol Hill," Hoegh noted in his private papers, "people tend to raise an eyebrow, before changing the conversation."[14] Now, at the end of 1957, the scales had tipped, for the first time, toward the OCDM policymakers. It was their moment to push discussions of civil defense to the front of the national agenda.

While Hoegh was looking for ways to make civil defense a more appealing prospect to DC's movers and shakers, Eisenhower was embroiled in his own institutional battle. As the historian Stephen Ambrose notes, in the months preceding the launch of *Sputnik*, the president had faced numerous demands to increase military spending yet "refused to bend to the pressure, refused to initiate a fallout shelter program, refused to expand conventional nuclear forces, refused to panic."[15] *Sputnik*'s launch had been, according to the Cold War scholar John Lewis Gaddis, "a deliberate effort on Khrushchev's part to extract political advantage from the demonstration of long-range missile capability," and it was forcing Eisenhower to work tirelessly to "dampen hysteria and resist militarization."[16] This was no easy feat. News coverage was claiming that the president's relative passivity was analogous to the situation before the attack on Pearl Harbor, when executive inaction had cost the nation dearly.[17]

Writing for the *Washington Post*, the journalist and DC insider Stewart Alsop sardonically compared Eisenhower's response to the *Sputnik* launch to Franklin D. Roosevelt's 1938 hesitation as Britain began implementing a policy of appeasement toward Germany.[18] Eisenhower's Democratic rivals, expertly riled by Senator Johnson, worked to gain political capital as they attacked the president's lackluster defense program. With the 1958 midterms approaching and no clear Democratic frontrunner for the 1960 election, Johnson launched a series of scathing public attacks about a "weak willed" and "passive" president who appeared to be impotent in the face of Communist scientific advancement.[19] Calling for a reactivation of the Preparedness Subcommittee, the senator made it clear that both the nation and the president were ill-prepared. In the pages of the *New York Times,* he lambasted Eisenhower's "record of underestimating the Soviet program" and his historic "lack of willingness to take proper risks."[20] In this new missile age, Johnson argued, vigor, determination, zeal, and self-sacrifice were necessary. Now was "not the time for a failure of nerves. It [was] a time for action." While members of Congress offered little concrete evidence of what exact form this "action" should take, they were clear that the Eisenhower administration needed to disseminate a public message about the state's obligations to ensure its citizens' survival. Eisenhower's inner circle tried to downplay *Sputnik*'s impact but had little success. When Percival Brundage, a key ally and the director of the Bureau of Budget, mentioned to the Washington socialite Perle Mesta that *Sputnik* would be "forgotten in six months," she simply said, "Yes, dear, and in six months we may be dead."[21]

In the months following the launch of *Sputnik*, do-it-yourself survival became the watchword of civil defense, and in the winter of 1957–58 various policy positions began to solidify around the idea that private shelter construction was the most cost-effective solution for the dilemma posed by the growing Soviet nuclear threat. Eisenhower's stance was not just a product of the *Sputnik* moment but was rooted in a long-running discussion within the national security establishment about what exactly comprised the state's duty to protect its private citizens.

Throughout the early 1950s discussions about what to do if the bomb dropped were a persistent, troublesome refrain in U.S. strategic thought. In the symbol-driven politics of the Cold War, the desire to strike a balance between toughness and aggression made civil defense a contentious topic during NSC meetings. In this new missile age, what should the American home front look like? More importantly, how should it differ from the Soviet Union's? Several politically savvy members of the FCDA—among them, Edward Lyman, the director of civic affairs; William Heimlich, the head of public affairs; and Katherine Howard, the agency's vice-chair under its director, Val Peterson—had long claimed that, if presented correctly to the public, family shelters would project both peace and domestic strength. They would symbolize a society composed of prepared and patriotic families rather than a fully militarized state. Describing national civil defense as a "volunteer effort," these policymakers based their visions of a protected nation not around the practicalities of survival but around the more cost-effective principles of individualism, self-reliance, and freedom of action. Home shelters, as Howard stated at a 1953 civil defense conference in New England, offered a space for both domestic security and the performance of patriotism, thus balancing the paradox of the nuclear state. They would be "a direct answer to [the] sword rattling of Mr. Khrushchev" and "a chain reaction for peace."[22] In other words, civil defense was to be built from the basement up.[23]

Since the early 1950s civil defense had been pitched as a national endeavor from the ground up, rooted not in the actions of the state but in the local and the familial: for the "belief and spirit of the American people . . . survival must be an individual experience."[24] Privatized shelters were a powerful symbol of the Cold War's unique new home front, a combination of middle-class militarization, home-ownership acquisition, consumer culture, family values, and leisure time. The FCDA's 1954 annual civil defense report, closely edited by the public relations specialist Edward Lyman, borrowed language that Eisenhower himself later used in public addresses on the matter, agreeing that the "problem [of civil defense] lies . . . outside the realm of money and material preparation" while reminding skeptical NSC readers that the age's weapons of "terrifying power" made "civil defense . . . an issue of growing public interest."[25] The report, which was more than two hundred pages long, argued that U.S. civil defense efforts must differ from the Soviet Union's. Where the Soviet state system was organized "from [the] top to [the] bottom... requiring *all* the population [to] be trained," the U.S. system was formed of "volunteers," "of men and women willing to fight."[26] Katherine Howard agreed: "While in the Soviet Union, duties are thrust upon a nation of men and women who have no choice as to whether or not they wish to participate," in the United States "we have the choice to protect ourselves and our families."[27] In theory, civil defense—if done correctly—had the potential to be a powerful tool in America's Cold War propaganda arsenal, resolving the contradictions of home-front militarization, recapturing a frontier spirit, affirming the nation's vitality, and countering Soviet aggression and state control with a uniquely American vision of family-oriented, democratic, middle-class citizenship.[28]

In 1957, the 1954 FCDA report, with its low-cost solutions and rhetoric of volunteer efforts, still chimed with Eisenhower's own thinking.[29] Although the rising Republican star Nelson Rockefeller was insisting that federal commitment to a strong national civil defense position would strengthen America's hand in matters of foreign policy, his arguments seemed to find few sympathetic ears among members of Eisenhower's inner circle.[30] What is clear is that when civil defense officials pitched nuclear survival as a volunteer effort, they found a receptive audience, especially with Eisenhower, who noted that this might be the political compromise his administration had been looking for. Speaking to Henry Luce, the publisher of *Time* and *Life* magazines, during a Washington summit on civil defense, the president reiterated his belief that "unless the private citizen does become interested [in civil defense] and has a definite sense of responsibility for himself and his family, there is little the government, by itself, can do."[31] The traditional household head, not the politicians, were to be at the center of civil defense.

By the end of 1957 the family-oriented nature of civil defense became even more pronounced. Interestingly, the public relations campaign redefining the American family as the custodian of civil defense coincided with the birth of an increasingly vocal transatlantic anti-nuclear movement. By 1958, international disarmament activism led by Bertrand Russell, Albert Einstein, Norman Cousins, and Linus Pauling had solidified under the banners of the Campaign for Nuclear Disarmament (CND) in the United Kingdom and the National Committee for a Sane Nuclear Policy (SANE) in the United States and was beginning to lobby for a moratorium on all nuclear testing.[32] Fueling this growing anti-nuclear sentiment was a series of blunders made by FCDA's director, Val Peterson, who, when asked about the best way to survive a hydrogen bomb attack, replied that one should simply "not be there."[33] During Peterson's tenure at the FCDA, he made a number of mistakes in front of congressional committees, and the vigilant editors of the *Bulletin of the Atomic Scientists*, who recognized the fallacy of asking ordinary families to build shelters, were keen to use his words to damage the credibility of civil defense policy.[34] While roaming the streets and halls of DC, one of those editors, Ralph Lapp, would spring questions on Peterson whenever he saw him and then publish Peterson's fumbled answers in the *Bulletin*. At one encounter he asked point-blank how the FCDA was preparing to protect the nation from fallout; at another he asked about what life would be like after a nuclear attack. Peterson's reply was revealing: "[W]e are just not ready for that kind of hell."[35]

Peterson may have been honest, but he was ill-equipped to steer civil defense during this time of increasing scrutiny. His loyalty to Eisenhower's hands-off approach to civil defense led him to make a number of awkward or contradictory statements that embarrassed the administration.[36] For instance, when standing before a congressional committee in 1956, he declared, "[W]e believe in shelters but we don't want to mislead people." When pushed for more information about what he personally believed might make America safe again, he replied, "[A] tremendous sum of money."[37]

Peterson was frequently lambasted in the pages of *Newsweek*, the *Nation*, and the *New Republic*, and his signature civil defense initiative—an annual evacuation exercise known as Operation Alert—was of little use to an administration that was concerned about its alleged inability to protect its people. Today, it may be difficult to understand exactly why Peterson decided to endorse Operation Alert, given that every annual mock air-raid drill around the nation seemed to "confirm the impossibility of protecting civilians from nuclear attack."[38] Yet for Eisenhower these pointless exercises were a way to test the emergency preparedness of various government branches.[39] During these yearly exercises, described by Guy Oakes as a form of "elaborate national sociodrama," huge swaths of the urban population across sixty cities were told to take cover for fifteen minutes.[40] Derided as "fumbling and inconsistent"[41] by Merle Tuve, the chair of the National Academy of Science, and "worse than no program at all" by General Otto L. Nelson, Operation Alert clogged highways and confused and exasperated both officials and the public. Reportedly, many office workers ignored the drills, and civil defense officials often did not know where urban residents were supposed to be evacuated to.[42] According to DC's civil defense spokesman, John Garrett Underhill, the officials running Operation Alert were "so inadequate they couldn't cope with a bush fire threatening a doghouse in the backyard."[43] Although Operation Alert was praised publicly as a "pretty good show," private recollections affirm that it revealed the nation's woeful lack of preparation.[44] Rather than being perceived as too aggressive or too weak in the face of nuclear threat, the U.S. civil defense efforts looked ridiculous.

While the government eventually embraced the policy of do-it-yourself survival, there was one final charge in favor of mass community shelters, this time led by U.S. Representative Chet "Mr. Atomic Energy" Holifield.[45] A Democrat from California, he had been at the forefront of the U.S. nuclear debate since witnessing the attacks on Japan in 1945. In Congress he had worked on the Joint Committee on Government Operations, advised the U.S. House Committee on Government Operations, and by 1956 was a member of the U.S. House Subcommittee for Civil Defense, which became known as the Holifield committee. The committee's work framed a pivotal moment in the history of civil defense, illustrating that valid national alternatives to do-it-yourself survival existed as late as 1956.[46] In a hearing that opened on January 31, Holifield argued that "effective civil defense measures can be taken if the need for them is sufficiently understood by the public, . . . financially supported by Congress, . . . and congruously administered by the Executive."[47] Citing public apathy, congressional cynicism, and various bureaucratic failings, he and his colleagues then spent four months searching for solutions to the nation's civil defense problem. Their resulting report to the Eisenhower administration was the era's clearest and most coherent version of a nationwide shelter construction program, going so far as to state that the best hope for nuclear survival lay in "both self-help, and federal sacrifice."[48] According to Holifield, costs for a program of community shelters could be kept to $20 billion.[49] "A shelter program," he stated, "is an acid test of a national will to build an effective civil defense."[50] His report itself can be seen as an "acid test" for both Eisenhower's commitment to domestic national security and the will of the American people. It repeatedly emphasized that for civil defense to have any real domestic utility it had to be both a federal obligation and a citizen's duty. Survival could not and should not be simply left to private citizens. Funding issues, regional variations, and the practical questions of home-shelter construction posed "as many problems as [they] did solutions."[51] If Eisenhower were not careful, Holifield concluded, civil defense might become a "phantom" program of American defense, existing as little more than a placebo for its citizens.[52] To truly function as America's shield, it needed funding, research, and presidential support.

Despite gaining bipartisan and popular support, the Holifield committee's recommendations were sidelined. Peterson, in a last-ditch attempt to salvage his political career, did an about-turn, trying to cash in on the committee's political momentum by presenting Eisenhower with his own plan for a $32 billion national shelter program.[53] Eisenhower, however, rejected both suggestions, claiming that costs were too high.[54] In the administration's eyes, the problems of civil defense were "virtually unsolvable."[55]

In the summer of 1957, more than a hundred scientific experts, industrialists, and nuclear strategists, including Paul Nitze and Herman Kahn, gathered in Washington, DC, for the first meeting of the

Gaither committee. Their intent was to conduct yet another comprehensive review of U.S. defense priorities, and their actions have been well chronicled by historians.[56] Now, in the wake of *Sputnik*, the committee pushed for incremental militarization in matters of national security, concluding that with the Soviet threat "civil defense becomes of the utmost importance." For Nitze, "the freedom of the United States Government" was rooted in its ability "to give the perception we are willing to take strong actions, which may carry with them the serious risk of Soviet reaction."[57]

The members of the Gaither committee faced the sobering prospect that, in the age of the intercontinental missile, warning times were now a fraction of what they had been. Gone were the days when volunteers could take to the roof, binoculars in hand, to spot incoming planes. As early as 1955 a lengthy two-part report, *Meeting the Threat of Surprise Attack*, had raised concerns that the acceleration of ballistic-missile programmers would soon render any hope of urban evacuation obsolete.[58] Now, in 1958, reports authored by the RAND Corporation called for military investment to be shifted toward rapidly increasing the number of *Thor* and *Jupiter* intermediate-range ballistic missiles (IRBMs) deployed in Europe.[59] The missile age offered both possibilities and dangers. On the one hand, the growth of missile technology gave Eisenhower far more power to flex the nation's nuclear muscles. On the other hand, the increase created pitfalls. Once again it fell to Val Peterson to try to explain the inconsistencies in civil defense planning, this time in a meeting requested by the visiting West German chancellor, Konrad Adenauer. When asked by the chancellor "if thinking on civil defense by means of evacuation from the cities has shifted," Peterson replied, "[N]ot entirely." Then he quickly noted, "Evacuation is practicable today only because we believe we can count on 3–5 hours warning against attacks other than from submarines. The coming of the inter-continental ballistic missile, which will cut warning time down to 15–30 minutes, will clearly mean that evacuation is impossible."[60]

Peterson's answer to Adenauer did little to address the problems still being debated by the Gaither committee. If the executive branch were to win the Cold War, it needed the citizenry on its side and thus must implement "measures to firm up public morale."[61] In the discussions of the Gaither committee we see the paradox of nuclear survival in full effect. On the need for shelters the committee noted:

> Of itself, a shelter program would, in the Panel's opinion, forcibly augment our deterrent power in two ways: first, by discouraging the enemy from attempting an attack on what might otherwise seem to him a temptingly unprepared target; second, by reinforcing his belief in our readiness to use, if necessary, our strategic retaliatory power.
>
> Further, a shelter program might symbolize to the nation the urgency of the threat, and would demonstrate to the world our appraisal of the situation and our willingness to cope with it in strength. It would symbolize *our will to survive*, and our understanding of our responsibilities in a nuclear age.[62]

Experts from the Gaither committee, much to Eisenhower's disappointment, recommended another $25 billion shelter policy. Yet in the wave of public concern that followed the launch of *Sputnik*, the administration recognized that more direct action was needed. As Eisenhower said, "we have before us a big a job of molding public opinion as well as avoiding extremes."[63] The president was not ready to bankrupt the nation for shelters, nor was he willing to remove nuclear weapons from the nation's arsenal. A compromise had to be struck. Families, not the state, must shoulder the burden of Cold War militarization. Every home would become a fortress.

THE POLITICAL STYLING OF SHELTER FATHERHOOD

While it is true that the family-centered civil defense program emerged as a political compromise—the Eisenhower administration's attempt to strike a balance between fiscal responsibility and state militarization—its distinctive emphasis on fathers as shelter builders reflected long-held cultural ideals equating active fatherhood with domestic and national stability. In the increasingly suburbanized world of middle-class America, the notion of fatherhood as an anchor of masculine identity had become a staple in popular and political culture.[64] Evidenced in the rise of the family sitcom, the popularity of parenting magazines, and the wave of public intellectuals debating the social implications of male suburbanization, this new version of fatherhood seemed to be an inevitable and logical shift within a society that was increasingly preoccupied with its domestic identity. The new fatherhood of the 1950s combined emotional maturity with domestic responsibility, encouraging war veterans who were entering the white-collar work force to find a balance between a strong social work ethic and tough individualism, traits that would supposedly help them guide their children smoothly into adulthood. Of course, as K. A. Cuordileone argues, this domestic ideal was a social paradox that ignored the vast racial and class divisions still plaguing society.[65] Nevertheless, the era's cultural emphasis on active fatherhood slipped into the realm of civil defense policymaking.

At the end of 1957, with *Sputnik* orbiting the earth, the family fallout shelter was primed to take center stage in the nation's defense effort. Yet questions of how to "educate and inform the public" about its new civic obligations remained up for debate.[66] In the first half of the 1950s the private shelter was seen as a "companion piece to a public shelter system," according to Laura McEnaney.[67] Now, with the home shelter set to function as the cornerstone of civil defense policy, OCDM policymakers had to ensure that all public education efforts mirrored this new vision of privatized survival. Writing to Ed Lyman, now the director of OCDM public affairs, in a memo dated March 5, 1957, civil defense spokesman John Kirby said, "The objective of defense now is simply, we need **awareness** and **action** [emphasis in the original]."[68] By early 1958 the OCDM's task was to convince ordinary families across the United States to convert their basements and backyards into bunkers. "All noteworthy, radio-TV coverage of regional, State and local civil defense efforts must be directed towards family shelters," Leo Hoegh wrote in a memo to William Heimlich shortly after assuming office as director of OCDM, adding, "[W]e need 'meaty' stories."[69] "Home owners have to be sold on this," Heimlich replied. "[W]hat we need is narrative."[70]

At OCDM headquarters in Battle Creek, Michigan, Hoegh, a former governor of Iowa, was setting out to make his mark on civil defense. Between July 1958 and October 1960, the agency, under his direction, launched a new program of public education designed to place families at the forefront of public-defense policy.[71] As McEnaney notes, this was a time when "policymakers clumsily escorted shelter policy towards the single-family home."[72]

Yet this was no haphazard shift; OCDM policymakers, under the direction of public relations companies in Chicago, New York, and Los Angeles, embarked on one of the era's most extensive political marketing campaigns.[73] Advertising the family shelter as "the quintessential home improvement exercise of post-war America," they produced a steady stream of pamphlets, posters, and exhibitions aimed at selling civil defense to the public. Although the practice of home-shelter construction remained decidedly imperfect and a host of technical questions were left unanswered, OCDM put forth a strikingly coherent campaign message stating that homes with private shelters had a better chance of surviving the next war. As the United States entered the missile age, the agency made it clear that fathers were the best custodian of the American family.

Without federal funding and with presidential support for a network of community shelters a distant dream, the OCDM directed the majority of its funding and administrative energy toward the production and distribution of home-shelter construction booklets. In a move that Holifield later compared to building "an army, or a navy or an air force by advising each one to buy a jet plane," the agency actively encouraged a new domestic protection plan premised on principles of government "guidance" and "stimulation" rather than direct federal intervention.[74]

It was one thing to endorse the idea that families across the United States should build shelters; it was another task entirely to convince homeowners to practice do-it-yourself survival. In Ed Lyman's view, the situation was a public relations exercise as much as a problem of logistics. In a series of remarkable briefing documents, he detailed the new direction that national defense efforts needed to take: "[I]t is essential that civil defense speak with a voice that is respected if not loved. . . . [W]e need to emphasize the personal responsibility of the individual citizen in building total defense."[75] Noting that it would take an impressive marketing effort to get families to turn their basements into bunkers, he wrote, "[We need] the force of frequent repetition to make it stick."[76] OCDM policymakers had to convince citizens that their performance in the home was a valuable addition to national security efforts. For Lyman the objective was clear: "[W]e need to clothe civil defense in the same mantle of popular and national necessity that our military defense wear. . . . [B]uilding a family shelter is more than an isolated gesture of self-protection. It becomes something that is bound up with our international mission as leaders of the free world."[77]

Through 1958 and into 1959 the staff members who were producing OCDM publications followed Lyman's suggestions to the letter and framed home-shelter construction as the heroic male do-it-yourself project of the Cold War. Understanding all too clearly that a policy of privatized survival lived or died on the whims of public support, Hoegh, too, set about making the private acts of civil defense part of everyday life.[78] Fusing the priorities of the national security state with the consumer culture of the suburbs, he framed the construction of the family shelter as a natural and positive extension of the domestic duty of men in the home.[79] Describing the American middle class as the "target audience" for newly revamped civil defense efforts (because, as William Heimlich cynically noted, that group had "the income and temperament" needed to undertake do-it-yourself projects of "international significance"), the OCDM embarked on a series of public talks and exhibitions aimed at engaging fathers to pick up their tools and build bomb shelters.[80] While Hoegh did not exactly exclude the urban poor, the disenfranchised, and those who did not have an available basement, he did not cater to them either. OCDM officials admitted privately that a policy of home-shelter construction meant that certain "individuals may desire to undertake the construction of home shelters" but would be "unable to do so due to lack of available finances," yet they appeared to have little internal incentive to remedy this.[81]

The internal discussions at OCDM and between agency officials and the president reveal that the privileging of white middle-class masculinity was a deliberate choice. During a tense meeting with Eisenhower, Hoegh tentatively suggested that more might be done to expand public access to civil defense. Armed with a Gallup poll, he argued that creeping nuclear tensions had created an audience primed and ready for home survival: "Mr. President, over 71% of citizens now favor fallout shelters."[82] Pressing his point, he claimed that "more than a million people had already built fallout shelters and 13 million families had chosen the safest place in the home in case of nuclear attack." He continued: "Surely the President might make the statement regarding fallout shelter in a press conference, or in the State of the Union Message, or might announce that he was building a fallout shelter at Gettysburg."[83] Eisenhower, however, was rightly suspicious of the data and balked at taking a more active stance. When pressed about providing more access to families by addressing "incorrect local building codes" and offering "tax credits" to spur male homeowners into action, he called such steps "illogical." "People take a great many actions for their own welfare without claiming tax credits," he said. Buckling, Hoegh noted that he still "believed that people would build their own fallout shelters as indicated by the Gallup poll." Eisenhower quickly retorted, "[I'm] wondering whether a large number of people in the Gallup poll . . . favored shelters because they thought the Government would pay for them."[84]

During these sessions Eisenhower cited a persistent truism, one that appears again and again in the political history of civil defense—namely, that collective defense was "too expensive."[85] He was an ardent believer in the principles of fiscal conservatism; and because he saw risks in government expenditure, he made the case that expectations should be kept low to avoid promoting the idea that every citizen had an "inherited right . . . to have his life insurance risk approved."[86] According to one policy document, "[the] home fallout shelter is a weapon for peace" built by "the patriotic citizen who takes it upon himself to provide welfare for his family."[87] The "patriotic citizen" in this context was defined by his privilege, access to economic power, self-reliance, property ownership, and physical prowess. The shelter builder was a unique home-front combatant who, through his purchasing power and physical actions in the domestic realm, was ready to fight a war that was in many ways nonphysical in nature. The economic doctrines of civil defense entrenched this vision of selective patriotism, and it unsurprisingly became linked with white and middle-class suburban identity.

How aware were civil defense policymakers about the class and racial dimensions of their policies? To answer this question, it is useful to turn to the public education campaigns launched under Hoegh's watch, which reveal the airbrushing of societal diversity through a narrative of individual choice. If, as Lyman frequently said, fallout shelters were to be "products" of the Cold War, then the messaging had to be streamlined. For him and others at the OCDM the true power of home survival resided in its simplicity: "[I]f we start to put in too many factors . . . cities vs. rural, renters vs. owners, even who you want in and out of shelters then it becomes tricky." Of course, "there will be letters, but any federal body might be crippled trying to firefight those issues." He suggested, "Let's leave that to local officers with a better sense of their people."[88] In practice, then, public education campaigns trumpeted the ideals of democratic citizenship while being anything but.

In a dramatized radio show broadcast by CBS in 1959, we see the streamlined narrative of survival in full effect: "We Americans have a better chance than many people for survival of our system and our values. The reason is that Americans are self-reliant. They are used to taking part in government. . . . Above all, the basic means to survival is practical knowledge, the knowledge that each individual must have to protect himself and his family."[89] After tying the nation's contemporary situation to its revolutionary heritage, the broadcast went on to answer a host of questions from preselected white suburban audience members; they ranged from shelter costs, to equipment, to the nature of radiation. Never once did they turn toward issues of race or class. Such conspicuous absences tell us a great deal about the world inhabited by civil defense policymakers. Again and again, their propaganda erased distinctions of race, class, and gender expression outside of the rigid heteronormative binary of the nuclear family.

Instead, it emphasized straightforward solutions to an inherently complex problem.

The social makeup of the late 1950s suburbs, built on the racialized lending policies of the Federal Housing Administration, which had routinely denied minorities an equal level of access to housing or credit, had created a target audience for the family shelter. Thus, instead of creating a civil defense program that reflected an accurate portrait of American society, Hoegh decided to focus the agency's efforts on the middle class, specifically by appealing to fathers and mothers. At the 1958 civil defense conference, for instance, he declared that the "nation's homemakers are the traditional custodians of the family.... [T]his responsibility goes hand in hand with the aims of the family shelter."[90] In the lexicon of privatized survival, white women framed as mothers would serve as "child nurturers, food prepare[r]s, and hospital workers," while the physical task of shelter construction would be the purview of white suburban fathers.[91]

Past generations of historians studying gender and civil defense have emphasized the role of women in national defense efforts, exploring how the OCDM presented women as "true civil defenders . . . with the feminine courage, and strength of mind and heart" critical for defending the nation.[92] But with do-it-yourself survival at the forefront of public policy, ideas about white middle-class fatherhood and shelter construction also permeated the American cultural imagination. Between 1957 and 1960 the OCDM produced several detailed guides designed to translate the rhetoric of do-it-yourself survival into reality by providing homeowners with a step-by-step illustration of how to construct a family shelter.[93] The booklets are remarkable Cold War artifacts that normalize the terrifying idea of preparing a family for nuclear war and tell us a great deal about the intersection between the politics of civil defense and late-1950s conceptions of fatherhood. In them, the act of shelter construction and participation in civil defense was presented as an opportunity for men to develop their skills as effective fathers. Time and again in civil defense literature, men were encouraged to think of both their paternal duty and their obligations as private citizens of the United States, to embrace their dual role as father of a family and defender of the free world (see figure 3).

Hoegh recast the American man as part of a tradition of male service as old as the nation itself. "Protection of our people is not new in the United States," he said in 1958. "[W]hen a free America was being built by our forebears, every log cabin and every dwelling had a dual purpose as [both a] home and a fortress." On the Cold War home front "citizens should be called upon to make the same contribution . . . not for building a free America, but for sustaining a free

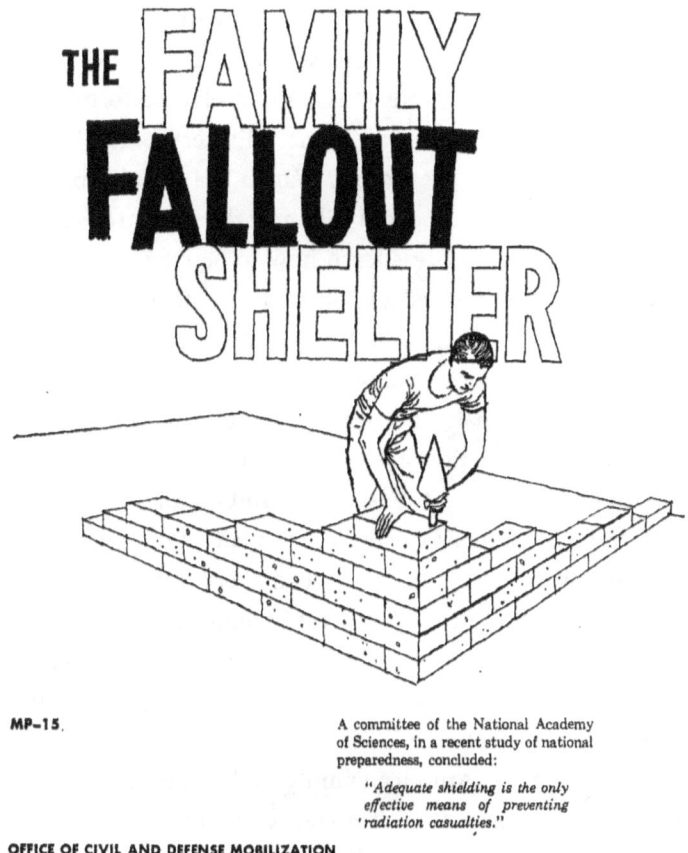

FIGURE 3. Office of Civil and Defense Mobilization, "The Family Fallout Shelter" (Washington, DC: Government Printing Office, 1959). Courtesy of the National Archives and Records Administration, College Park, Maryland.

America."[94] The family fallout shelter—the log cabin of the nuclear age—provided a space for American men to reaffirm and recapture a frontier spirit and become pioneers of self-protection.

Hoegh was not alone in using pioneer mythology to hone the language of do-it-yourself survival. For Vincent Wilson, Jr., a civil defense advisor, the task was "no more than the nuclear age's equivalent of keeping your powder dry."[95] The family shelter, according to an article in *Life*, was the "modern stockade" of the suburban middle class, a comparison that revived old conceptions of American self-defense and self-reliance. OCDM public education programs stressed that the threat of nuclear war required only a slight revision of traditional masculine social scripts, that civil defense was a chance for every father to protect his family and to perform small acts of heroism in his own suburban home.[96] Ex-servicemen, returning from World War II and the Korean War to live in suburban worlds of conformity and comfort, could still meet the standards set by their forefathers and in the process learn how to be effective fathers and husbands. The shelter created a space in the home in which the Cold War and ideals of frontier fatherhood intersected, normalizing the prospects of nuclear war and allowing men to position themselves as domestic experts on matters of survival. Of course, the lived experience of shelter construction was far different from the political ideal. But at a time when ideas of masculinity and manhood were in considerable flux, the pioneer/shelter father analogy served the OCDM exceptionally well. Critically, its policymakers framed male acts of do-it-yourself survival not as a "retreat underground" but as a "positive form of security" that provided a generation of suburban fathers with a new purpose. They insisted that fathers had agency in the face of total nuclear devastation.[97]

The idea that the all-American family could build shelters and prepare for war had great symbolic resonance, capturing the imagination of social critics, writers, and politicians in remarkable and diverse ways. Yet their reaction was far from positive. Despite the potent marketing of do-it-yourself survival, practical questions as well as the policy's social implications on the nation's character and community ethic remained unanswered. Moreover, the actual practice of do-it-yourself survival differed greatly from its framers' predictions. Nevertheless, if Hoegh's goal was, as he stated, to "raise awareness and readiness," then he succeeded. From 1957 to 1959 the OCDM took the message of do-it-yourself survival on the road, dispatching mobile shelter displays to cities, towns, and state fairs across the United States. The Model Fallout Shelter Display Unit—or LYN, as it was commonly called—"served as a guide to home-owners planning shelter protection in their basements."[98] Transported inside an "all-Aluminum trailer," the LYN was a "completely self-contained unit, including its own gasoline operated electric generator, Public Address System, and all important reception area." Its manufacturers had created a product "geared" to "illustrate just how simple survival is." During a 1959 pitch to renew his OCDM contract, New York LYN Shelters's managing director, J. R. Sanchez, claimed that the mobile shelters were central to the agency's public relations campaign because "they can present 'the survival story' in a dramatic and convincing manner . . . making survival a personal experience."[99]

For those "interested in survival," model shelter exhibitions were aimed at showing them just how "easy it would be for families to survive the next war."[100] Visitors were offered the chance to pick their preferred model shelter from government-approved catalogues. Once they had decided on a base model and selected a do-it-yourself construction kit, they could choose how to furnish the structure.[101] As McEnaney writes, shelter construction was "a form of militarization that could be purchased, handcrafted and even tastefully decorated."[102] Homeowners could pick backyard, basement, or above-ground shelters, with blueprints designed by OCDM experts working in tandem with civil engineers and architects.[103] While the marketing literature never directly said these shelters could withstand a "direct nuclear blast," it did claim they would be the "perfect space for the family to wait out the dangers of radiation in comfort and security."[104] According to guidelines printed by the OCDM and handed out at model shelter exhibitions and performed by state politicians such as Governor Ernest Frederick "Fritz" Hollings of South Carolina (figure 4),

FIGURE 4. Governor Ernest Frederick "Fritz" Hollings of South Carolina and Mrs. Hollings and a child in the newly constructed nuclear fallout shelter below the governor's mansion. The underground shelter is equipped with an air intake system, beds, food, and medical supplies in the event of a nuclear meltdown or attack. Fallout Shelter at the Governor's Mansion (1960), The State Newspaper Photograph Archive, Box 4, Governor's Mansion, Fallout Shelter, Richland Library, Columbia, South Carolina. Courtesy of Richland Library, Columbia, South Carolina.

a family living in a shelter might emerge after two weeks "ready to start anew." The narrator of a 1960 OCDM promotional advertisement for a construction booklet titled "The Family Fallout Shelter" asserted that "a home shelter could save your life in a nuclear war. This is a fact you have to accept." Still, not everyone did accept these OCDM "facts."[105]

In the new language of do-it-yourself defense, the idea that male breadwinners should be able to choose their own shelters made logical sense to the OCDM, which saw consumer choice as a vital way to encourage middle-class families to engage in civil defense efforts. Within this framework of choice, the patriarchal underpinning of men as their families' primary economic providers remained firmly in place. As I will discuss in more detail, do-it-yourself survival linked the disparate worlds of male consumption, suburban living, and Cold War patriotism. On the home front the act of purchasing and building a shelter and preparing a family for war was a patriotic form of consumerism rooted in the historical imperatives of the age.[106] While the family fallout shelter, once built, might have all the "comforts of modern living" (booklets often pictured women and children decorating the shelter space), the physical act of constructing the shelter and training the family remained the duty of men.[107]

By prompting families to reconsider their most intimate domestic spaces and arrangements, the act of building the family shelter was an important way for fathers to impart ideas of manhood and masculinity to their sons (see figure 5). In keeping with the OCDM's effort to frame civil defense as "positive home protection," fathers were encouraged to use this opportunity to spend "quality time with their boys" and, in so doing, set a "fine example to their sons."[108] As the historian K. A. Cuordileone notes, Cold War culture placed a premium on this new fatherhood, which saw men at home as role models for teenage boys who, according to parenting magazines of the 1950s, were at a "high risk of juvenile delinquency and homosexuality."[109] The act of shelter construction encouraged a generation of men to abandon the model of the father as a distant authoritarian figure and instead provide a positive, domesticated variant for their sons that was both masculine and affectionate. Drawing on ideals of the "heroic artisan," OCDM publications frequently displayed men holding or instructing small children, thus transmitting ideals of paternal duty and compassion by preparing their family for nuclear war.[110]

During the publicity drive that followed the October 1958 launch of the National Shelter Policy, the OCDM saturated U.S. culture with

FIGURE 5. Shelter literature frequently characterized shelter construction as an appropriately masculine activity that fathers and sons could do together. Source: Office of Civil and Defense Mobilization, *Fallout Protection: What to Know and Do about Nuclear Attack* (Washington, DC: Government Printing Office, 1961), 20. Courtesy of the National Archives and Records Administration, College Park, Maryland.

accounts of men who were discovering "a new-found respect" for their families through their participation in civil defense.[111] Project Hideaway, a 1958 OCDM-sponsored psychological experiment at Princeton University, introduced the public to the Powner family, a white, suburban, middle-class couple with three small children who accomplished the "heroic feat" of spending fourteen days in a fallout shelter. Widely reported in newspapers such as the *Los Angeles Times* and *Washington Post*, the story helped bring the ideal of the fallout shelter father into the mainstream.[112] Coverage of the experiment focused on how the family unit had reacted to time spent in close isolation. In interviews, Mr. Powner spoke "for the family," saying that he had found the experience positive because it had given him the "opportunity to get to know his children better." "More families," he noted, "ought to try to plan vacations when they are alone together."[113]

An OCDM television spot distributed to major television networks shared the story of the Brown family, who, like the Powners, decided to spend a week in their recently constructed family shelter. According to the narrator, Douglas Brown, who lived with his wife and eight children in a two-story brick colonial outside of Topeka, Kansas, first met with architects and other planners to determine the ideal location for his home's latest addition. He is described as having "foresight," "planning," and "willingness to get the job done." The task of construction is a relatively complex, but the film guides viewers step by step. First, with the help of a small fleet of trucks, he digs a deep hole in his yard, carefully measured to ensure that three feet of earth will remain on top of the shelter as a fallout shield. As one of Brown's sons looks on and learns from his father, the homeowner pours and reinforces a concrete base for the shelter. All the while whimsical musical plays in the background. The film does fail to mention that Brown was a professional contractor who specialized in building fallout shelters, and a modern audience may be surprised at just how complex the task seems to be—clearly far more suited to a professional contractor than to a do-it-yourself amateur. Nevertheless, the narrator stresses that this is a project that "any American family might be able to partake in."[114]

The Brown family became a minor media sensation when they volunteered to spend a week underground in their new shelter to test the viability of shelter living. During this time Brown fully embraced his role as a shelter father. "We have talent shows, we have plays, we did it all together," he stated. "[I]t was the children who got us through the experiment."[115] One scene in the film depicts him holding his youngest child as he introduces viewers to his children one by one and talks about how much he enjoyed his time underground.

By linking successful fatherhood with efficient survival, the OCDM created a powerful marketing tool. Instead of sharing coherent urban dispersal plans, it flooded the nation with pamphlets, booklets, television spots, radio broadcasts, and educational events, all aimed at persuading ordinary families to follow in the footsteps of these civil defense pioneers. Families like the Browns and the Powners were placed on the front line of the nation's survival efforts, representing a powerful political role model and a potent form of domestic militarization.

By 1958 discussion of fallout shelters and fatherhood was firmly embedded in public policy. On the eve of the National Shelter Policy announcement, the NSC announced that "the . . . policy is based *firmly* on the philosophy of the obligations of each property-owner to provide protection on his own premises [emphasis in the original]." It was a "policy based upon actions by individuals, primarily individuals who are heads of families."[116] Its success or failure was therefore tied to the actions of millions of fathers and families across the United States.

GOLF COURSES AND FALLOUT SHELTERS

In September 1961, Eisenhower, now retired and looking forward to weekends of golf and fly fishing, received a letter from Mary Florsheim Jones asking for his support for the building of a fallout shelter at the Eldorado County Gold Club in California. In the letter Jones expounds on her plan for survival: "[M]y husband and I originally thought we would build the shelter ourselves. This seems selfish and I though perhaps we could ban[d] together and ask for a piece of land and make this a community project that might set a good example." Before responding, Eisenhower wrote to one of his golfing buddies, the comedian Freeman F. Gosden of the *Amos 'n Andy* radio show, to ask for advice on how to "not offend the lady." In this letter he spoke freely, perhaps more so than at any other time, on what privatized survival had done to the nation and how it still ate at his conscience: "[E]ven if I were persuaded that the building of a shelter would be good, I would most certainly insist that it would take care of all the caddies, the workmen on the golf course, including waitresses, maids, janitors all the rest."[117] No fallout shelter was built at the Eldorado County Gold Club, though reports do mention that when

Eisenhower later "shot a golf ball through the window of the Jones' family house," he "got an earful when he tried to retrieve it."[118]

When Eisenhower left the White House, the bomb-shelter craze was just starting to take shape. During the next two years, 1961–63, the former president remained on the periphery of civil defense policy while the public openly discussed stocking shelters with guns, fly-by-night shelter salesmen became a national talking point, and the nation was embroiled in the Cuban missile crisis. Out of office, he remained ambivalent about the entire practice of civil defense. During a campaign event in February 1961 for New Jersey gubernatorial candidate James P. Mitchell, an Associated Press reporter asked Eisenhower to share his views on private shelters, and, Ike spoke his mind: "If my family were not in the shelter with me, I would just walk out. I wouldn't want to be left in that kind of world."[119] What had begun as an internal debate about how to protect ordinary citizens was now steadily morphing into one of the most contentious issues of the nuclear age.

Caught at the center of this evolving shelter narrative were the American family and American fathers, and their story would grow even more intense in the years after Eisenhower's presidency. The Soviets resumed atmospheric testing, crises escalated in Cuba and Berlin, and a young presidential candidate named John F. Kennedy spoke with intensity about missile gaps, new frontiers, and the need to recapture an American spirit of independence and sacrifice. Meanwhile, for fathers such as Edward Hazel, far removed from the halls of power, the rhetoric of do-it-yourself had become a far more intimate experience. In his letter to the OCDM, he grappled with the political language of civil defense and its self-deterministic conviction that he was a capable defender of his family. "It is my duty to protect them," he wrote. Yet he admitted, "I have the booklets and I attend the local meetings but it just doesn't seem to stick."[120] As he worked to perform this task of home survival, Hazel was also grappling with a host of contradictions that had, during the past decade, been imperfectly swept away. He was not alone in his struggle and his confusion.

CHAPTER TWO

The Fallout Shelter Father on the New Frontier

> The monstrous gods of the ancient world have all reappeared, hugely magnified, demanding total human sacrifice. To appease their super-Moloch in the Nuclear temples, whole nations stand ready, supinely, to throw their children into his fiery furnace.
>
> —Lewis Mumford, *The City in History,* 1961

> Want a quick way to survive nuclear fallout? The FHA has the answer.
> —"FHA Loans Available for Family Shelters," *Sarasota News,* August 4, 1961

At 7 P.M. on July 25, 1961, more than 25 million Americans tuned in to watch the president of the United States inform the nation that the time had come to construct fallout shelters and prepare for the possibility of nuclear warfare in the missile age. "In the event of an attack, the lives of those families which are not hit in a nuclear blast and fire can still be saved," President Kennedy proclaimed, "if they are warned to take shelter and that shelter is available. . . . [W]e owe that kind of insurance to our families and to our country."[1]

Kennedy had cultivated his image as an intellectual Cold Warrior during his successful presidential campaign, and during this televised broadcast, known as the Berlin Address, he was continuing to call on that trope. He informed the American people that the battle for Berlin would be fought on both "the endangered frontier of freedom" that ran through the divided city and the frontier of the American home, where each family must "bear the burden" of the Cold War conflict "if freedom is to be defended." At the center of Kennedy's domestic frontier was the suburban family and its fallout shelter, a structure that, while "new to our shores," reflected a "distinct vision" of the American character. "In the coming months," the president reassured the nation, "I hope to let every citizen know what steps he can take without delay to protect his family in case of attack. I know you will want to do no less."[2]

The Berlin Address ended, the camera lights cooled, and suddenly the switchboards of local civil defense offices lit up.[3] Phone lines that had formerly received only an occasional call were now jammed as worried citizens tried to reach an authority who would tell them exactly how they were supposed to protect their homes.[4] For Frank Fields, a forty-two-year-old resident of Jacksonville, Florida, the impact of the president's address was immediate: "I had a sinking realization that building a shelter was going to cost."[5] On living-room couches and across dining-room tables, householders discussed their finances and made swift calculations.[6] Families started to wonder if "every citizen" was truly equal on the home front. The family fallout shelter was about to become one of the "biggest political headaches" of Kennedy's New Frontier.[7]

In 1961, the Kennedy administration made several institutional attempts to solve the problem of nuclear survival, but its introduction of fallout shelter loans was a particularly curious emblem of its bureaucracy and one that shaped everyday life on the nuclear home front. While historians have yet to document the form, function, and social impact of shelter financing, the process mirrored the smaller, subtler, and less visible practices in which men engaged as they set about preparing their homes and loved ones for a nuclear strike. The intent of the program was straightforward: fathers would not have to dig into their own pockets to purchase shelter walls and survival supplies but would have the opportunity to apply for a small personal loan from the Federal Housing Association (FHA). By providing tax breaks and financing options for home improvements, shelter loans offered middle-class homeowners a federally sanctioned economic way to participate in civil defense. Kennedy seized on the idea, believing that such economic incentives would stimulate and nurture a new pioneer class ready and willing to stand up to Soviet aggression. Yet within his administration, there was considerable internal cynicism about the wisdom of embracing a policy that favored middle-class homeowners over other kinds of citizens.

The idea of shelter loans may have been straightforward, but in reality the program was fraught with contradictions. First, shelter loans did little to address longstanding issues of discriminatory lending and prejudicial realty practices that structurally excluded non-white communities from equal access to the suburban housing market. Second, they became tangled in a web of practical and regional obstacles involving building permits, bureaucratic battles with local housing authorities, and construction complications. The shelter-loan program co-opted local financial institutions such as savings-and-loan firms, banks, and citizen trusts into State Department efforts to domesticate nuclear war, thus linking the masculinized rhetoric of do-it-yourself survival to institutional politics that privileged middle-class families who could access private capital. Building a shelter depended, in part, on personal interactions among fathers, local lenders, and housing authorities. Rather than creating a nation of suburban frontiersmen taking survival into their own hands, shelter loans highlighted the inaccessibility of civil defense and the impotency of the many fathers who were unable to provide meaningful protection for their families.[8]

A NATION OF SHELTER BUILDERS

In August 1961, Rex Hydron, a schoolteacher from San Diego, received the first FHA home-shelter loan: "$4,550 for a reinforced concrete shelter, 24 feet wide and 14 feet long, to be built in the front yard and covered with three feet of soil." The moment was the culmination of a protracted process of discussion and formulation over how best to prepare the nation for a potential domestic nuclear catastrophe.⁹ Initially, the Kennedy administration approached civil defense as an "insurance policy" should the nuclear balance of power tip in an "unfavorable direction."¹⁰ However, as the president's advisors became aware of the cost, scope, and difficulties involved in creating a comprehensive program of public shelters, their discussions shifted to the practicality of having the middle class convert parts of their homes into private shelters, despite growing institutional awareness of their futility.

Documents prepared early in the Kennedy presidency reveal why the administration chose to embrace a policy of privatized survival. Even before he was sworn into office, the president-elect was given a detailed brief cataloguing the issues besetting the nation's civil defense effort. Compiled by Herbert Jolovitz, an administrative assistant to Senator Stephen M. Young of Ohio, the brief lambasted the OCDM as an expensive, bureaucratic, bloated agency that had "failed miserably" in its most basic and obvious functions. The report argued that during the previous decade civil defense intellectuals had "offered no realistic solution to the problem" of nuclear survival. Instead, citizens "had been fed psychological pabulum" and "lullabied into complacency with plans bordering on fantasy." "Civil defense today is a myth," the brief concluded, one characterized by concepts and programs that are "completely outdated and inadequate." It was "failing to reach most Americans" and, among those it did reach, was met with "indifference and apathy."¹¹ Yet, as the brief noted, these problems seemed to have little to do with the nature of the policies themselves. Rather, the report blamed the issues plaguing the OCDM on ineffectual management and the impotent actions of Val Peterson and Leo Hoegh. Envisioning the suburban father as the subject and target of civil defense campaigns was still appropriate. All civil defense needed was a change in management style.

Thus, instead of allowing the home-shelter concept to recede into obscurity, Jolovitz advocated a new approach that would emphasize a "vigorous and continuing campaign of education on [nuclear] self-protection" using all "media of communication at our command—TV, radio, newspapers, magazines, and schools." An awareness campaign should be "instituted immediately."[12] While the "scientific reality" of a domestic nuclear strike did lead to "unpleasant answers," dread could be moderated by vigorous leadership, active fact finding, and "moral courage."[13] A nation of shelter builders might embody the burgeoning aspirations of a new active presidential style. If survival were to be a viable insurance choice, then it needed to remain firmly grounded in social mobility, homeownership, and disposable income, which at the time not everyone had access to. Civil defense might be an expensive, problematic, mismanaged mess, but it was still a necessity in the nuclear age.

Remarkably, Jolovitz's report is rarely mentioned in historical accounts of Kennedy's civil defense policy.[14] Yet his brief, filled with pithy sentences, cynical interpretations, idealistic goals, and bullet-point summaries of vast and complex issues, offers insight into how the president's New Frontier operated as the administration began to debate the theories and procedures of nuclear survival. It suggests that if civil defense were to be taken seriously, nuclear crisis planning needed to be brought directly into the Oval Office. Jolovitz proffered no new information about the logistical problems of sheltering the American people, nor was he deeply concerned about the social questions that the shelter-loan program would soon inspire. However, he did offer an initial solution to fostering public support for civil defense (and, by extension, a policy of nuclear deterrence): namely, collating as much information as possible about the current level of nuclear threat and OCDM's policies before changing the way in which civil defense information was disseminated.

Between January and May 1961, the administration intensified its interest in a civil defense program that would offer some form of immediate financial encouragement to economically prosperous middle-class homeowners. As a federal policy, shelter loans reflected two strands of political culture: fiscal liberalism at home and masculine toughness abroad. Support for the program was filtered through a prescriptive set of gendered assumptions that tied the economic strength of the middle class to families' individual agency when facing total devastation. Supporting families through financial incentives was seen as a "pragmatic solution" to the impossible question of how to survive a nuclear war. It married the belief of "vital center liberalism" in limited state intervention to a decade's worth of civil defense literature that told families they had the means to protect themselves.[15] Limited economic state invention had its supporters in the OCDM, especially from the agency's newly elected director, Franklin B. Ellis, who thought that allowing local civil defense officials to "target protection towards the home owning public" (depicted in all shelter construction manuals as white, suburban, and middle class) might bind communities together under the common banner of hometown survival.[16] How households would access this support remained vague and undefined.

Over the next few months the concept of shelter loans faced growing resistance from vocal critics both inside and outside the White House. To those who viewed civil defense communities as almost exclusively suburban, supporters made the case that, while more "inclusive solutions were sought," it made sense that "those sections of society who had the social and economic mobility to access shelters should be encouraged to do so."[17] To shift the mood of these select few from apathy to engagement, the New Frontier manufactured a narrative of survival suggesting that the perceived toughness of families at home had strategic value abroad. Rather than emphasizing a democratic vision of collective survival, policymakers focused on the willingness and ability of suburban fathers to pay, with limited federal support, for their families' safety.

In 1961, the idea of introducing small-scale loans or tax breaks for potential shelter builders was not entirely new. Throughout the 1950s, planners working for the FCDA and the OCDM (soon to be reformed into the Office of Civil Defense [OCD]) were acutely aware that embracing a system of private home survival risked stirring up public questions about the accessibility of civil defense, particularly in terms of race and class, that officials were ill-equipped to answer. Not only would they alert the public to "inconvenient truths about housing inequality," they would also give local financial institutions a level of autonomy over a community's nuclear preparedness.[18] Clearly, if the politics of civil defense became too reliant on suburban action, then sharp divisions might be created around the tricky questions of who had the means to access shelters and whose loan applications were approved or rejected. "This is a balancing act," wrote William Heimlich, the director of the OCD's department of civic affairs. "[M]anaging expectations is key. Promoting equal access is key." He continued: "Families need to construct shelters, but the messaging over these trusts must be carefully managed."[19]

For more than a decade, civil defense planners had tried to minimize the glaring inequalities of a home-shelter system and the implicit whiteness that characterized much of their public literature. By 1960, however, an increasingly cynical view had taken hold, one arguing that those in charge of national survival were faced with a no-win scenario. According to Ralph Lapp, the paradox was the terrifying fact that "you can't in this age afford security for everyone."[20] Yet the question of how to manage public anxieties, especially following an election campaign run on the rhetoric of missile gaps, required something more substantial than slogans and cynicism. A solution, however imperfect, was needed.

Since the publication of Irving Janis's *Air War and Emotional Stress* in 1951, policymakers had been toying with the idea of introducing a small government subsidy, a federal income-tax credit of $25 per household, and financial incentives to private contractors to help "equalize the opportunities" in civil defense and encourage fathers to build shelters. While the system itself was still prefaced on structural access to private property, Janis argued that financial investment in civil defense would give families a sense of reassurance and agency: "the feeling that 'I am really able to do something about it.'"[21] His suggestions, while often cited internally, were never implemented, partly because FCDA and OCDM officials knew that they might tie the success or failure of national survival to the whims of local lenders and the politics of the housing market.

Private finance was a concern, but even more important was the fact that by the time Kennedy took office, 62 million Americans—mostly white, working-class families and non-white communities—still did not own their own houses. Among those Americans who did own property, only 54 percent had a basement unit that might be adapted to fit OCDM shelter specifications.[22] But if the government was rejecting community shelters due to their astronomical costs and shelving urban evacuation plans due to reductions in advance-warning time, then policymakers had no choice but to deal with the political optics of individual survival and to make the social dynamics of the suburbs even more pronounced than they had been.

In the early months of 1961, as Jolovitz's brief was circulating among the administration's inner circle, Kennedy was not overly concerned about the inequalities of a private shelter-loan regime. Between January and June, he found himself inundated with memoranda from civil defense officials and pro-shelter governors, Nelson Rockefeller foremost among them, who were seeking executive action on the matter.[23] Concerned about meeting the expectations of his own rhetoric and fearing the political and personal implications of a "Civil Defense Gap" in the 1964 election that might "showcase weakness inconsistent with his general stance," he turned to his national security advisor, McGeorge Bundy, a political scientist and a former Harvard dean. Bundy had been a protégé of Henry L. Stimson, an elder statesman of U.S. foreign policy who had served as secretary of the War Department (1940–45). In theory, Bundy was well suited for the task of reconsidering how private and public shelters might serve the New Frontier diplomatically and domestically.[24] He was a vocal critic of atmospheric testing and vehemently opposed nuclear brinkmanship, and he offered a skeptical and at times indifferent voice on matters of civil defense. As the historian Andrew Preston has argued, he viewed the entire question of mutually assured destruction with something close to revulsion. For Bundy, "nuclear weapons were simply too terrible to use or even contemplate used except as a theoretical abstraction for the most extreme."[25] Nevertheless, despite his disdain for hawkish approaches to nuclear diplomacy, he was troubled by the question of what to do if the bomb dropped: who would get to live and die?

Since 1958, the notion of "every home a fortress" had been framed as an opportunity for men to become better fathers while defending the "moral aspects," "spiritual freedom," and "toughness" of the domestic front through the performance of patriarchal leadership at home.[26] Eisenhower's policymakers had believed that home shelters, if marketed to the public correctly, could avoid the negative implications of turning the nation into a garrison state while alleviating public anxieties about nuclear protection. Yet questions remained regarding the government's role in turning citizens into shelter builders. In the waning years of his presidency, Eisenhower was reluctant to endorse a loan program for private shelter construction. Bundy saw wisdom in that stance. He, too, was uneasy about the ideological implications of civil defense and the logistics of a system that left so much responsibility to the whims of the housing market. When asked if home shelters truly fitted into a heroic narrative of civic service and sacrifice in pursuit of national survival, he argued that civil defense was limited as both a "tool of crisis management" and a way to "demonstrate [national] will or superiority." Still, Bundy saw it as a prudent, if imperfect, insurance policy for a few citizens, a "way of mitigating a possible disaster, not a way of avoiding it or making it acceptable." "If protection was to be offered," he reasoned, "then it might as well be provided to private residences while we fix the other problems."[27] Arguing that a scaled-down solution was better than nothing, he managed to earmark $2 million to be used as federal assistance for private shelter loans.

With such internal cynicism, why did Kennedy decide to throw his personal support behind private shelters? Why did civil defense play such a central role in his Berlin Address? Why did the White House endorse *Life*'s fallout shelter issue? And why did the president advocate the introduction of private loans to shelter builders? It is easy to dismiss these decisions as the political mistakes of an inexperienced first-term president. But in fact, the policy vision of shelter fatherhood took central stage because policymakers decided to ignore the warnings of past planners and place the local power and political fortunes of civil defense into the hands of suburban homeowners and their faith in private capital.

During a 1964 interview, Kennedy's speechwriter Theodore Sorensen was asked if, "given the history of lack of action in this area, . . . was civil defense one of the first things the President did pay some attention to?" Sorensen replied that "for the President shelters were a 'matter of moral conscience and moral responsibility.'"[28] As Robert Dean has argued, the political world inhabited by Kennedy and his imperial brotherhood was defined by the pursuit of masculine self-affirmation at home as the solution to geopolitical conflict. Indeed, when it came to the question of nuclear war, the "moral responsibility" of a president to protect his nation clearly affected Kennedy personally. Yet in practice the language of "moral consciousness and moral responsibility" was both limited and exclusionary. When the president set out to solve the problem of national survival, he did so by normalizing and strengthening the power imbalances and gender dynamics that had long defined private survival.

Within the confines of the New Frontier's inner circle, composed of people who had emphatically stated they were not the cookie pushers of the Eisenhower years, private shelters offered a powerful, if not convincing, cultural narrative of political action and heroic frontiersman. Under Kennedy's watch, shelters became cultural shorthand for a population ready to confront any threat. A nation of shelter builders might, in theory, demonstrate will and nerve and, critically, the agency of a bold new administration ready to face the Soviet Union. The fact that 62 million Americans did not own property did not play as important a factor as it should have for an administration that was looking for bold action. "Civil Defense can never be used as a tool to construct new residence[s]. Congress won't buy it," Bundy noted to Kennedy. "[W]e have to work with what we have."[29] Potentially, the FHA and the Housing and Home Finance Agency (HHFA) might induce local lenders and contractors to invest in their communities' residential shelters without the need for political intervention into the construction of new houses with shelter spaces already built into them.[30] The plan would create very little risk for the president or his reelection chances and would shift the burden of survival from the state onto fathers applying for home improvement loans. For a brief moment, a model of nuclear survival prefaced on the predictions of elite white men who were simplifying and generalizing the suburban experience had reached the center of national strategic thinking. Within this narrow intellectual frame, the narrative of a nation of shelter-building fathers, implicitly white and explicitly middle class, had gained an intellectual and institutional foothold that would prove hard to shift.

A DO-IT-YOURSELF PROJECT OF INTERNATIONAL SIGNIFICANCE

In the spring and summer of 1961, institutional support for shelter loans continued to gain ground, and the way in which the program was put into practice strengthened the masculine hegemony that came to define shelter fatherhood.[31] In April, as the Kennedy administration was reeling from the Bay of Pigs fiasco, Bundy delegated the task of reviewing the latest OCDM proposal to two assistants: Marcus Raskin, an expert in disarmament negotiations and a member of the special staff of the National Security Council; and Carl Kaysen, a Harvard alumnus and an international security specialist.[32] During the months leading up to the Berlin Address, both men were persistent and pragmatic dissenters in discussions of the president's civil defense privatization ambitions, frequently advising him to avoid making any direct announcement about a program that they saw as a "waste of money" and "socially abhorrent" with the potential for "dire political consequences."[33]

Initially, Kaysen, who had published a 1954 article on civil defense in *World Politics*, was receptive to the idea of shelters. However, after combing through more than a decade's worth of civil defense literature, he grew progressively more skeptical. He was concerned about the numerous "troublesome social questions" attached to the OCDM's current civil defense proposals limiting the accessibility of survival to the suburbs.[34] Raskin, in contrast, had been opposed to civil defense from the start, criticizing Jolovitz's suggestions for encouraging a major propaganda effort that would be "authoritarian" in style and "questionable in substance."³⁵ "At worst," he wrote in a memo to Bundy, civil defense "will change our society and reinforce misperception and distort awareness of reality more than our senses are distorted already."³⁶ Raskin worried that notions of social reform, nondiscrimination, and inclusion were not being discussed in any depth. He questioned the claim that shelter loans would make survival available to "all" and pointed out the risks of leaving the program's day-to-day operations to local authorities and the conservative lending practices of the HHFA.³⁷ Together, Raskin and Kaysen composed a carefully written report for Bundy, which they ironically titled "A Modest Proposal for Civil Defense."³⁸ Unlike many government reports, it is a striking read. While it is intensely critical of civil defense, it also does its best to offer some form of workable solution as a federal duty to protect the population.³⁹ Nonetheless, it firmly concluded that Kennedy "should not approve any civil defense plans" in the foreseeable future.⁴⁰

Although the report was prophetic, its impact on policy was decidedly limited. In early May, with a congressional meeting on the horizon, Bundy, Raskin, and Kaysen met with Sorensen and his deputy, Elmer Staats, from the Budget Bureau to share their findings. During the session Bundy remained quiet as Raskin and Kaysen offered a flurry of "dissenting points" about the proposed executive plan for private and public civil defense. Nonetheless, Sorensen informed them that "the President has made up his mind about civil defense": he would make a direct appeal to Congress to appropriate more funds for shelters in public spaces and federal buildings and for individual loans for shelter builders. Raskin's response was blunt: "[I]t would be a political disaster." Sorensen's reply was equally direct: "[W]e *have* to do it. You have to prepare a program." At this point Bundy, who had shown up at the meeting in shorts and with a racket, said, "I have to go play tennis," and left.⁴¹

During this meeting, Raskin had said that private shelter construction ran the risk of lulling the middle class into a false sense of security.⁴² Why did Kennedy decide to turn his back on the logic of Raskin and Kaysen to embrace a policy that, in hindsight, seems to have inevitably reinforced the impossibility of survival? The historian Garry Wills offers one plausible suggestion—namely, that to understand the New Frontier and the decisions that were made during this era, we must recognize that the high rhetorical gestures of the early 1960s were fundamentally about style, not substance.[43] By applying Wills's observations to the issue of civil defense, we can see that the image of willing and active suburban fathers rushing out to build and buy shelters fit a specific stylistic mode of heroic leadership. For Kennedy and his elite advisors, social problems were "isolatable, to be removed from prior context and given a neat technical solution."[44] A key dynamic of the loan program's political symbolism was the way in which it allowed policymakers to reform and contain the unstable, contradictory, and deeply problematic social dynamics of nuclear warfare into a unified national discourse that could be presented at multiple levels: at home, in the workplace, and in local communities. Middle-class affluence, domestic unity, and heteronormativity allowed policymakers to make nuclear war seem familiar and thus solvable. For an administration caught between crises in Cuba and Berlin, the solution suggested by Kaysen and Raskin—inaction—was deemed unviable. It seemed that constructing a politically palatable symbol that both engaged the public and projected American toughness abroad was a task better suited to speechwriters than to scientists.

Raskin's critical study, *Essays of a Citizen: From National Security State to Democracy* (1991), offers considerable insight into how the masculinized discourse of civil defense gathered support. Central to the "civil defense madness" that swept through the New Frontier was the administration's willingness to accept a concept advanced by the Stanford Institute of Research in 1953: that if a "will-stiffening" could be performed on the suburban class, American policymakers could be that much tougher at the bargaining table.[45] Raskin expands on this concept of will-stiffening, framing civil defense as an ideologically motivated program designed to "create a new martial spirit in the country and the bureaucracy." Once hardened, the suburban family would present an image of the United States that could be "advertised abroad."[46] A nation of active suburban shelter builders, in their fully equipped shelters, had the potential to be a powerful diplomatic tool, demonstrating national readiness. For Raskin, the dangers of this approach were all too apparent. In a memo to Bundy he warned that the concept of civil defense was being converted "to something much more broad, comprehensive and frantic."[47] By normalizing shelter construction as the job of private households, civil defense risked becoming one of the most dangerous social myths of the age.[48]

Nevertheless, on May 25, 1961, Kennedy took a major step in reinforcing the inequality of civil defense: he informed Congress that he was assigning responsibility for the program to the secretary of defense. He opened his statement by declaring that "one major element of the national security program which this nation has never squarely faced up to is civil defense. . . . [T]he problem arises not from present trends but [from] national inaction in which most of us have participated."[49] He overlooked the fact that for more than a decade civil defense planners had been routinely abandoning urban areas, discriminating against non-white communities, ignoring residential renters, and paying scant attention to those who did not fit into a heteronormative vision of family life. Instead, he conflated *national* with *suburban citizen*, clearly linking the inaction of a property-owning class with the failure of the nation as a whole.

The president then shifted his focus onto the failures of the middle-class public, calling out their "apathy, indifference and skepticism" while also noting that "many civil defense plans have been so-far reaching and unrealistic that they have not gained essential support." He amplified the limitations of civil defense, something that Eisenhower had never been bold enough to state publicly: "[T]he administration has been looking hard at exactly what civil defense can and cannot do. It cannot be obtained cheaply. . . . [I]t cannot deter a nuclear attack." However, "the history of the 20th century sufficiently reminds us of the possibilities of an irrational attack. . . . Once the validity of the concept is recognized there is no point delaying a nationwide long-range program."[50] In this way, he implicitly laid the new nationwide program at the feet of suburban householders, a segment of whom took up that responsibility with conviction.

One of the most significant aspects of Kennedy's congressional message was its incentive plan: to offer FHA loans, matching grants, and income-tax breaks to suburban homeowners who were willing to construct shelters in their residences. In effect, the plan privatized survival. Framing shelter construction as a middle-class civic duty, the president declared that "no insurance is cost free; and every citizen must decide for themselves whether this form of survival insurance justifies the expenditure of effort, time and money. . . . For myself I am convinced it does."[51] Although the introduction of FHA loans would not be formalized for another few months, Kennedy's instructions were clear: those who had the means should get ready to build shelters.

FINANCING FAMILY SURVIVAL

The FHA proposed that fathers who wanted to apply for shelter financing might do so in one of three ways. First, for ambitious builders who were planning "comprehensive rehabilitation" of their existing homes, sections 203(k) and 200(h) offered a path toward family survival. Projects qualifying for these sections had to show evidence of being "substantial home improvement task[s]"—for instance, dilapidated homes that needed foundation work or extensive remodeling.[52] Homeowners who received funding under these sections had to provide blueprints of the planned work before construction and agree to FHA inspection after completion. Second, property owners could "refinanc[e] their home through existing FHA mortgages" to pay for shelters. Third, fathers could apply for a property improvement loan under the provisions of Title 1, which could be applied to either new or existing private residences. Under these provisions, domestic fallout shelters fell into the category of "home improvement" and could be framed as "dual-purpose rooms" built along with a new laundry space or a family den.[53]

With this range of options at their disposal, homeowners gradually began applying for loans, and the number of FHA-approved shelters reached a high of 869 in November 1961.[54] Yet the language framing these loan offers reveals much about the faltering and often exclusionary ways in which they affected communities across the United States. For example, in theory, Title 1 loans democratized civil defense: they offered applicants up to $3,500 with no down payment, and they could be repaid in monthly installments for three to five years at an interest rate of 6 percent. Title 1's terms and conditions note that, in all but "'special cases,' . . . collateral, co-signers and prior FHA approval are not deemed necessary." But what constituted a "special case"? That was left vague, thus giving local lenders incredible levels of discretion in deciding who was and was not an "unreliable borrower."[55] The situation was soon to have visible social consequences.

Insuring home-shelter loans under Title I provided a level of protection for local lenders who were working with civil defense officials. With the incentive of matching federal funding, banks could lower interest rates for moderate-income households, and civil defense officials could reach their target group with new levels of efficiency. Protection of capital was also enshrined in the FHA's stipulation that all "shelter construction would have to meet Department of Defense specifications."[56] In practice, as we will see, quality control was tricky, to say the least. However, in the meantime, local lenders worked to reinforce the visual style, social values, gender divisions, and inequality that had been defining fallout shelter construction guides and manuals for the past decade. The difference was that worried residents could now open the pages of their local papers and see civil defense being advertised by their local bank. "Protection made easy with an M & S Fallout Shelter Loan," advertised the Merchants and Saving Bank of Janesville, Wisconsin. "Now you can add a fallout shelter to your loan at minimal cost! There's no time to lose!" announced Citizen Trust, a savings and loans bank in Albuquerque, New Mexico. "If you are planning to build a fallout shelter, we'll loan you the money. You just need to have an account here," declared the

First Federal Savings Bank of Syracuse, New York. "Don't be half safe. Build a shelter and invest in your family's future!" counseled Savings Bank, a local savings firm in Miami, Florida.[57]

Many regional papers featured local-interest stories about fathers who had received shelter loans and were thus becoming pioneers of protection. In Michigan, the *Herald Press* revealed that "two local heroes" from Benton, John A. Kollath and Bob Phillips, had received loans and building permits for their shelters. The paper detailed the costs of the shelters ($400 and $200, respectively) and published the story alongside an advertisement for "Homes for Americans" and a half-page editorial about FHA shelter-loan applications.[58] The coverage clearly linked Kennedy's rhetoric with local finance and affordable survival, mapping out how local readers might join the ranks of these suburban frontiersmen. The *Herald Press* was not alone; similar stories appeared in the *Baytown Sun* in Texas, the *Sarasota News* in Florida, the *Nashua Telegram* in New Hampshire, the *Beckley Post Herald* in West Virginia, and in many other papers around the country.[59] "Cheer up!" the *Las Vegas Daily* told readers in October 1961. "There's no need to put off building that shelter until 'tomorrow.' We live in an age of buying. Just be sure to check the people you deal with are reliable. Not sure? Ask your local OCD officials for advice."[60]

While most local papers framed shelter construction as a suburbanite task, some emphasized that these enterprising fathers were also being good neighbors. Applying for loans was seen as a sign of a householder's community spirit. Take, for example, the story of Robert Faust, a resident of Churchview Avenue in Baldwin, Pennsylvania, near Pittsburgh, who decided to buy a shelter not just for the five members of his family but for all of the twenty residents living on his street. "I pray," he told reporters, "that we'll never have to use it. But the way I see it . . . this is the best kind of life insurance a man can buy."[61]

Reportedly, Ray Parks, an FHA builder inspector, asked Faust to explain why "this shelter is going to be big enough for 20 people."

Faust replied, "I figured it could hold about 25, maybe a few more if we squeeze them in."

"But why so many," Parks persisted. "[T]his is supposed to be a family shelter."

Faust shrugged and said, "[T]hat depends on the way you look at things. My wife, Alberta and I like our neighbors." His community generosity in the face of privatization highlights the reality of civil defense. "It was a luxury out of our reach," Faust's neighbor Mrs. Yeo told reporters. Another neighbor, Mrs. Boyle, the mother of "two boys and a girl ranging in the ages from 2 to 6," called it a "wonderful thing for him to do." For Faust, sharing his fallout shelter was the same as "lending his lawnmower to the man next door."[62]

Media stories depicted shelter builders almost exclusively as white men, yet this did not mean that non-white communities were invisible or uninvolved. A few accounts in the OCDM's public letters and in the black press detail how people of color were also attempting to participate in the shelter-loan system. Again, these anecdotes were often framed as local human-interest stories. For instance, articles in the *Chicago Defender* featured African American fathers who were attempting to finance do-it-yourself shelters—among them James Ditto, who "did not regret his loan being turned away . . . after hearing about the struggle to build them." The *Pittsburgh Courier* tells a similar story about a war veteran named William Bell, who had "a lucky escape from the shelter madness."[63]

As civil defense intertwined with the social politics of local housing authorities, it became increasingly clear that survival strategies were primarily aimed at white suburbanites who could easily access financing. While FHA records hide many of these complex exclusionary practices, the black press recognized what was happening. Responding to the growing civil defense hysteria, *Jet* and *Ebony* ran articles about home shelters, describing them as a "white craze" that demonstrated the irrationality and neuroses of white citizens.[64] The voices of African Americans were prominent in debates regarding the integration of community shelters, and many also mentioned private shelters as white middle-class spaces. OCDM records do contain a few letters from African American families (often filtered through local religious outlets that were working with the OCDM), and, like the newspaper articles, the writers often commented on their good fortune in escaping a poor investment in shelters.[65] More often than discussing private shelters, however, these letters raised questions about the integration of public shelter spaces.[66] David Lock, a New York father of two and a Korean War veteran, did mention private shelters in his letter, noting that "getting a contractor to build one is the first issue, getting credit towards it is the second." Another correspondent, Percy Hamner, wrote that "after the trouble it took getting this house a fallout shelter is the last thing on my mind."[67] Lawrence Hank was even more direct; he complained that Kennedy's Berlin Address had "worried the kids ... [but] the battle and expense doesn't seem worth the effort. One bomb drops and we are all goners anyway."[68] Such comments do not mean that African American communities were disengaged from the politics of the nuclear state; as Vincent Intondi argues, this was far from true. Nevertheless, when it comes to the specific act of domestic shelter construction, the inherent whiteness of the cultural narrative is striking.[69]

The political vernacular of civil defense may have normalized the idea that middle-class fathers should be applying for shelter loans, but this did not mean that receiving financing was straightforward. The loans had to be approved by both the FHA and the OCDM before they could be officially processed. As I have mentioned, blueprints for large projects had to be drawn up, often by a professional contractor, and then approved by local civil defense officials to make sure they met specific guidelines. Homeowners then took these blueprints to a local lender, who had to approve the loan option and set the interest rate. After the shelter was constructed, a local civil defense official, acting on behalf of the Department of Defense and the FHA, visited the site to check that all regulations had been followed before authorizing a "certificate of eligibility."[70] Typically, homeowners repaid their shelter loans over the course of the next three years, remitting money directly to their local lender, who was covered by FHA insurance if the payments faltered.

In short, fathers who wanted to become pioneers of protection faced a slow, complex process composed of numerous steps, any one of which could affect the status of the application or require additional work. Moreover, regional variants added many more hurdles. For instance, if a homeowner applied for a home improvement loan, he still needed to obtain a local building permit, frequently at extra cost, before starting construction. In Florida, as soon as "[you] dig 4–5 feet you gunna hit water," so local housing authorities often needed to approve expansive above-ground construction sites that required additional wall cladding, typically steel, to meet OCD specifications.[71] By October 1961, no local shelter loan had been approved in Portland, Oregon, because county building codes dictated that all structures needed to have windows.[72] Fathers' letters to the OCDM are filled with frustration about the bureaucratic complexities in what they saw as an emergency project. "Hopefully war will wait until your reply," wrote one Chicago resident.[73] "[As] I look at these forms," wrote James Scott of Las Vegas, "coldness goes through my military mind."[74] In practice, the regulation of the marketplace was far from formalized, and both fathers and businesses frequently acted outside the federal guidelines. Yet the fact remains that building a shelter was extremely difficult. Rather than inspiring a nation of domestic pioneers, loans created a barrier between the political ideal of civil defense and the social practice of do-it-yourself survival. Art Carlson claimed that he and his son spent just a few weekends turning their home into a fortress, but for most citizens the process required a surprisingly in-depth knowledge of architectural planning and considerable patience with local authorities and bureaucracy.

A successful loan application, especially during the height of the shelter craze, often took months to process. And even when an application was eventually approved, fathers sometimes lost their motivation. The various hiccups in the loan process might lead to them to the notion that building a shelter would be a mistake, and this connection between citizenry and regret became another major signifier of the shelter father. As retired brigadier general Robert L. Scott, Jr., wrote in an open letter,

> [I]t is folly for something so foolish to be apparently encouraged by our government—by FHA approval. . . . Last Sunday . . . I was able to read what was said by a writer who calls himself a "family financial counselor." He states that residents of Valley Sun are now eligible for

financing under FHA. Yes sir. A family can obtain protection with nothing down and have many years to pay it off. Where—down under, living like a mole.⁷⁵

Home shelters may have offered insurance for the anxious, but the prospect of applying for a civil defense loan sparked questions as to what sort of society families were investing in. Local papers debated whether financing a shelter was a sound or an irrational decision. An editorial in the *Tucson Daily Citizen* "argue[d] that shelter owners are not moles! The moles are those who deny the need for shelters, crawling blindly in their own ignorance."⁷⁶ But not everyone agreed.

Controversy arose, too, as family shelters became status symbols for the affluent men who built them. In Pennsylvania, the *Morning Call* reported that "landowners are holding subterranean soirees, showing their digs to friends and business associates as proudly as if their survival headquarters were a new baby, or more currently impressive, a new swimming pool."⁷⁷ In New York papers, there were stories about shelter parties in which owners showed off their new spaces to their wealthy friends. One upstate journalist overheard a conversation between a host and his guests: "How do you like it?" the host asked. The reply was a thoughtful pause followed by "[I]t is the end."⁷⁸ On the West Coast, Lucius Beebe, a columnist and food critic for the *San Francisco Chronicle,* was stocking his bomb shelter with champagne and caviar.⁷⁹ In southern California, local manufacturers were offering a shelter that they falsely claimed was "OCD and FHA approved!" One half was a swimming pool, the other half a bunker with a glass window through which to take pictures of the swimmers. Any gullible suburban family "looking to impress" now had a suitable space "if the weather, or the war, gets hot."⁸⁰

While local lenders and businesses embraced the idea of the family shelter, many people were repulsed by the social inequality of the private system of survival. In a letter to the editor in the *Morning Call*, Phyllis Battle wrote, "I don't know what phases of the family shelter business [are] more disturbing—the emotion[al] controversy over whether men will turn into beasts to protect the entrance or this . . . evident fact that such a desperately basic life and death commodity should be treated by some members of modern society as a symbol of ego or affluence." She asked readers, "Which type of animal do you prefer, the primitive kind which claws, or the over-civilized kind that cloys?"[81]

Amid these grassroots tensions, the international stage was being set for a confrontation in Vienna with Soviet Premier Nikita Khrushchev.[82] The Vienna summit, which took place in June 1961, was a pivotal moment in the evolution of Kennedy's civil defense stance because it shook the New Frontiersmen's notions of their masculine character.[83] At the summit, Kennedy was hoping to "ease" Soviet-U.S. relations by way of a series of "responsible and reasonable" policy solutions designed to "respect Soviet interests." Yet over the course of the three days the leaders spent in Vienna, Khrushchev physically dominated and rhetorically outmaneuvered the president on almost every occasion, even openly laughing at this "young man who had a great deal to learn and little to offer." When Kennedy tried to press his agenda about western access to Berlin, Khrushchev chastised him and then erupted into a series of long and often rambling diatribes about the theoretical underpinning of the Communist system.[84] In one of those polemics, the premier, who was well aware of the impact he was having, described Berlin as the "testicles of the West," and said, "[E]very time I want the West to scream, I squeeze."[85]

Kennedy left Vienna, in his own words, "upset," describing his performance as weak and saying that he had been "unprepared for the brutality of Khrushchev's presentation."[86] Trying to present himself as flexible had made him look and feel vulnerable. Even during lunchtime exchanges, Khrushchev was dogging Kennedy about nuclear weapons, boasting that "the Soviet Union had nuclear-armed submarines, short-range, medium-range and intercontinental missiles in production."[87] The New Frontiersmen shared their leader's sense of vulnerability. One of his advisors, Eugene Rostow, described Vienna as a "testing of our nerve."[88] Another, Dean Acheson, believed that the "result" of the summit was "an appearance of weakness," and he called it a "failure."[89]

The New Frontier saw Vienna as a loss, and that attitude is crucial to understanding the climate in which the Berlin Address was written.[90]

Now the administration's internal discussions of civil defense took on a frantic new urgency. According to the historian Fred Kaplan, "as Kennedy grew more concerned with Berlin, he became increasingly enthusiastic about civil defense."[91] More New Frontiersmen joined Bundy, Raskin, Kaysen, and Sorensen in debates about the need to offer the public robust options. Among them was the president's brother and attorney general, Robert Kennedy, who was "an extreme enthusiast for civil defense." Robert Kennedy urged Kaysen and Raskin to outline a new policy that would mobilize suburbanites into "join[ing] a citizens' corps that would practice evacuation-and-shelter drills once a week."[92] Robert Kennedy's call to militarize the suburbs was echoed by the hardliners Paul H. Nitze, Foy Koler, and Walt Rostow, who advocated a "rapid increase in civil defense capabilities."[93] Trapped in a dilemma over Berlin, Kennedy wrote to Secretary of Defense Robert McNamara, who had by now taken direct personal control of the nation's civil defense program: "I am concerned that we move as quickly as possible on Civil Defense."[94]

During discussions, Acheson aggressively argued that the United States respond to Soviet actions in Berlin with both fever and force. The historian Lawrence Freedman writes that the advisor pressed Kennedy to "boost American credibility," advocating a tough military stance to show that American's suburban residents were "ready and willing to risk nuclear war." But Acheson's suggestions worried the president.[95] In search of a moderate stance that would avoid direct threats to Soviet national security while demonstrating that the United States took its commitments to West Berlin seriously, he sought the advice of less bellicose advisors such as Dean Rusk and McNamara. In a memo, Arthur Schlesinger, Jr., advised Kennedy to carefully consider his response to the Berlin crisis—to detach nuclear diplomacy from the question of "are you chicken or not?" while avoiding an appearance of being "soft, idealistic, mushy etc." on matters of national safety.[96] Kennedy took Schlesinger's advice and set out to broadcast a message to the nation that would tread a fine line between diplomatic efforts and domestic militarization.

The Berlin Address offered a composite picture of the internal policy discussions that had shaped civil defense for more than a decade even as it emphasized that preparing suburban families for nuclear war was normal and desirable. It was written by Sorensen, whose rhetorical skills and influence were significant.[97] In the address, he dovetailed the shelter construction narrative with the president's personal beliefs while evoking the sense of historic purpose that had characterized the 1960 campaign election campaign.[98] Sorensen wanted to construct a speech that "underlined our commitment to the people in Berlin" and demonstrated that the domestic front had the "required endurance."[99] To do this without causing mass panic required care, and Bundy advised, "[T]his speech should be full of information, and should leave Americans with the feeling they know what to do and why they need to do it."[100] In Bundy's view, Kennedy should maintain a "cool tone" that indicated "a willingness to explain lots of things. . . . [T]he President will in a quite literal sense speak softly."[101] The role of civil defense and white paternalistic duty would be presented as an "insurance policy" for not just America but the world. The domestication of the message would have the added advantage of combating what *Newsweek* had called the "biggest obstacle to civil defense": the "apathy, complacence, and contempt" of the middle class.[102]

The Berlin Address presented a specific vision of the nation's masculine character by way of the fallout shelter father. During the thirty-minute speech, 25 million Americans heard that Kennedy had requested and received $207 million in additional civil defense funds to identify and stock potential shelter sites, a figure that amounted to 60 percent of the total funding that civil defense had received in the previous decade.[103] This combined amount of federal funding, legislative support, and executive commitment was more than any other president would ever enjoy. Although Democratic senators Stephen Young, Wayne Morse, and Ernest Gruening blasted the civil defense agency as a "bunch of hacks" who talked "vaguely about survival, planned alerts to annoy their neighbors, and distributed countless reams of literature," Kennedy had successfully brought the discussion of civil defense into the heart of Washington politics.[104] As the *Washington Post* noted, "the lean years are over: Now civil defense is the success story of D.C."[105] But these halcyon days were short lived. Almost as soon as the speech ended, agency phones began to ring, with families on the other end of the line, begging to know what they could do to protect themselves.

THE RESTYLING OF CIVIL DEFENSE

After the Berlin Address, politicians and families found themselves grappling with the limitations of shelter fatherhood. It had been simple enough to create a political rhetoric of do-it-yourself survival, but translating a model of paternal action and self-determination into concrete solutions for everyday families was another task entirely. While FHA loans gave fathers an economic pathway, financing options alone could never solve the question of nuclear survival. So shortly after the speech, the Kennedy administration pledged that, within the next few months, it would distribute a free booklet to every household: a new definitive civil defense pamphlet provisionally titled *Fallout Protection and You: What You Can Do About a Nuclear Attack* (1961). Conceived as a companion piece to the rollout of FHA loans, the booklet would have a print run of more than 60 million copies; as Raskin waspishly noted in a memo to Bundy, it would be "the most circulated piece of literature in Man's history since the Bible."[106]

Fallout Protection and You was in production between July and December 1961. In this same period families were applying for their first FHA shelter loans, and the administration's internal shelter debate was evolving into something more than a protracted theoretical discussion about the merits of patriarchal civic duty, liberalized economics, tax breaks, and financial incentives. Raskin, Bundy, Schlesinger, and the office of the president were engaged in an exhausting public relations task that required an active partnership with pro–civil defense sections of the American press. The goal was to facilitate a new domestic education program for civil defense. In

July, Bundy, aware that Kennedy was keen to delegate oversight of civil defense to the Department of Defense, asked Raskin and Kaysen to find a "point of contact" in the Pentagon.[107] Raskin went looking for someone who "shared his opinion" about the problematic nature of shelter loans and settled on Adam Yarmolinsky, a special assistant to McNamara, as a potential ally. To Raskin's surprise, however, Yarmolinsky embraced the FHA plans and treated civil defense as a serious proposition that deserved his full attention. As summer advanced and the nation's bomb-shelter craze took hold, he emerged as the spokesman of national readiness. He made public appearances and answered press questions. To show his commitment to the cause, he even constructed his own do-it-yourself shelter.[108] Yarmolinsky had once served as a law clerk for Supreme Court Justice Stanley F. Reed, and he was now known as one of the Department of Defense's whiz kids, recruited during the New Frontier's early talent drives. He was acutely aware that the administration needed a party line to support FHA loans for civil defense.[109]

By late July, McNamara had appointed Yarmolinsky to assistant for civil defense and charged Steuart L. Pittman with coordinating state and local civil defense efforts.[110] Yarmolinsky spent the next six months trying to find a middle ground on civil defense—somewhere, he cynically noted, between "nuclear holocaust and surrender."[111] Between October and December he recruited a team to produce the first draft of *Fallout Protection and You*. In his seminal study of the Kennedy years, *A Thousand Days*, Schlesinger mentions an unnamed Pentagon official—undoubtedly Yarmolinsky—who "reached out to Madison Avenue experts" for help in writing the new public manual.[112] In fact, Yarmolinsky wisely decided to commission the six-member editorial team behind *Life*'s September fallout shelter special edition.

The team was headed by the magazine's managing editor, Edward K. Thompson, who was also Bundy's close personal friend. Thompson was well versed in the message of civil defense, and his memoir, *A Love Affair with "Life" & "Smithsonian"* (1995), details the writing team's internal dynamics and recalls the intellectual climate in which the booklet was produced. He recalled that one of the first ideas pitched by the Pentagon was to open the booklet with an illustration of "a frontier family besieged by Indians in a log cabin. Of the ten family members, five would get scalped because they had no blast shelters, and five would not because they did have a shelter." Thompson felt that this depiction of frontier violence was overkill and worked to take creative control away from the Pentagon and tone down the opening. He also recalled that a section in an early chapter, one detailing how to treat nuclear burns, drew McNamara's ire; the assistant secretary commented in a terse memo, "[K]ill it."[113] The booklet was shaping up to be a disaster, and Raskin, who was in frequent contact with Yarmolinsky, attempted to stop the first draft from being circulated. Writing to Bundy, he asked him to end the project: "I have read the document and feel very strongly that ... [it] should not be sent around.... [T]he effects per se of sending the documents [to the public] are incalculable."[114] Despite Raskin's best efforts, however, in mid-October the first draft was finished and circulated throughout the Pentagon and the White House for comment. In the words of Frank Kaplan, "nearly everyone who saw it, especially outside the Pentagon, was aghast."[115]

In discussions and policy memos, the New Frontiersmen had created a thoughtful metaphor for civic engagement that evoked a heroic narrative of presidential leadership and a politically viable call for domestic masculine commitment to a wider Cold War conflict. But it was not easy to translate the rhetorical ideal of male shelter construction into a printed booklet that outlined citizens' specific duties during and after a nuclear attack. It did not help that the dense, heavily illustrated draft (more than 140 pages long) also incorporated every problematic historical trope that had defined civil defense literature during the past decade.[116] For instance, the log-cabin shelter, frequently ridiculed in the *Bulletin of the Atomic Scientists*, appeared in the form of a father guiding his family into a cabin structure that doubled as a makeshift boat for escape from key coastal zones.[117] The draft also failed to make any reference to shelters in urban spaces: every illustration depicted either office spaces with large shelter structures in the basement or shelters for suburban homes and families. Factories, apartments, and tenant buildings were invisible.

In an attempt to be practical, the *Life* writing team had simplified the narrative of nuclear survival to the point of absurdity—claiming, for instance, that "communities that are well organized and hav[e] planned their decontamination actions will be able to return to normal life conditions" within two weeks. This optimistic two-week schedule appeared in a section titled "Shelter Living Will Be as Healthy as You Make It." Suggesting that shelter living might "strengthen the bonds of the American family," it made no reference to safe levels of radiation dosage, blast radius, or the potential contamination of foodstuffs and glided over what was becoming a growing public concern: the notion of survival as a business. In fact, in a later section, readers would learn that civil defense was good for maintaining the American pioneer spirit of male entrepreneurship: "the anticipation of a new market for home shelter is helpful and in keeping with the free enterprise way of meeting the changing conditions in our lives."[118]

White House staffers began to refer to the booklet as the "Fallout Is Good for You" guide. Fred Dutton, an assistant to the president, wrote in a memo to Bundy that "the feel of the pamphlet, especially the drawings, is not reassuring. I suspect a poor public reaction to this."[119] His response was mild compared to the reactions of other New Frontiersmen. John Kenneth Galbraith, the ambassador to India, criticized the Department of Defense for allowing so many factual errors to appear in the booklet. In a memo to the Pentagon prefaced with "I regard this as a matter of high importance," he declared that it was seemingly designed to "sav[e] Republicans and sacrific[e] Democrats" and called it "absolutely incredible and particularly injudicious." He continued: "There are survival plans for people who have individual houses with basements in which lean-to fallout shelters can be built" but "no design for civilians who live in congested areas, tenements, low cost apartments." Like the shelter-loan program, the pamphlet in its current form "seeks to save the better elements of the population, but in the main writes off those who voted for you."[120]

Schlesinger agreed, stating, "[T]here is particularly nothing in the pamphlet with which workingmen can identify."[121] Raskin took specific aim at the fallout shelter father, noting that the booklet "assumes that the paterfamilias has some objective tool to ascertain what protection he'll need to survive. This is nonsense. This part also gives the impression that the booklet is something to 'study' since it's the key to survival. This is also nonsense."[122] Raskin offered one piece of editing advice: "[O]n page 12 there is a woman who looks like Mrs. Kennedy. We might want to change her so that she looks like Mrs. Rockefeller."[123]

During a 1985 interview, Pittman recalled the "extraordinary number of man hours" that senior officials spent on the pamphlet: "the President, Bundy, Wisner, Kaysen, McNamara—all these kinds of people were crawling all over this piece of paper which was to be a booklet, arguing about whether you should show a boat as a fallout shelter because it might offend poor people that don't have boats."[124] This remarkable anecdote captures the way in which the executive branch found itself grappling with the class dynamics inherent in the privileging of middle-class fathers. In recollections of the debacle, Kaysen noted what he called a "real Kennedyism": "I was going over the pamphlet with him, which he insisted we do word by word. He wanted to be sure of what was said, and this again reflected the Berlin incident . . . the feeling that all of this was terribly sensitive."[125] Sorensen, too, worried about public reaction to the booklet as it "forc[ed] the issue even further out of perspective" and provided "ammunition to SANE and hard-line militarists." He wrote, "Sending it out to every home is justified only as a means of clarifying the confusion and saving lives in case of attack, but this means considerable revision and stripped down text with different pictures."[126]

Finally, the administration decided to redraft the pamphlet and gave the task to Schlesinger, who in November 1961 received a copy of the original draft with the words "Art let your light shine over these pages" written across the top.[127] On November 22 Kaysen told Bundy that, "after consideration, Arthur and I think there is no point in trying to put the [original] papers together. His will be along."[128] Schlesinger's report, "Reflections on Civil Defense," written in December, worked to negotiate the contradiction between the need for civil defense and shelter hysteria. In the document, Schlesinger depersonalized the political discourse of survival, recognizing that the spirit of individual shelter construction had turned ugly, "at war with morality and at war with the sense of community cooperation which will be indispensable in the case of attack. It is an invitation to barbarism."[129] Kaysen supported this point of view, telling Bundy that "the central question in making this decision is whether it is possible to continue to rely mainly on individual action. In the light of the present high level of concern about civil defense domestically I do not think it is possible to do so." His solution? *Fallout Protection and You* would be "made available on request through local civil defense offices. . . . [O]nly those specifically interested in the civil defense problem get the pamphlet."[130] The New Frontiersmen liked this concept of a targeted release. The booklet's print run was reduced to 25 million copies, and copies were placed in regional civil defense offices without any accompanying executive statement or publicity effort. Discussion of shelters disappeared from the front pages of the nation's newspapers. Kennedy's input into civil defense messages was also reduced: the pamphlet now opened with a letter from McNamara.

The content of the booklet had also changed by the time its final version was published in January 1962. It was slim, down to forty-eight pages, with fewer illustrations and no historical images of America's frontier past. The title was shorter: *Fallout Protection: What to Know and Do about Nuclear Attack*. The text made direct reference to shelters in tenant buildings and urban spaces, with an emphasis on community projects and medical training rather than individual financing options. The family shelter did make an appearance, with illustrations of men building bunkers and fortifying homes and women in supporting roles. However, these images did not reinforce the pioneer spirit of male entrepreneurship and self-sufficiency that had dominated the original draft. The revised version advised citizens that "before writing in [to the OCDM] try to answer your own questions with the help of your neighbor." It also advised people who planned to build a shelter to "put a large letter S on the front" of their letters if they required a design catalogue or the letter B for more copies of the booklet.[131]

The Kennedy administration underwent a noticeable learning curve in its understanding of civil defense. Yet that is only half the story. Individuals at both the top and the bottom of the power structure struggled with how to perform the masculine political ideals inherent in shelter construction. The introduction of private shelter loans triggered many of these confusions on the Cold War home front. Certainly, their history confirms the conclusions of the historian Andrew Grossman: that civil defense was a social blueprint for survival that favored the suburbs over the city. But it also reveals the way in which local financial institutions cooperated in the structural exclusion of non-property owners from civil defense. Shelter loans were part of the inequality that lay at the core of the Cold War home front, an era when 62 million Americans were told to rely on finding survival in their community. Civil defense officials told fathers to be willing actors in the nuclear state. Yet the growing backlash against private shelters demonstrates that resistance to a state-directed model of masculinity manifested itself in many different forms.

CHAPTER THREE
Fatherhood in the Target Zone

> You hear thunder. You watch a 700-ton concrete lid blow itself sideways; you say "Oh!"; you see a woman run for the telephone; you see the Titan rising through orange and yellow gases—there's still that wind and that Kansas sun and that grazing cow—and you gawk and rub your eyes—not disbelief, not now, it's belief—and you stand there and listen to the thunder and track the missile as it climbs into that strange smiling crease in the sky, and then, briefly, you ask yourself the simple question: Where on earth is the happy ending?
> —Tim O'Brien, *The Nuclear Age*, 1985

> The average American is willing to concede that a hole in the ground could be his ticket to survival.
> —Frank Cartwight, "Everyone Is Talking About Shelters," *Colorado Gazette*, January 15, 1962

During the Berlin Address President John F. Kennedy offered little in the way of concrete solutions to the dilemmas of nuclear survival. Instead, going against the advice of his civil defense experts he simplified and dramatized the narrative of nuclear survival, actively linking the actions of individuals in the domestic space to the fate of the nation. For Marc Raskin, Berlin had given the public a message that was paramilitary in tone, void of technical details, and offered little more than a "hodgepodge grab-bag series of suggestions and non-sequiturs" that had "little to do with creative problem solving."[1] Yet the public was increasingly urgent for answers.² For Arthur Chase, a Denver father of five, questions of war and survival had never seemed so close to home. In a letter to Kennedy, he wrote:

Dear Mr. President,

I listened to your speech last night and after hearing it have decided to build a fallout shelter. I got a fallout pamphlet showing plans on how to build . . . it.

I called my civil defense co-coordinator, but they could not give me any information that I [could not] already get from the pamphlet. I asked him a lot of questions about his shelter but [he] could not give me any answers. Here are the questions that I wanted to know.

1. Could I use water from my well after an explosion and [for] how long?
2. Could I put my water tank on the outside of the shelter in the ground?
3. Where could I get a filter for the air intake?
4. Could I use a small gas engine to power the fan?
5. Could I get any finance to help build it?

He said for me not to worry about it for he didn't think that I would have any use for it. He sure is a good defense officer to have in charge telling people that. I don't care what he says for I am going to build it anyway for I think I may have to use it. Please advise me where I can get the information that I need. For I want protection for my wife and five children. Just in case.³

Chase's letter is a reminder that shelter fatherhood was as much a personal performance as a politicized model of citizenship. Though he and other fathers had been suddenly spurred to action, the actual work of preparing a family for nuclear war was laborious and tedious. Chase's particular understanding and performance of the task reflected his socioeconomic background, his access to private accommodation, his willingness to accept the premise of civil defense policy, and the fact that he was a father present in the home. Such men had to purchase materials, reinforce walls, and secure ceilings; they had to read, internalize, and implement shelter literature. In other words, they had to perform numerous individual steps, not simply accept or reject a single, overarching, militarized domestic chore. As Laura McEnaney has shown, the doctrine of do-it-yourself survival required citizens to reconstitute themselves into autonomous paramilitary units to present an illusion of unity in the face of overwhelming destruction.[4] This was how policymakers saw the civil defense family, but it was not always how fathers saw their own actions.

Fathers practiced home survival in ways that were intimate, unexpected, and deeply personal. They were never passive actors. Some reached out to their government, seeking aid and assistance; others started building shelters but never finished them; some wrote angry letters to local agencies demanding to know why they had to take survival into their own hands; others made no effort to prepare their families for nuclear war. These varying reactions allow us to see beyond the political stereotypes of the civil defense family and consider how ordinary citizens came to terms with the meanings and manifestations of safety and national security in their private lives.

Civil defense is best understood as the unfinished home project of the Cold War, often started or considered but never completed. These half-built shelters mark the difficulties fathers found in performing the masculine ethos of home survival. In the archives, we rarely encounter tales of men who easily performed the idealized, state-sanctioned model of shelter fatherhood. Instead, we read of burst water pipes and collapsed shelter ceilings, pleas for financial aid, applications for building permits, questions about practical safety, and domestic disputes. These stories not only give us greater insight into the local and regional worlds of civil defense but also personalize the microhistories of the nuclear age.[5]

In her study of atmospheric testing, Sarah Alisabeth Fox emphasizes that the nuclear arms race is a story of many perspectives."[6] Each version has been shaped by where the storyteller decides to begin: perhaps in the world of nuclear strategists and the dossiers of physicists as they made calculations in secretive laboratories, perhaps with the oral testimonies of people who watched images of mushroom clouds erupt on television and wondered exactly how the world was changing around them. Fox's work demonstrates how important it is to study the local networks of state and non-state actors that came to define the nuclear everyday.[7]

By considering civil defense as a domestic performance, we start to see shelter fatherhood as a local phenomenon that radiated from the home and affected all aspects of life. For instance, at the time of the Berlin Address, Colorado was on the frontline of national security. As the home of the North American Aerospace Defense Command (NORAD), the nation's first line of defense against a sudden nuclear strike, it was the nerve center of homeland security. Expanding military installations meant that the region would likely be a first-strike target zone in the event of war.[8] In other words, if the Cold War turned hot, the families in Colorado would feel it first, and the stories they told showed that they recognized their proximity to destruction. Did rural and urban fathers react differently to the prospect of nuclear survival? How did the location of military complexes affect fathers' perceptions of vulnerability? A study of Colorado shows us that, regardless of how similar or different local experiences were, fathers struggled to balance the practical experience of fallout shelter construction with Washington's politicized Cold War rhetoric of survival.

IN THE SHADOW OF NORAD: MILITARY LIFE AND SUBURBAN DEVELOPMENT

Colorado has long been versed in the rhetoric of do-it-yourself survival, and the violent reality of the nuclear age was readily stitched onto the social fabric of life in the American West.[9] According to the urban theorist Edward Soja, "life stories have a geography too, they have milieu, immediate locales, provocative emplacements with affective thought and action."[10] To fathers in Colorado, the bomb brought not only thoughts of destruction but also thousands of jobs and millions of dollars of federal investment into the region; it changed the built environment and turned small towns into thriving communities. Such growth meant more than new housing developments; it was, for many fathers, the foundation of work and family life.

Low humidity, uranium deposits, and easy access to railroads made Colorado the heartland of the nuclear age, and the military-industrial complex transformed the fortunes of families in the region.[11] This change began in 1942, when the government built the Rocky Mountain Arsenal, a center for the construction of chemical weapons. In 1952, the Rocky Flats Nuclear Weapons Factory opened its doors and went on to produce more than 70,000 plutonium triggers for America's nuclear arsenal during the next four decades.[12] In 1958, the headquarters of NORAD became operational under Cheyenne Mountain, further cementing homeland security operations throughout the state.[13] Despite the secrecy that surrounded the functions of these sites, newspapers celebrated every new plant, airbase, and complex and the new jobs that were soon to follow.[14] By 1965, Colorado's defense industry, its research and development contracts, and its dense manufacturing facilities were enriching the state's coffers by $1.15 billion per year.[15]

The military-industrial complex had a noticeable impact on the built environment and residential life in the Rockies. Grand Junction and surrounding towns on the Colorado Plateau lay at the center of the Manhattan Project's uranium-mining efforts; more than 2.6 million pounds of uranium oxide were extracted here between 1943 and 1946.[16] Remote hamlets such as Uravan, once the home of gold prospectors seeking fortune in the hills, now became hubs of Cold War growth: in Uravan, the population spiked from thirty residents to nearly eight hundred by 1960.[17] The region's cities also transformed. Housing booms in 1955 and 1958 turned the sleepy metropolises of Denver and Boulder into bustling urban centers, with 420,000 new residents mostly settling in the ever-expanding suburbs statewide from 1955 to 1958.[18]

To contemporary observers, the scope and scale of the growth was awe-inspiring. One person wrote: "Today Denver is something of a sleeping beauty among cities. . . . She is beautiful beyond doubt. She is growing. The town and its suburbs are bursting out at the seams. Building is under way everywhere, and still the roofs are not numerous enough to meet the demand. Many of the newcomers are ex-GI's who discovered Denver when they were stationed at Lowry and Buckley Fields, and now have come back to make homes."[19] Between 1945 to 1965, the population of the five counties that formed the Denver metropolitan area increased by 146 percent, with the number of inhabitants reaching just over 1 million.[20] In less than a generation, Colorado had changed forever.

Given that more than 80,000 residents in Denver alone drew paychecks from federal, state, and municipal employment, fathers who were working and raising families in the state's new Cold War industries were clear that their homes would likely be on the front line of a full-blown nuclear exchange.[21] For instance, Henry J. Frank, a steel manufacturer who had been involved in the expansion of the military academy on Lowry Air Base, recognized that his job influenced how he perceived the risk. Writing to his regional OCDM branch in 1958, four years before the nation's shelter mania truly took hold, he spoke of how his proximity to military industries had spurred him to design his home shelter:

> After watching current events from day to day, I have realized for some time that it is pertinent that we prepare ourselves for the greatest task of survival known in history. It is quite obvious that Communism has won about all the conquests it can through negotiation and infiltration. So therefore it leaves but one choice and that is the use of force so that Communism can fulfill its dreams of world conquest.
>
> I have been watching and appreciate the stand you have taken and the promptness and expediency that you have exploited in preparing the country to defend itself. I feel that it is up to us as Americans if we have an idea or technical developments that will aid you in your work. To cut a long story short, [thanks to] the experiences that I gained in war, in foxholes, dugouts and air raid shelter[s] and the experience I have gained in the steel fabrication business since the war I have come up with an idea which the government and private citizen can afford.[22]

Yet as Frank's letter continued, a sense of skepticism entered. While he was satisfied with his initial blueprints for a model shelter, he was not fully convinced that the design would "withstand a nuclear blast." He asked if the army might consider building and testing his model shelter against various levels of explosives and expressed his uncertainty about this "new war," which was in almost every way "different to my time fighting in Europe." Attaching a photograph of his prototype shelter with his family inside, he reiterated, "I want to see the taxpayer get his money's worth and the family have the maximum protection" (see figure 6).[23]

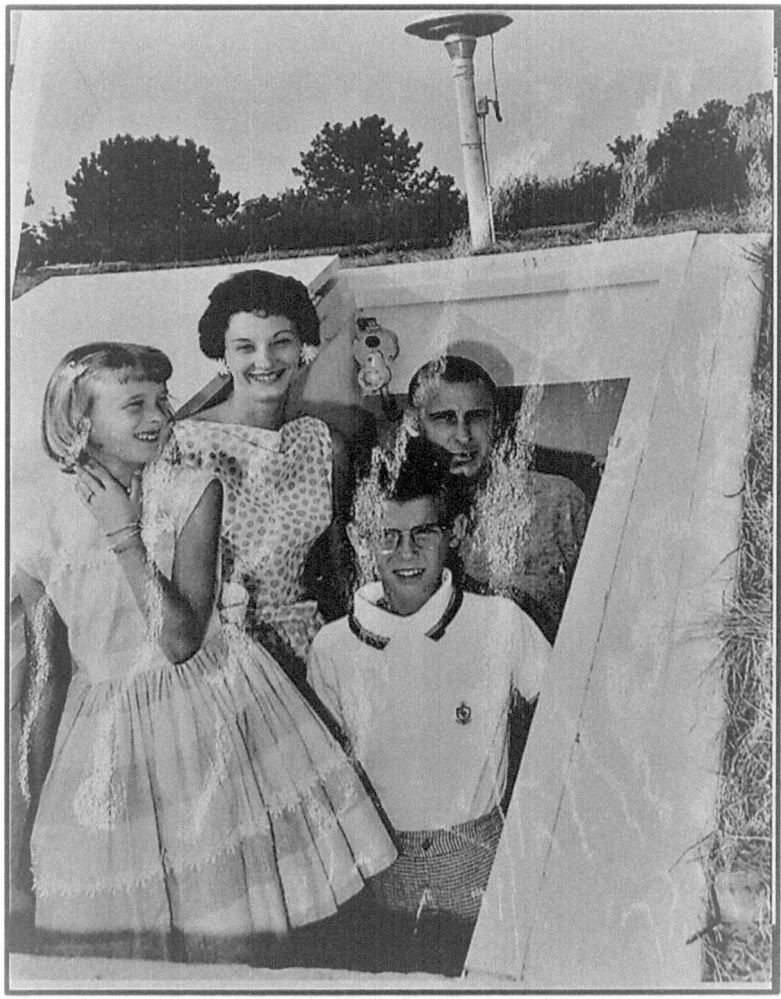

FIGURE 6. Henry J. Frank and his family pose in their prototype "Blast Shelter," 1958. Office of Civil Defense, Central Files, 1958, Records of the Defense Preparedness Agency, RG397, box 29, National Archives and Records Administration, College Park, Maryland.

The OCD booklets encouraged fathers to follow their preset guidelines, but Frank interpreted the ethos of home survival in a personal way. In this way, he was like every working father in the Rockies, each of whom tackled the question of home survival slightly differently. Jeremy Knox, a Boulder construction worker who had paved the roads leading into the Rocky Flats complex, took a more maverick approach. In a letter to OCDM headquarters in Battle Creek, Michigan, Knox requested additional civil defense booklets to distribute at work, noting that he was planning within the next week to "nail sandbags to the basement ceiling and floor.... Logically I know this will work."[24] We will never know when he realized that poking holes in a sandbag might have unexpected results. We do know, however, that other fathers took a more fatalistic approach. Stewart Parks of Denver, writing in 1961 after the publication of *Life*'s special shelter issue, complained about the glaring inequality between the protection of military sites and the protection of family homes: "[W]e know those sites have shelters deep and vast to protect the important ones, . . . government officials and the like. I know they are there . . . [but] there is nothing I can do. Clearly my family and I are not important enough to save."[25]

In Colorado, the two extremes of civil defense existed side by side: one typified by the grand underground shelter complexes built eighteen meters into the rock face of Cheyenne Mountain, the other by Knox's sandbag-covered ceiling.[26] The contrast between these public and private worlds made the hopelessness of home survival more visible, especially when one adds the awkwardness of local civil defense officials trying to convince families that basic household solutions were the best response to nuclear war. In 1955, after William Nicholson was elected mayor of Denver, the regional presence of the FCDA expanded exponentially. Nicholson's public statements chimed with William Heimlich's efforts during the late 1950s to shift away from costly urban evacuation programs toward a privatized vision of individual domestic survival. Nicholson recognized the potential for federal investment in the region and encouraged the OCDM to maintain a "strong presence." In response to that support, Leo Hoegh decided to relocate the agency's western base of operations (Region 6) to Denver.[27] By 1958, civil defense had become deeply embedded in neighborhoods across Colorado, and local municipal meetings, PTA events, and town hall gatherings featured discussions of civil defense literature.[28] The region's strategic importance, coupled with the cooperation of state officials and the fervor of Edwin C. Johnson, Colorado's fiercely anti-Communist governor, meant that local residents were at the forefront of some of the OCD's most ambitious civic-educational campaigns.[29] People who lived in Denver's University Park and Lake neighborhoods, southeast of the city center, could attend civil defense meetings on the third Wednesday of every month. They could hear lectures on what to include in a household survival kit, go on field trips to Civil Defense Headquarters in Colorado Springs, tour prototype home shelters, and take part in PTA projects such as making nuclear survival identification tags for the region's children.[30] Colorado Springs to the south and Boulder to the north, as well as rural areas to the east such as Pikes Peak, Hartsel, Guffey, Cripple Creek, and Florissant, were also at the forefront of these extensive public awareness campaigns (see figure 7).[31]

In Colorado, the intersection of family life, regional employment, and military installations complicated the topic of home survival.[32] The state had an exceptionally high level of employment in Cold War military industries, a factor that shaped conceptions of family vulnerability. In the mid-1950s, as the FCDA was finding its foothold in the region, Denver had the nation's second-highest percentage of federal employees after Washington, DC.[33] As a result, Colorado was targeted with several region-specific nuclear survival guides and films that were never disseminated in other states. One film was aimed specifically at Denver housewives, with the goal of teaching them how to shop during a nuclear war. Produced by the Colorado Civil Defense Agency, the film, *Food for Thought* (1956), was screened at civil defense lectures throughout the state and made nuclear war a familiar experience. It focused on four local women who shopped at Mountain View Market, a landmark retail outlet on the city's outskirts, and it followed them as they purchased food and dealt with

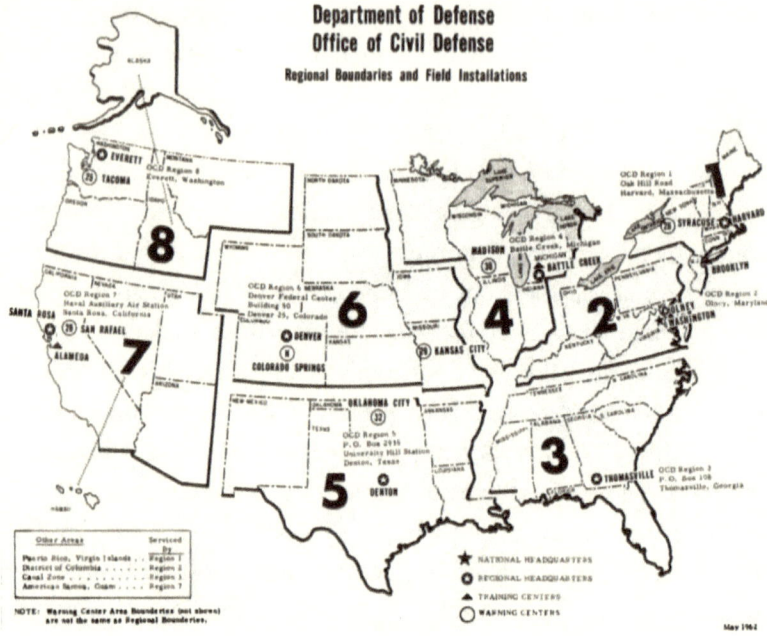

FIGURE 7. A map of the regional breakdown of Civil Defense, May 1962. Source: Department of Defense, Office of Civil Defense, "Regional Boundaries and Field Installations," *Annual Report of the Office of Civil Defense for Fiscal Year 1962* (Washington, DC: Government Printing Office, 1962), 92, figure 2. Courtesy of the National Archives and Records Administration, College Park, Maryland.

shortages following an atomic attack. One housewife was shown taking in survivors from downtown; in another scene, an emergency kitchen was set up in the northern suburb of Brighton.[34]

The region-specific nature of civil defense was especially important when it came to buying a home, and realtors in Colorado kept nuclear survival firmly in mind. In 1953, the Denver Association of Home Builders sponsored the first of what subsequently became an annual event, the Parade of Homes.[35] Two years later, the Parade of Homes exhibited the first new residential developments with fallout shelters prebuilt in each model.[36] Soon thereafter, the United Construction Company announced that it was building 179 houses on a sixty-acre tract of land in Denver's Inspiration Point, a development with long curving streets and mountain views, located between West 50th and West 52nd avenues from Harlan Street to Sheridan

Boulevard. New homes at Inspiration Point were priced between $14,000 and $35,000, depending on size and location and whether residents wanted a bomb shelter in the basement. The company marketed the homes as "the last word in modern living."[37]

Buying a home, starting a family, and finding a well-paying job were key markers of Cold War masculinity and were often depicted as transitional moments in a man's life. Their primacy was reinforced by a gender-biased economic system (through credit plans, mortgage policies, tax codes, and educational opportunities) that had historically undermined women's ability to become breadwinners or even have access to their own money.[38] Popular television shows such as *Father Knows Best* (1954), *Leave It to Beaver* (1957–63), and *The Adventures of Ozzie and Harriet* (1952–66) suggested that men who directed their consumption toward the home would reap domestic rewards.[39] But this promotion of white, middle-class, suburban, domestic masculinity was not extended to include racial minorities and the urban poor.[40] Residential redlining, periodic layoffs, discriminatory mortgage lending, and low wages meant that suburban homeownership was mostly limited to white males.[41] Equally important was the Interstate Highway Act of 1956, which, through infrastructure projects, made the Denver suburbs, like those throughout the United States, more accessible by car.[42]

Over time, white men's monopoly on breadwinning would be challenged. But for Denver residents during the nuclear crisis years, home survival and male ownership were built into the vocabulary of the home retail market. In the pages of the *Denver Telegraph-Gazette*, the *Denver Post*, and the *Greeley Daily Tribune*, fathers read that they could buy a home with complete confidence, safe in the knowledge that their decision to purchase a house in the suburbs meant they were buying a vision of community security and that they would be safe from a nuclear strike. Safety, however, came at a cost. In an irate letter, Martin Richards complained that the new model homes being built in the Denver suburbs were offering survival at an unreasonable price:

> I am writing this letter because I feel it is necessary. There is a worry in my family and I want it dealt with. The home we have up here suits us

nicely. We do not currently have a shelter but I am contacting you to get necessary advice. I do have an issue I feel others around here feel likewise about. If you thought this was necessary for new homes to have shelters why is there nothing in place for us? Every home must have a shelter not just the new fancy ones which seem to cost more.[43]

Richards had a point. On average, prices for new suburban houses ranged around $14,000, depending on size, location, and style. The same sort of home with a shelter cost at least $17,300, a significant addition to the standard price.[44] This markup is surprising, given that the United Construction Company estimated that building a shelter in the new models should cost about $300. In any event, buying a family home in Denver meant paying extra money to ensure that security was built into the foundation.

In 1959, the *Denver Post* covered the opening of the "nation's first fallout shelter in a housing subdivision."[45] The project, which Hoegh oversaw personally during his last years at the OCDM, was the ideal opportunity to turn the rhetoric of do-it-yourself survival into reality.[46] The United Construction Company was not the only contractor involved. Jack Hoerner, the owner of a new subdivision known as Allendale Heights, offered shelters in fifteen out of forty houses built in 1960.[47] According to Hoerner:

> The model includes a 20 x 14 ft. basement "radiation fallout shelter." Eight hanging bunk beds "provide a safe and practical haven" in case of nuclear attack. The shelter is a standard feature which includes "an air blower system, 40-gal. water tank, complete first aid and household supplies," a bicycle which has the dual purpose of operating an electric generator and providing exercise, and even a shotgun for "protection against the enemy" (and relatives or neighbors who try to "take over.")[48]

Mention of a shotgun in the shelter appeared in publicity materials for the 1959, 1960, and 1961 Parade of Homes, seemingly a way to reframe a defensive position as something active and manly. Whether this was a poorly phrased joke or a deeply serious social commentary, the issue of violence and retreat was becoming central to shelter fatherhood.

Among fathers who did not want to buy property, home shelters nonetheless remained a visible part of their residential communities, in contrast to the surprising "invisibility" of most public shelters, with their discreet signs and unadvertised entrances.[49] The Parade of Homes turned home shelters into a public spectacle. For instance, in July 1960, Martin Sherman, who lived at 1939 Chelton Road in Colorado Springs, demonstrated to his friends and neighbors how easy it was to build one. During Parade of Homes week, he proudly displayed the shelter he had built in the basement of his two-story colonial house to anyone "interested in survival." The shelter matched the archetypal OCD model: six feet, ten inches wide and fifteen feet, seven inches long, with concrete walls eight inches thick. Colonel L. T. Vickers, the city council chairman, was impressed, telling the *Colorado Springs Telegraph-Gazette* reporter that it had been built by a "true patriot." Not only was Sherman's shelter "civil defense approved," but it also "contain[ed] everything the modern family needs from fruit juice to first aid kits." Even equipped with these modern luxuries, it was a bargain, costing "only about $250." Vickers considered that price "dirt cheap," especially given that the "house itself [was] only 200 yards from a warning siren." He added, "I am sure the government would feel more secure to deal with potential enemy countries if more residents acted like Mr. Sherman."[50]

Visitors to Martin Sherman's model shelter immediately noticed the refurbished air-raid siren that stood imposingly at the intersection of Chelton Road and Pikes Peak Avenue. All that July, during the Parade of Homes event, neighbors watched a frenzy of activity around the family home. Participants included a small army of self-styled survival experts recruited from the local branch of the Toastmasters Club, a women's reading group from High County Baptist Church, representatives of the county's building and home associations, and a few "amateur radio operators." All were "eager" to bombard passersby with information about sensible home survival. Orchestrated publicity events like this one turned residential homes into stage sets. As one local resident wrote to the *Gazette-Telegraph*, the situation seemed "artificial, . . . like watching a play I wanted no part of."[51]

In Colorado, the performance of civil defense became a feature of daily life, and few people could escape from it. One local resident, John Parker, wrote to Vickers after "seeing the siren" and visiting Sherman's shelter on his way to work as a high school teacher. He told Vickers that he knew now that the time had come for him to build a shelter. Spurred to visit by a mixture of "worry and instinct to see what the fuss was about," he felt as if he were "waking up to the reality."[52] But turning this realization into action was tricky. Correspondence between local residents and the regional OCD office was dominated by complaints about shelter construction tasks that had gone terribly wrong. Like many Colorado fathers, Parker became mired in frustration. In his case, he was unable to build an effective ceiling for his shelter:

> From the literature I deduced that protection is keyed to the weight and mass of the structural material and the only material recommended is a concrete block.
>
> This kind of construction is not practicable for me is there is any other material that is effective. I do not have the cellar head room as the model over at Chelton. Therefore, I would appreciate your comment on this problem. I have considered the following: (I am not interested in protection other than from fallout)
>
> 1. Lining ceiling with sheet lead or other material
>   a. Do you estimate this to be prohibitively expensive?
>   b. Please give me protection information for various thicknesses of lead. I believe your standard is 1/100 of some factor
>   c. Is there any other material that will work?
> 2. Store sufficient concrete blocks on hand to be able to cover the desired area by arranging them on floor above cellar shelter and filling cracks with sand. I assume I would have 10 minutes. Is this practical? What would be the result of not filling the intersections with sand?
> 3. Next, I would like to know where I can get a radiation detection device. I would like a "masters" or something that would advise on degree of personal exposure.
>
> Finally, please send me a list of government publications that will give me data and general information about the entire problem.

The OCD office did reply to Parker, sending him a detailed letter and a number of helpful publications. But the reply was not timely: Parker had written in early August and did not receive an answer until mid-November. That gap in response time had an enormous effect on the project. In a return note, he wrote, "[A]fter some careful thought and time speaking to my wife I have decided to no longer pursue this project."[53]

THE HALF-BUILT SHELTER

Parker's letter reveals the practical constraints of building a shelter and the opportunities and dilemmas of nuclear-age fatherhood. Again and again, fathers started shelter projects but did not finish them. Tales of half-built shelters litter the public records in Colorado, and each provides subtle clues into how fathers tried to engage with the process of home survival. Generally, their letters mentioned some or all of the following concerns: (1) their position as economic providers, (2) their ability to act as role models for their children, and (3) their skills as successful home improvers.

The ability to afford a home shelter was a clear barometer of men's success in inhabiting their role as shelter fathers. To protect their families, fathers had to spend money, whatever the type or scale of the project might be. Throughout the 1950s, FCDA and OCDM policymakers had done little to challenge the underlining assumption that men's primary civil defense role was to finance their families' safety. Thus, in addition to struggling with FHA loan applications, shelter fathers had to wrestle with tax credits, direct loans, and one-off payments. Take the case of William Simonds, a father of three who lived in Park Hill, a residential suburb northeast of Denver. One 1960 brochure described it as an area in which "you can be pardoned for feeling quietly pleased with yourself . . . just a bit smug."[54] Park Hill was a center for affluent white families as well as a neighborhood shaped by racialized lending practices. These had made Colorado Boulevard (just one street away from Park Hill) a clear dividing line between white and black Denver.

When it came to private shelters in the suburbs, the wealthy, home-owning, white families of Park Hill were the ideal audience for the message of self-funded survival. Yet even here, fathers were reluctant to pay. Writing to his regional agency in September 1961, Simonds noted that the shelter literature he was reading would be pointless unless financial assistance were made available. He asked, "[W]ould it be possible to divert some of the Federal funds, funds that are being spent on the printing of pamphlets etc., to some down to earth, realistic measures like me building a shelter?"[55] Mark Jenkins, also a resident of Park Hill, bluntly requested "an immediate cash investment to help make my family's safety secure," and another unnamed resident suggested that "assistance be set aside for those who work around here."[56] After making an oblique reference to the military industry that employed him, the letter writer stressed that having spent "long hours . . . working for this country . . . I want to know my family is safe at home."[57]

The Cold War demanded unparalleled levels of military spending and organization at a national level. For Park Hill residents such as William Simonds and Mark Jenkins, it also required buying into the state illusion that home shelters were their keys to survival. Although local officials announced that "with proper reworking of tax relief a family could build a fallout shelter with virtually no cost to the man bringing home the weekly pay check," this did not ring true for many men. Instead, building a shelter at "virtually no cost" seemed impossible to manage.[58] Park Hill was just one example; correspondence from residents of other Denver suburbs—Montclair, South Denver, Highlands, Berkeley—reveal a similar attitude. Many wrote letters to the local newspapers demonstrating that they framed shelter construction as both a material and a political consideration. Fathers' concerns spread among other members of their families. "Do you realize how much a private shelter costs? And how much for a public one for a city the size of Denver and its suburbs?" asked Linda Evans, a sophomore at Greeley High School, in a letter to the *Greeley Daily Tribune*. "Would your parents enjoy their taxes being doubled or tripled when they are to have shelters?" In his study of midcentury fatherhood, Ralph LaRossa notes the importance of economic power as a marker of fatherhood. But even wealthy fathers rarely accepted the idea of buying a shelter outright without any form of financial reparation.[59] Indeed, a few Colorado fathers went so far as to request money back for materials they had already invested in survival. Writing to the OCDM during the week of the Cuban missile crisis, Luke Gardner, a resident of Montclair, asked if he could send the agency receipts from his planned shelter project to be reimbursed in the event that war did not break out.[60] The idea was a novel one, to say the least, but it demonstrates that shelters were a cumbersome expense that some fathers sought to avoid. Frank Vivian, a father of three from Boulder, noted that he was not alone in thinking that the government must "subsidize the men around [here] having to spend our wages to do the right thing."[61]

As Vivian and Gardner were compiling their receipts, Jason Murphy of South Denver was worrying that he couldn't afford to buy a shelter. Writing to the OCDM in October 1962, he began by praising "those who are responsible for Civil Defense in this area"; they "have done a wonderful job." He affirmed that both "the public and my family are in a mood for shelters." Yet when his children asked him, after "civil defense lessons in school," if they were going to have a home shelter, Murphy could not give them a confident answer. "[T]he models that seem to be the most effective cost more than I earn in a year." He was wondering now if there were "installment plans" available.[62] Charlie Coates, another South Denver resident, also reported that his children had become concerned about home shelters following "conversations at school." In his letter to the OCDM, he expressed frustration and anger about the lack of financial assistance. He believed the agency should immediately "issue a statement" about financing, though he acknowledged that "this late time may be too late." "**UNLESS** you have some scheme by which the federal government is going to finance shelters and pay for them," he thundered, "it may be completely impossible in this area." Coates gave agency officials a deadline: "In 30 days will you show us how exactly to build radiation protection above ground for $100 to $150?"[63] He received no such assurance.

In letters such as these, fathers were turning to local authorities in hope that they would ease the tension between their roles as breadwinner and shelter builder.[64] Yet as the historian Alice George has noted, at a time when "most Americans lacked the will or resources to run and hide" and were seeking "answers, however tenuous in their own communities," there was a distinct paralysis in U.S. civil defense.[65] This was especially apparent in regional offices. Citizens who wrote with urgent questions frequently received neutral responses such as "Fallout shelters are insurance for the civilian population in the event of a miscalculation. Fallout shelters that meet most of the standards set by the Office of Civil Defense could save most survivors from the blast and heat of nuclear attack. You apparently are sufficiently aware of the need for safety for your family and yourself. One possible solution is to encourage your local government to provide shelters in existing public buildings."[66] This standardized response was notably passive, given that it was coming from an organization whose primary aim was to mobilize and sustain the support of the American public. In Colorado, this disconnect was enhanced by the logistical problems that beset local civil defense offices throughout 1961 and 1962. During the months between the Berlin and Cuban missile crises, they were "swamped" and "overwhelmed" by public inquiries. They were also ineffective at providing specific information to local letter writers. A Colorado resident who sent the OCD an inquiry in July 1961 was not likely to receive a reply until the end of September.[67] This gap got wider between October and December, when the president's press secretary, Pierre Salinger, ordered that all shelter correspondence addressed to Kennedy be redirected from the federal Public Affairs Office to regional OCD branches. Letters addressed to senators and representatives were also redirected to local OCD offices, and the result was gridlock.

During the fall of 1961, the *Greeley Daily Tribune* ran an article suggesting that residential shelters might increase housing values for families thinking of selling. By now householders were losing interest in such projects.[68] Yet local papers were still publishing letters from those who were looking to fund community shelter projects. A local resident named Eileen Gleason wrote the following:

> I saw a picture of an underground community fallout shelter in Life Magazine, so why couldn't our community get together and build one deep enough to withstand the blast? I know it would cost a lot, but if everyone shared the cost, wouldn't it be possible to build it right? Couldn't we consolidate our money for other buildings and use them for other things than just a fallout shelter? They could provide partitioning for schools, etc. So many kids talk that they want a fallout shelter that I think we should give them a chance for hope and security, since we grown-ups are so darn ornery we can't get along.[69]

Letters such as this one show that communities were seeking alternatives to the private rhetoric of home survival, finding strength not in fathers alone but in townspeople working together to reach a common goal.

THE TESTING OF THE FAMILY

Paying for a shelter was a family's first hurdle; learning how to interact with the new space was the next. As Jack Lynn considered building a shelter, his primary concern was not cost. Rather, he wondered how to explain the function of their bomb shelter to his children. In a letter to the OCD, he wrote that his long commute to work meant that "family time was limited" and that he and his wife were confused about how to educate their six-year-old son about civil defense protocols: "I know it's important and school does part of this . . . but to tell him without scaring him is tricky, [so] we have thought [we might] make a game we could play. Do you have any advice to share?"[70]

Lynn was not alone; many shelter fathers were seeking professional parenting advice. In *Cold War Hothouses*, the historian Beatriz Colomina argues that Cold War culture was defined by such "conflation[s] of the public and private." The suburban home, "equipped with every imaginable appliance, projected the image of the lifestyle of prosperity and excess that was the main weapon of the Cold War."[71] Political messaging around the family fallout shelter echoed this point, bringing the military logic of the security state into the domestic sphere and treating the family shelter as yet another capitalist commodity in the fight against communism. On a private level, raising and sustaining family awareness meant reconstituting the private space of the home and the actions of the family unit within it. Each member had to be taught a new role that blended the discipline of a military unit with the consumer culture of everyday family life. The task was far from the straightforward process that civil defense experts had hoped for.

Like Jack Lynn, James Hayes wrote to his regional OCD director to ask for civil defense booklets that would help him resolve the tensions in his household. Both were ex-servicemen who had fought in Korea, and both found it difficult to instill discipline in their family. Hayes said, "I struggle. [The children] don't take this seriously... [but] it keeps me awake."[72] For these parents, being a shelter father was a tricky role to inhabit. Far from authoritarian figures, they found it difficult to negotiate their new entwined paternal and civic duties.

Other fathers did not find their new parenting situation so challenging. Frank Miles wrote to the OCD in October 1961 to ask about the best way to turn his garage into an above-ground shelter. He told officials that his family members "already know their duty.... [T]hey are ready. When I give the word they know what to do."[73] In a November 1961 letter to President Kennedy, Michael Ellis said that building his shelter had "brought my family together to fight Khrushchev."[74] David Brown wrote to the president January 1962 to ask for a federal loan to help finance his shelter: "I assure you, Mr. President, I have taught my boys a fighting spirit."[75] Time and again shelter fathers fused ideas of military service with family responsibility. Harry Taylor, writing in December 1961, and Jason Booker, writing in March 1962, both mentioned their time in Korea, and each closed his letter with the statement "my boys are learning."[76] In September 1961, Carl Hendel wrote, "Unless we build shelters, our nation may not survive as a first-class country." He assured his reader "that if the war gets hot my family is ready. The Russians will not be able to humble us."⁷⁷ Clearly, for some men, do-it-yourself survival allowed them to engage notions of military service, culture, and discipline.

Around the nation, veterans of the Korean War were struggling with their failure to achieve victory in that conflict. In their communities, they faced pervasive doubts about the fighting ability of American men. Thus, for many, time spent with a home-shelter project seemed to prove that they still had the fortitude for war. References to military service in Korea appear frequently in OCD correspondence, and men writing to Eisenhower and Kennedy about civil defense often introduced themselves as veterans of that war. Frequently their questions framed do-it-yourself survival as a continuation of their service overseas. Writing to Kennedy in November 1961, William Rowan, a resident of rural Jefferson County on the outskirts of Denver, said, "I am a Korean War veteran and have five children so I feel that in this time of crisis this concerns us [veterans] more than others." He admitted that "it may be that I am selfish as to the security of my family, but I feel that their security is my responsibility, just as it is yours to your own family." Rowan described a local civil defense class called "Individual and Family Survival" that he and other local veterans had attended. After telling the president about "a session entitled 'Modern Man's need to understand the Hazards of his Time,'" he recalled "the interesting and enlightening" conversation he had had with an unnamed civil defense official: "[He told us] it was up to us the civilian population, and our responsibility to organize our own unit [family] to the best of our ability. Well that was fine with us. We are used to surviving." Rowan and a few of his friends had banded together into a local disaster relief group. But after building some shelters, they learned that their construction efforts had not been "approved by the state." Now he and his friends were being called "renegades." Yet despite his sense of alienation, he had a strong desire to "protect his community" and was ready "to defend freedom any way possible."⁷⁸

In addition to protecting their families, shelter fathers had to call upon another military trait: the ability, both physical and psychological, to withstand the pressures of the nuclear age. Although the

OCDM claimed that a home shelter had the "potential to contain all the luxuries" of the modern home, life there was often seen as a test of strength and endurance.[79] Letters to the agency included accounts of families who experimented with spending long periods of time in a shelter, with no natural light, limited air ventilation, and shared chemical toilets. Most of these letters reveal considerable mental and physical strain. Yet such tests also gave men an opportunity to prove their manhood, and some wrote of hoping that time in a shelter might restore "tough mindedness" in an age of anxiety. Shelter living also gave fathers the opportunity to put the ideals of new fatherhood into practice. Under normal circumstances, most breadwinners could spend only limited amounts of time with wives and children, but shelter living proved whether or not they could put up with their families for prolonged periods.

Experiments with shelter living were not unique to Colorado. Kirt MacBride of Sacramento, California, spent a week alone in his shelter to "educate his community" that life underground was a chance to "prove one man's capacity to sustain." Throughout the week, MacBride transmitted hourly radio reports to the county directors of the California Disaster Office. These accounts of his "heroic ordeal" were sent to the *Sacramento Union,* which, in cooperation with local radio stations, then updated the community. In reality, however, MacBride's self-imposed trial was an OCDM-orchestrated publicity stunt designed to show "how any citizen can repeat Kirt's personal sacrifice," an "act that we should all salute." According to Hoegh, McBride's experience proved that "even outside of war the capacity to survive is within the spirit of every man."[80]

Not everyone approached civil defense as a chance to show strength and toughness. A number of fathers expressed confusion, hostility, and even a sense of emasculation over their inability to control their domestic surroundings. The 1944 Servicemen's Readjustment Bill had offered education and housing to more than 8 million, mostly white, middle-class veterans, and for some of them civil defense was an unwanted intrusion into suburban life. James Sauer of Boulder spoke for many when he wrote, "Nuclear war is unthinkable—biologically, socially, morally. . . . [T]his is not the same war, this is not a war we can win."⁸¹ Correspondence records at the OCDM reveal that an increasing number of individuals saw the construction of domestic shelters as an undesirable step toward war. In a detailed letter to President Kennedy in November 1961, Marvin Taylor, "a homeowner, an engineer, and the father of three children" in New York, explained that learning about do-it-yourself survival had awakened him to the inherent problems of the nuclear age. Recently, a local civic organization had invited him to speak with "authority" as both a civil engineer and a veteran about the benefits of domestic shelters, and Taylor had felt compelled to speak out: "I recognize the argument that some protection is better than none." Yet he wondered if "shelters offer any real protection in areas such as Long Island, which is so close to the prime target of New York City? If one did emerge alive from a fallout shelter, what would be left in the way of food, water, animal life?" His questions mirrored diplomat and historian George Kennan's concerns about the moral crisis inherent in civil defense.⁸² Taylor asked, "[I]sn't the entire concept of burrowing underground repugnant to our way of life as proud, free people? Wouldn't the psychological effect, especially [on] our children, be irreparable?" In conclusion, he told the president that civil defense, in its current form, had "left the survival of my children in the hands of high pressure automobile salesmen selling shelters, and political opportunists."⁸³

The boundaries of fatherhood around the family shelter were never static. While some men saw the private practice of survival as a means to reaffirm a code of manhood and legitimize their claims to domestic authority by associating it with military ideals, others understood all too clearly that the family shelter was an unwanted intrusion that brought the politics of the nuclear state into the private sphere. Public records show positions of acceptance, apathy, and protest, confirming that, whatever the reaction, the prospect of building a family shelter encouraged men to think about what it meant to be a father in the nuclear age. For the OCDM, survival required uniformity, standardization, and an almost blind adherence to the politics of civil defense. Yet rather than solving the contradictions of the Cold War military state, the family shelter seemed, in the eyes of many concerned suburban fathers, to exemplify the propagandistic excesses of their own government. Behind the OCDM's pamphlets and propaganda was a society trying to come to terms with a new and terrifying way of life.

A closer look at Colorado illustrates the diversity of family reactions to OCD policies. As the rhetoric of civil defense clashed with the reality of everyday life, what emerged was not a uniform policy of nuclear survival but a patchwork of local civic-educational efforts, exhibits, and mobilization programs.[84] In Colorado, one unintended consequence of this region-specific civil defense rhetoric was the emergence of tensions between rural and urban communities.[85] Rural and agricultural families were frequently described in civil defense literature as the "custodians of democracy." Unlike their urban and suburban counterparts, who, if the bomb dropped, were to be guided by civic leaders, "rural people—you, your friends and neighbors—will be in charge of reception centers for evacuees, have positions of responsibility and authority regarding feeding, shelter, sanitation facilities, first aid, welfare. . . . [T]his care for evacuees must be planned and organized." In 1954, Douglas and Jefferson counties, located close to Denver and home to numerous agricultural communities, were the testing grounds for Val Peterson's early rural civil defense initiatives.[86] A former governor of Nebraska, he now was collaborating with the U.S. Department of Agriculture (USDA), agribusiness leaders, and state cooperatives to launch a series of public campaigns to educate residents on their roles as "agricultural providers," shelter owners, and responsible citizens.[87] Rural civil defense propaganda efforts, repeated elsewhere with the help of state cooperatives in Iowa, Ohio, Missouri, and Kansas, advised rural male householders that they had a "unique duty" to construct shelters not just for their own families but to accommodate "evacuees from metropolitan centers in the aftermath of a nuclear blast."[88]

This trumpeting of the "charitable good will of rural residents" continued after Hoegh replaced Peterson as director.[89] Hoegh was a former governor of Iowa, another largely agricultural state. During his tenure, USDA/OCDM-sponsored propaganda swept through the midwest, emphasizing that "the principles of civil defense are not new to rural people. We have been taking care of our own, helping our neighbors and stay ready to help others."[90] By the end of Hoegh's tenure in 1960, the OCDM was reporting that "48 States had initiated rural civil defense programs and over 60 per cent of the counties in the U.S. have participated."[91] In Douglas County, whose largest town, Castle Rock, had only 1,152 residents in 1960, most of whom occupied "rural homes," expectations were high that residents would comply with the OCDM vision of homestead hospitality.[92]

For residents of agricultural communities in Jefferson and Douglas counties, the rural-urban dynamic proved to be a significant factor in how the gun-thy-neighbor debate unfolded. In September 1961, a few months after Kennedy delivered the Berlin Address, conversations about nuclear survival began to shift from a focus on adequate shelter spaces toward worries that during a nuclear attack urban residents might flock to their area and "take over our shelters."[93] In Douglas County these discussions took on an aggressive tone; at one point, the county's civil defense leader reportedly advised all local residents to be prepared to defend their shelters against urban refugees from Denver and Boulder, saying he had "equipped his own personal shelter with an arsenal to keep out unwanted visitors."[94] The actions of this official, who was quickly reprimanded by the OCDM's central branch, exacerbated tensions between Douglas County and Denver over the question of where urban refugees would relocate after a nuclear strike.[95] The *Denver Post* quickly publicized the violent rhetoric of this "voice of federal authority," and despite the OCDM's best efforts the gun-thy-neighbor debate exploded across Colorado in the fall of 1961.[96] The *Post*'s subsequent coverage of the Douglas County situation depicted the family shelter as part of both a national crisis over nuclear weapons and a neighborhood conflict much closer to home.[97]

When considering fathers' role in shelter construction, we have only individual stories, not a single unifying perspective, yet this fragmentation itself helps us understand how the nuclear age shaped and intersected with everyday life. The interplay between the masculine ideal of family protection and the practice of home survival drew sharp divisions between politics and social practice. In Colorado, there was a patchwork of individual stories, many revealing the unpredictability of human action and reaction. Yet despite their diversity they allow us to draw conclusions about how shelters came to inform regional ideas of Cold War masculinity.

On the national level, the image of a suburban father building a home shelter was promoted as a tool of deterrence—a powerful, if flawed, symbol of homeowners united in defense. Yet among Colorado homeowners, shelters were often discussed in terms of their material function and cost. In a state where investment and military-industrial upheaval were actively creating unpredictable change, practical concerns dominated the discussion. This made the low number of home shelters in the region truly remarkable, though we can never be completely sure how many were built or even started. Nonetheless, the consequences of do-it-yourself survival were evident in the ways in which fathers engaged with and debated the prospect of survival. Building a shelter was not just about rejecting or embracing a vision of domestic survival; it was a complicated story of individual agency in the face of total destruction. No Colorado father could have protected his family from nuclear strike, yet their faltering attempts reveal how ideas of protection and survival penetrated the mundane realities of everyday life. As the historian Paul Boyer has famously noted, the United States seemed to accommodate the presence of nuclear weapons in political life remarkably quickly.[98] In Colorado, however, private accommodation was not straightforward. Shelters were never normalized as either icons of paternal power or even a sensible solution to the question of survival.

CHAPTER FOUR

The Struggle to Sell Survival

> We all know how deadly and devastating radioactive fallout is to every living thing. When our enemy attacks, what will you do? Have YOU as the head of your family made adequate preparations so that you and your loved ones will SURVIVE? You carry life insurance—What have you done about LIFE ASSURANCE?
>
> —Florida Survival Shelters, September 21, 1961

> Why the hell would I want to buy a tomb for my wife and kid?
>
> —Tom Baulk, letter to the Office of Civil Defense, November 9, 1961

In September 1961, business was booming for fallout shelter salesmen. According to Frank F. Norton, the owner of the Chicago-based Atomic Shelter Corporation, profits had never been so healthy. "My best salesmen," he told a *Time* magazine reporter, "are named Khrushchev and Kennedy."[1] Since the Berlin Address, Norton and scores of other shelter suppliers across the United States, had been inundated with inquiries about how to purchase and build family shelters in backyards and basements.[2] One Chicago branch of Sears, Roebuck and Company estimated that four hundred shoppers per week had visited their model home shelter exhibition in September 1961. Meanwhile, Norton's crosstown rival, Leo Hoegh, now the vice-president of the Wonder Building Corporation, claimed to be selling two hundred shelters a week.[3] That autumn, as the Berlin Wall went up and the Soviet Union broke a moratorium on nuclear testing, fallout shelter salesmen stood primed to become the business-success story of the decade.

Demand for family shelters had reached an all-time high; and in light of an increasingly congested marketplace, Norton began running ads in the *Chicago Tribune*. Throughout the fall and winter of 1961 and into the summer of 1962, he pitched nuclear protection directly to middle-class homeowners, assuring them that "for just 200 dollars you too can have a fall-out shelter that you can enjoy!" Not only did his Atomic Shelter Corporation offer "affordable state of the art protection [that] every family needs," but these shelters also had a "dual purpose," providing "a year-round room for you to pursue your favorite hobbies, . . . woodwork, photography, you name it! . . . Or just think of it as a den to escape the wife and kids."[4] But Norton's vision was short-lived. During the course of the next two years, nearly six hundred shelter companies across the United States filed for bankruptcy.[5] By the end of 1962, Norton's firm had also collapsed. "The market is now dead," he told *Time* "[T]he manufacturers have had it."[6]

In this chapter, I chart the rise and fall of the fallout shelter business from its sudden boom in 1961 to its bust in 1963, considering how business records, trade publications, the personal histories of salesmen, and consumer reactions reveal new insights into the role of male consumerism on the Cold War home front.[7] Civil defense was, in essence, a capitalist process designed to convince male consumers to invest in their family's survival. During the Cold War, the physical act of buying, building, and maintaining a family fallout shelter was far more than a public policy or a national talking point. It was a site of consumer exchange. Fallout shelters were products designed by a national security state, and private companies then sold these products to fathers who were anxiously contemplating their own vulnerability. The politics and the social practice of nuclear survival were rooted in the willingness of fathers to complete this transactional exchange—to buy into, both literally and figuratively, a government strategy to save the nation from nuclear war that had been outsourced to local business interests.

In the development of civil defense, sales, salesmanship, and the creation of profit were not afterthoughts; they were central to its social function. As they traveled door to door, catalogue in hand and sales pitch at the ready, shelter salesmen were operating on the frontlines of national security. By asking suburban fathers how much they were willing to spend to ensure their families' survival, they promoted a vision of disaster capitalism that tied men's purchasing power to their ability to participate in the Cold War. In this way, they privileged a form of economic exchange that made the attainment of private profit a central and controversial platform for civic participation in national security. Yet the regional world that shelter salesmen inhabited was far from tranquil, and customers frequently accused them of profiteering, warmongering, and exploiting the fears of the vulnerable. As they questioned the validity of the product and the trustworthiness of its seller, homeowners challenged both the moral economy around the male consumer and the state-sanctioned vision of privatized survival.[8]

GET THE FAMILY ROOM OF TOMORROW, TODAY!

According to the *Saturday Review*, anticipating a "national fad" was one of the shortest paths to wealth, and during the summer of 1961 the home fallout shelter was primed to become one of the "[most-] demanded consumer products" in America.[9] Immediately after the Berlin Address, shelters became "the subject of every cocktail party and church social."[10] In small towns, shopping malls, and suburbs across the United States, businessmen quickly recognized their opportunity and rebranded themselves as survival specialists. Expectations for the new market were high, with one congressional leader going so far as to predict that shelter manufacturers and sellers would soon "achieve the magnitude and respect" of other federally promoted programs such as "highway building and urban renewal."[11]

To understand the history of shelter salesmen, we must consider exactly why nuclear survival developed into a consumer commodity in the first place. Since its inception, civil defense had been as much a commercial venture as a political message. Even before FHA loans formalized a consumer economy around shelters, private business had played a prominent, if problematic, role in the FCDA's and OCDM's national survival efforts. This commercialization was essentially a process of network building. In their efforts to manage public anxiety about a potential nuclear confrontation, policymakers had from the beginning worked closely with industrial suppliers, manufacturers, and designers. Shelter salesmen simply added an ingredient that was "part showbiz, part peep show and [all] hard sell" to the message of do-it-yourself survival.[12] It was another version of a national pattern, filtering responsibility away from the state and onto the shoulders of the suburban fathers. If it was the civic duty of fathers to purchase and construct shelters, then it was the task of the salesmen to match the product to the needs, wants, and peculiarities of those customers.

During the 1950s and into the early 1960s, shelter policymakers, manufacturers, suppliers, and promoters exchanged materials, blueprints, capital, and experience. While the variety and scope of this commercial network varied by region, the basic relationship among these stakeholders remained consistent.[13] Adding salesmen was the final step in a long process that had originated in the central OCD office in Battle Creek, Michigan, and then traveled through trade associations, industrial suppliers, and local financial institutions before finally reaching small-scale promoters (see figure 8).

Selling family shelters to fathers required considerable coordination between state and commercial actors. At the mass-manufacturing stage, the OCD worked closely with numerous trade associations, ranging from the American Concrete Pipe Association, to the National Lumber Manufacturers Association, to the Asbestos Cement Product Association.[14] Members of this collaborative public-private partnership developed shelter designs and even interchanged employees, creating internally approved models that were then franchised to regional dealers.[15] In this way, manufacturers and OCD officials invested in the standardization of their product and built a series of small regional monopolies. For example, Armco Steel

FIGURE 8. Office of Civil Defense Mobilization exhibit at a local civil defense fair, 1960. Photographs of Civil Defense Personneland Activities, 1956–2008, Records of the Federal Emergency Management Agency, RG311, National Archives and Records Administration, College Park, Maryland.

in Ohio, working with the American Steel and Iron Association, manufactured the steel needed in the seventy-three prefabricated walls of the Kelsey Hayes home shelter, which, in Oakland County, Ohio, was theoretically sold only by Kelsey Hayes's regional supplier, James Byrne of Michigan. This was the exact model of home shelter endorsed by President Kennedy, built by Art Carlson, and featured in the September 1961 issue of *Life*.[16]

As I have discussed in previous chapters, civil defense literature from the early 1950s framed building a shelter as a quasi-military act for the postwar family, one that would allow suburban fathers to participate on the home front as both a soldier and a civilian. By the late 1950s and into the early 1960s, shelter salesmen began softening that rhetoric of survival. In their advertisements, they pitched shelter construction not simply as a task of family protection but also as a standard Cold War home improvement option that would improve a father's suburban quality of life. "You are building a shelter and you are building your very own hobby room!" declared one salesman, Thomas Edwards, in the *Kansas Star* in 1959.[17] The American Institute of Decorators echoed this sentiment in a three-page advertisement, headlined as "designing for defiance," in 1960. Here, the construction of a fallout shelter was "not just about doing all you can to protect your family" but about reaffirming male agency in the home: "a shelter after all is also for you." Shelters were a "home improvement exercise" that let men take control in an age of nuclear anxiety, giving them a chance to create a room that might "double as an extra activity area for your fun and relaxation." The "nuclear bunker" was marketed for "daily use" as a "hobby room, music room, or recreation room."[18] Family protection was not all doom and gloom; it was an experience fathers might enjoy. Reportedly, one Wisconsin-based shelter salesman claimed that shelter owners would be able to "bring the buddies round . . . play some hands of poker . . . show off to neighbors."[19]

The message was clear: homeowners who bought fallout shelters were more than good citizens; they were also fulfilling their desire to consume.[20] "A family fallout shelter is a room with seven lives," noted David Feldman, an interior designer for the American Institute of Decorators, "card room, stereo hi-fi room, guest room and den." The shelter he designed offered the latest survival tools as well as an ottoman, a section bookcase, and a desk with a side chair and a lamp, all in "modern Danish style." The nine-by-twelve-foot space featured a "designer rug" that "unified the walnut and teak woods with harmonizing bright fabrics" and was accessorized with a "colorful abstract painting" to create a "room for the modern man to relax."[21]

Shelter advertisements appealed to a vision of masculine identity based on tasteful and appropriate consumption as it intersected with the politics of national security. Fathers could possess the latest survival equipment, from Geiger counters to emergency radios, and also enjoy well-stocked liquor cabinets, gourmet food, excellent stereos, the latest jazz recordings, and high-brow replicas of modern art. In the modern world of civil defense, they were suburban frontiersmen successfully navigating through the consumer republic. As one salesman touted at the 1961 Chicago Home Furnishing Market, personal shelters let fathers "battle the commies" while "waiting out radiation danger in pleasure and comfort, and relaxation."[22] The message was reassuring: with basic do-it-yourself skills and a cash investment, these men could make their homes robust and pleasant enough to survive a nuclear war. In the words of a Michigan-based shelter designer and seller, "why shouldn't the end of the world be comfortable?" (see figure 9).[23]

Salesmen also stocked the pages of newspapers and magazines with images of fathers and sons working together to construct shelters. In October 1961, at the height of public inquiries about civil defense, the Miami-based American Shelter Corporation filled its promotional material with such images.[24] In an endorsement for a Salt Lake City shelter company, Ben Smith, the city's OCD director, was pictured in *Time* cementing concrete bricks with his son while his daughter painted a large mural on a shelter wall.[25] The paternalistic act of construction that shelter salesmen invoked in their advertisements negotiated what K. A. Cuordileone identifies as the essential problem of midcentury fatherhood: finding the "appropriate balance between 'soft' and 'hard' fathering."[26] By building a shelter with his son, a father was modeling a version of male behavior that was seen as integral to nuclear survival. At the same time he was negotiating a balance between other kinds of male behavior. With his paternal warmth, he was fostering a compassionate and well-adjusted son; with his patriarchal leadership and authority, he was creating a bulwark against juvenile delinquency and deviance. According to a 1947 article in *Parenting* magazine, this "new fatherhood" was a benefit to society, a way to nurture "a boy who admires his dad and cherishes the time, the happy hours they spend together accepting his masculine role smoothly and easily." Simultaneously, "his sister will be forming, half consciously, her ideal picture of what a man should be and the kind of relationship she will one day have with her husband."[27]

Pioneers of Self-Protection in Barnyard and Patio

ATTRACTIVE ADDITION. In Orlando, Fla. Doug Bartholow built concrete-block shelter as annex to his house. Here family relaxes in patio as Mrs. Bartholow tends garden on roof.

FIGURE 9. "Pioneers of Self-Protection in Barnyard and Patio": "Attractive Addition. In Orlando Doug Bartholow built concrete-block shelter as annex to his house. Here family relaxes in patio as Mrs. Bartholow tends garden on roof." "Pioneers of Self-Protection in Barnyard and Patio," *Life*, September 15, 1961, 108. Photo by Ralph Morse/the LIFE Picture Collection via Getty Images.

Studies of American fatherhood have outlined the numerous ways in which lifestyle magazines such as *Good Housekeeping*, *Esquire*, and *Reader's Digest* and television shows such as *The Adventures of Ozzie and Harriet* popularized the cultural ideal of effective fatherhood as the most important occupation in the world. As the historian James Gilbert argues, it was something that men were told they had to "learn." Within the bounds of suburban domesticity and mid-century fatherhood, do-it-yourself projects had considerable cultural currency because they offered men the chance to teach their sons by means of tasks that felt like "small acts of heroism performed by frontiersmen on the suburban badlands."[28] Parenting magazines and politicians repeatedly encouraged suburban fathers to "relinquish the old ways of their fathers, and to instead share hobbies and have fun with son[s]," not primarily for reasons of companionship but to provide an appropriate model of masculinity.[29]

For the shelter business, however, do-it-yourself survival was less about cultural resonance and more about profit. The commercialization of civil defense coincided with the ascension of the do-it-yourself industry, which by midcentury had become the "new billion dollar hobby."[30] Its rise was predicated on the growing popularity of home improvement exercises during the Great Depression, sugarcoated as "necessary but fun" acts of American domestic life.[31] As homeownership rates skyrocketed after World War II, home improvement became a "national pastime."[32] According to *Life*, by 1959, U.S. citizens were spending "more on leisure than on new housing and automobiles combined," and much of that sum went to do-it-yourself hobbies—a "$40 Billion Bill just for fun."[33] The cultural historian Sarah Litchman points out that, by 1953, 11 million "do-it-yourselves—mainly men— sawed through 500 million square feet of plywood, brushed on 100 million gallons of paint, and applied 150 million rolls of wallpaper."[34]

Fallout shelter salesmen were operating in what *Business Weekly* called "the Age of Do-It-Yourself," and throughout the 1950s and into the 1960s the OCD increasingly looked to them to help sell the message of survival.[35] The sales strategies these men concocted displayed their detailed understanding of the masculine dynamics of the do-it-yourself industry, although their styles of selling varied. In training sessions, salesmen who worked for trade associations frequently engaged with OCD civil defense booklets and educational materials, while those who worked directly for shelter companies allowed themselves more creative license. Many commonly used color prints that depicted various shelter models and flip cards printed with price points to be memorized.³⁶ These flip cards, sometimes collected by local OCD officials, often included pithy quotations from politicians and key survival statistics published in popular magazines. But sales, not education, were the key goal. "Make no mistake! Family Fallout Protection is a serious business," declared an advertisement for Family Fallout Shelters, Incorporated, of Pottstown, Pennsylvania. "[I]nvestigate before you buy and get the facts from us!" The ad featured fifteen different shelter models, including one made almost entirely from plywood, demonstrating just how far the facts might be stretched to secure a sale.³⁷

Sales brochures were a primary prop for doorway interactions. Howard Shaw, the founder of Survive-All Shelters of Columbus, Ohio (the company reverted to its original name, Hollywood Pool, Inc., a week after the Cuban missile crisis), provided his salesmen with a version he had produced in partnership with Mort Kridel Advertising Agency. It opened with a letter written by Shaw offering a foundation for the sales pitch that followed.³⁸ Clearly, selling Survive-All Shelters meant blending scientific authority and popular culture with blurry evidence that shelters would work and inserting handy quotations from political supporters of civil defense. The result was a striking and apparently logical, if not fully convincing, composite of the masculinized rhetoric that dominated the politics of home survival. Discussion of the post-apocalyptic film *On the Beach* was treated as a test of survival readiness; references to *Life* magazine and the names of prominent civil defense supporters such as Governor Nelson Rockefeller and the atomic scientist Edward Teller were slipped into the pitch to add a level of authenticity. The act of purchasing a shelter was made familiar and relatable, and a final exhortation urged fathers to bravely confront the issue.

According to letters sent to the Federal Trade Commission from citizens complaining about unscrupulous business practices, face-to-face shelter pitches were marked by two prominent themes: salesmen told customers to man up to the atomic threat, and they touted shelters as a new space for male retreat in the suburban home—in the words of one salesman, "[t]o put your hard-earned money into your family's safety" and "to face the threat and make something for yourself."³⁹ Using these dual themes of male consumerism—escape and conformity—salesmen developed an exceptionally malleable language for customers in which the fallout shelter receded from its original function of protection and became an imagined suburban space awaiting homeowners' needs and desires. Again and again, the male-dominated world of the salesman intersected with the domestic ideology of Cold War fatherhood as local shelter businesses, which had considerable autonomy in controlling how their communities participated in the home front, presented male consumers with a carefully constructed national purpose.⁴⁰

Price played an important role in the social experience of selling and buying survival. As I have already discussed, many potential shelter builders were anxious about their economic instability and their lack of adequate construction skills. Thus, the notion of affordable survival became a key weapon in the linguistic arsenal of shelter salesmen. Costs varied wildly, from the suspiciously low price of $150 for a model shelter kit to more than $10,000 for a multiroom deluxe shelter complex.⁴¹ Options in size, type, and scale gave male consumers the comfort of agency as they chose how to protect their families. "Think of it like a new car," argued Frank Hopkins, a one-time car dealer but now, in 1961, a full-time shelter salesmen. "[T]here are a range of models. But pick any one and it will get the job done."⁴²

Negotiating price gave salesmen another strategic advantage: the option to upsell their products. The sales brochure of Shelter, Inc., displayed a range of options, from "basic models" that claimed to offer all the "necessities of survival" to spacious luxury models decorated with rugs and "expensive indoor paneling." While working for the Fallout Shelter Company, Robert Ambley noted that if buyers balked at the initial cost of purchasing a shelter, he might discuss a range of financing options and a "lowering of costs . . . if it meant closing a sale." If customers thought a shelter was a necessary purchase and agreed to the initial cost, then he would encourage them to spend a little more to make their spaces as "impressive and comfortable as possible." "After all," he noted, "war or not, it'll make a pretty dandy extra room at a price you can afford."[43]

"ENTER THE SURVIVAL MERCHANTS"

According to *Consumer Reports,* a total of 200,000 home fallout shelter assembly kits were sold in the United States in 1961 and 1962.[44] This figure is probably not accurate: an unrecorded number of homeowners kept their shelters a secret from neighbors and the authorities, and many construction jobs were never completed.[45] Nevertheless, if we consider that the nation in these years had a population of 180 million, the estimate illustrates a fundamental truth about the consumer culture of civil defense: when given the opportunity to purchase, construct, and furnish their own shelters, most American families declined to do so. *Consumer Reports* analysts blamed the commercial failure of shelters on the product itself: "Fallout shelters of the type widely proposed to date" were too "costly and complex in their requirements [for oxygen supply, water, power, heat, food, and sanitary arrangements] . . . limited and unreliable in usefulness . . . dependent on variants and unknowns."[46]

The recorded testimonies of salesmen tell a more complex story, one of failed expectations and declining profits, of fathers trying to make sense of a federal policy that encouraged them to take survival into their own hands. These recollections suggest that quality, cost, and feasibility factors do not entirely explain why most male consumers refused to purchase backyard bunkers. Steven Heck, a sales representative for the Michigan-based shelter company Gricar-Anderson, remembered, "One guy shouted at me—actually *shouted,* '[D]on't you know that the more shelters we have the more likely someone is about to start a war? Why do you do this to us?'"[47] In other words, far from being received with respect, salesmen were often seen as unwanted intrusions, even as hucksters who were exploiting private citizens and profiting from community fear.

Still, the records of shelter companies make it abundantly clear that their sales failures were not due to a lack of public interest. According to many salesmen, people continued to be curious about home shelters, though they were often more attracted to the consumer spectacle than to the actual products. The recollections of James Cline are typical. Like many shelter entrepreneurs, Cline, the manager of a lumber company in Royal Oak, Michigan, decided to try selling survival after reading *Life*'s fallout shelter special issue in September 1961. He was struck by the bunker's "elegant design" and the "ease" with which the Carlsons had constructed it. Because he had little technical or design experience, he became a regional dealer for Kelsey Hayes, the company whose model had been featured in *Life*. Cline constructed a model Kelsey Hayes shelter in his lumberyard and began advertising shelter kits priced at $725 each. At first he was shocked by the volume of people visiting his display: during an eight-week period, 2,500 shoppers viewed and discussed his model.[48] Yet only one customer purchased a shelter kit. Not only was Cline's new business venture a commercial disaster, but it also alienated members of his community. "People were confused, frightened, angry," he recalled. "I was accused of profiteering, war-mongering—you name it." For the people of Royal Oak, Cline had become a symbol of nuclear disaster and an unwelcome reminder that survival had a price tag.[49]

Salesmen's recorded testimonies are filled with similar anecdotes that reveal the inherent contradictions of civil defense as a capitalist venture.[50] Yet even when homeowners bought into the civic expectations of civil defense, they often discovered that building a shelter was no easy feat. Social histories of the Cold War typically frame the creation and maintenance of domestic spaces such as garages, workshops, and barbecue pits as a means to affirm conventional ideas of masculinity in an increasingly suburbanized world.[51] According to Steven Gelber, do-it-yourself activities allowed postwar American men to create a male space in their homes while "actively participat[ing] in family activities."[52] Yet in salesmen's recollections, this narrative of domestic masculinity, which dominated the marketing culture of home shelters, was in practice complicated and muddy. Rather than typifying what D. B. Holt and C. J. Thompson call the "man-of-action" consumer, potential fallout shelter builders were often portrayed as confused, incompetent, and skeptical.[53] Even their own letters make this clear. John Boyd, a father from Oklahoma, wrote to the OCD in July 1961 about his experience with a shelter salesman: "[I]f I build a shelter, if it even works, then what? I ask the sales guy this very question. He just shrugged and told me 'better than doing nothing at all.' I didn't trust him; the whole thing left a bad taste in my mouth."[54] Jake Willis, a father from Boston, asked the OCD in November 1961, "Why would I take out a loan to bury my family underground, what sort of father would do that?"[55] Far from affirming domestic masculinity, the family shelter was, for many men, a grim reminder of their vulnerability and impotence.

In this uneasy atmosphere, door-to-door shelter salesmen often found themselves engaged in complex interactions with families. In a letter to her local OCD office, Michelle Pomerleau, a San Diego resident, wrote of her experiences with a traveling shelter salesman, noting that she had spotted trouble right away: "I don't know who this salesman thought he was. Clearly a huckster." Although she admitted "my husband was keen for the extra space," she herself was convinced that "this fly-by-nighter meant no good." She begged local officials to exert more control over who exactly was allowed to sell shelters: "[T]his business is bad for your publicity."[56] Other families had similar reactions to shelter salesmen. Linda Hope of New Jersey invited a salesman into her home and quickly recognized that his product was a "bad way to waste a pay check."[57] Alice Laurel from Los Angeles pointed out that a shelter would be useless "unless the bomb drops when my husband is home and my kids are back from school.... Think about this for more than ten seconds and the logic falls apart."[58] Sales rhetoric promoting the consumerist ideal of the bachelor pad bunker was constantly undermined by realistic discussions of household finances and appeals (often by women at home talking to these salesmen) to basic common sense.

Children, too, played an important part in undermining masculinized sales rhetoric. The archives contain a trove of letters that schoolchildren sent to President Kennedy on the topic of nuclear survival, often at the behest of their teachers. In several cases, they mention their discomfort with the notion of shelters. Charlie Wilkins, age twelve, told the president that "personally I don't like shelters. They make me feel odd. Not sure why we need them."[59] Archie Bowers, age fourteen, said, "[T]he [shelter] display at school worries [me]. I agree with my teacher that it should go away."[60] Their personal stories reveal far more than government records do about families' complex reactions to shelter salesmen.

Clearly, salesmen had trouble pitching a product that represented not conformity and security but anxiety and revulsion. They also encountered other problems on the job. One of the most detailed accounts came from James Byrne, a Detroit-based plywood salesman, who, like others, faced considerable animosity from customers about do-it-yourself survival. At first, he saw home shelters as a "can't miss proposition"; every statement from the Oval Office, every copy of *Life*'s special issue was a "million-dollar free advertisment."[61] The potential profit margin was also attractive: he could purchase one Kelsey Hayes shelter kit at the wholesale price of $433 and sell it for $725.[62] The representative from Kelsey Hayes had been quick to tell him that not only had Sears, Roebuck and Company already "agreed to test-market" the product, but a "national 'saturation' advertisement campaign" was in the works.[63] The quality of the product could also, in theory, be trusted. Byrne said in an interview that he had "believed" the Kelsey Hayes agent who "assured" him that "two men could assemble [the shelter] in two to four hours."[64] On paper, it seemed like the perfect way to make a profit, perform a patriotic duty, and offer a do-it-yourself project to any homeowner with basic manual skills.

Byrne bought fourteen unassembled Kelsey Hayes shelter kits and immediately sold thirteen to other aspiring regional dealers in Michigan. Reserving one shelter from his original purchase to serve as a model display, he then placed an order for another fourteen shelter kits. Confident about his new business venture, Byrne spent $20,000 on a local advertising campaign, assigned two employees to construct the model shelter, and eagerly waited for customers. The first problem emerged when Byrne found his workers struggling to put together the model shelter. Rather than taking two hours to build, it took ten.

The second problem appeared after the walls were erected. Reinforcing them to OCD specifications required "dumping a small mountain of sand—four to five cubic yards—into eight-inch hollows between the walls and ceiling panels," a task that Byrne realized would take yet another ten hours to complete. Faced with these complications, he started to doubt the validity of the spokesman's claims. If Byrne and his workers were struggling with these basic construction problems, how would an ordinary homeowner overcome them? As he pointed out in his interview, "[Y]ou will be filling a space nearly seven feet high, and there are only a few inches of clearance between the shelter and the basement ceiling. . . . [H]ow are you going to get the sand in there? With a spoon?"[65]

As Byrne's experience makes clear, a Kelsey Hayes fallout shelter was far more complicated than a typical do-it-yourself project. This became a persistent problem for both salesmen and homeowners as they struggled to assemble shelter kits. The consumer message of do-it-yourself survival was devolving into an almost comical narrative of families and salesmen trying and failing to build shelters. Letters sent to the OCD during the week of the Cuban missile crisis are littered with accounts of failed shelter construction projects. Problems included water leaks, prefabricated walls that did not fit into basements, shelter ceilings that collapsed, and local authorities who refused to issue building permits. Miami residents complained that high groundwater levels were making basement shelters almost impossible to complete; in Ohio a farmer who was attempting to build a shelter accidentally cut a water pipe, flooding his home and creating a local water shortage.[66] In place of "every home a fortress," the OCD was facing, in the words of its director Steuart Pittman, "a national DIY disaster."[67]

Shelter entrepreneurs found themselves having to make the best of a difficult situation. In the case of James Byrne, despite his personal misgivings, he remained convinced that shelters had the potential to turn a profit, and he had already made a substantial capital investment in that hope. He assigned his best sales representative, Sal George, to recruit a team of door-to-door salesmen, offering them a $100 commission for every sale made. "They went out with high hopes," George recalled. "[T]hey pointed out [to homeowners] how shelters were useful not only as shelters, but also, when paneled, as a spare room, study or photo lab. They really wanted those $100 commissions."[68] But not a single shelter was sold. According to George, two factors were at play. The first was the cost: "we can't afford it now" and "we will see how things turn out in Berlin" were common responses to sales pitches.[69] The second was the message of do-it-yourself survival itself: "People listen to the sales pitch, take all the literature, . . . ask questions and then just walk away. . . . [T]hey just didn't buy it." Even during the Cuban missile crisis the public refused to buy Byrne's shelters. On October 23, 1962, the day after Kennedy announced that missiles had been discovered in Cuba, George and Byrne loaded the model shelter onto the back of a flatbed truck. In a last-ditch attempt to attract sales, they reduced the price by $100, posted a display sign on the model touting "FALLOUT SHELTERS—WHILE THEY LAST," and parked the truck outside "shopping centers and veteran halls." Despite a steady stream of foot traffic, there was not even the "nibble of a sale." According to Byrne, "That shelter was out there day and night unattended . . . [and] not so much as a bolt was stolen. . . . [E]ven vandals weren't interested." Eventually Byrne placed an advertisement in a local paper offering to give away the shelters free of charge. A family in Westphal, Michigan, took him up on the offer. "Last I heard from them they were having trouble assembling it. But I'm not asking questions."[70]

Although shelter entrepreneurs shared many stories of failure, a few shelter companies did have limited success in selling their products. The reasons behind the disparity in successes and failures are difficult to discern, partly due to the inflated rhetoric in salesmen's testimonies and the scattered nature of private business documentation. We can, however, draw some conclusions. First, in 1961, salesmen such as Frank Norton and Leo Hoegh reported a profitable year in part because they had strong, preexisting, institutional contacts with civil defense policymakers. Thus, unlike Byrne, they were able to work through federal channels when plying their trade.[71] Hoegh, as a former head of the OCD, was able to keep his company, Wonder, Inc., afloat by adjusting quickly to shifts in administrative policy and public sentiment, which led him, for instance, to move from selling individual home shelters to constructing public shelters in schools. Few shelter salesmen had such close governmental affiliations.

Many of the shelter companies reporting limited success stayed solvent by taking on the responsibility of home protection themselves. They made a profit not by selling construction kits to homeowners but by building the shelters themselves. In place of a do-it-yourself model, a new service industry had started to take hold. "For two years I've starved in this business," said an Orlando-based shelter salesman named Douglas Bartholow. "[S]ince Kennedy's defense talk," however, his shelter construction company was "average[ing] two sales a day at $2,195."[72] In the last quarter of 1961, sales for shelter construction services appeared to be healthy.[73] In October, a Boston contractor reported that he was "overwhelmed" with orders and was turning down requests from "panicky citizens" who were willing to spend nearly $800 each to have him build a shelter "the next day."[74] In Sacramento, business was booming for Atlas Shelters, which was selling six-person, OCD-approved, thirty-five-ton prefabricated shelters for $5,000 to $6,000 each. According to the company's owner, Frank Ringer, "[W]e haven't done any advertisement yet, there's so much demand we hardly keep up with it."[75]

"SUEDE-SHOE BOYS": THE DECLINE OF THE SHELTER SALESMEN

During the height of the bomb shelter craze, the infant shelter industry, unregulated and chaotic, was struggling to translate the consumer language of do-it-yourself survival into direct sales. However, its potential for market growth was being rapidly undercut by a new issue confronting potential buyers: claims that the industry was steeped in fraudulent business practices. By 1962, shelter companies and salesmen who were conscientiously working within OCD guidelines were competing against unscrupulous hucksters falsely "claiming to sell government approved shelters."[76] According to an article in a February issue of *Time*, one of the biggest problems for the home fallout shelter market, aside from issues with the products themselves, was the fact that swarms of non-experts, from "swimming pool contractors to car dealers, ... [were] claiming to be authorities on bomb shelters."[77] Reports to the Federal Trade Commission indicate that shelter salesmen in Los Angeles, New York, and Chicago were "posing as civil defense officials" to boost faltering sales.[78] As the year progressed, the biggest challenge facing shelter companies across the United States was not the usefulness of their products but their own credibility.

In an early 1962 issue of the *New York Times*, the syndicated columnist James Reston sardonically declared, "No group of citizens is showing more solicitude for the well-being of the nation" than the fallout shelter salesmen who were trying to turn a profit out of national fear. In his view, their existence exposed the inequality inherent within civil defense, a government policy that favored "the rich over the poor, the single house dweller over the apartment dweller, the homeowner over the renter."[79] Rather than providing a public service, shelter salesmen offered gullible homeowners a chance to be "evaporated in style."[80] Reston was not alone in his criticism. William L. Shirer, writing for *Good Housekeeping*, derided the "true barbarity" of the family shelter. For him, shelters exposed troubling aspects of class and racial inequality that had long gone unmentioned. "Are only the well-to-do among us to have a chance of survival?" he asked, accusing shelter salesmen of "threatening to make a racket out of the bewilderment of the American people."[81] "The entire sales pitch of civil defense," Walt Goodman wrote in *Redbook*, is based on "the happy image of father, mother, children, sitting snugly together in their new convertible game room shelter, first aid kit ready but unused." To Goodman, the home-shelter market was "based on several grossly inaccurate assumptions."[82]

Against a backdrop of public unease, press scrutiny, and growing distrust, the consumer civil defense market began to decline. Acting after a series of citizens' complaints about shady shelter contractors appeared in the *New York Times* and the *Washington Post*, the FTC moved to sort out "official shelter manufacturers" from those operating "outside of OCD guidelines."[83] While its primary task was to catalogue the number of shelter firms operating across the United States, its reach clearly extended beyond the logistics of the market; for during the early months of 1962, it launched an investigation into the advertisement of home shelters. Do-it-yourself nuclear survival, already falling out of favor in the Kennedy administration, was suddenly experiencing a new level of scrutiny from a federal agency that had little vested interest in seeing the shelter market succeed.

Throughout 1962, Paul Rand Dixon, the chair of the FTC, took a hard line against salesmen who were operating outside of OCD approval—"suede-shoe boys," as they were dubbed by Roy Hoover, the director of the Los Angeles OCD office.[84] "Ideologically, we're at war with communism," Dixon said, adding that promoting "worthless shelters . . . comes pretty close to being treason."[85] Already, with the goal of curtailing "fraudulent and dangerous advertisement[s]," he had instituted new guidelines in late 1961, which would "limit the layman's language" in interpreting OCD protocols.[86] Shelter firms caught operating outside of these guidelines risked fines and potential criminal prosecution. The goal was to "root the exploiters of human fear out of the picture" and provide "a detailed, clear cut and nationwide civil defense program under the leadership of the federal government."[87]

The tightening of FTC guidelines around shelter advertisements demonstrated a new level of sophistication in the federal government's approach to the political management of nuclear survival. Since the early nineteenth century, as Helen Tangires writes, local U.S. markets have been controlled by the actions of city planners and officials who police and manage the impulse of private businesses to exploit their communities.[88] It is useful to consider this pattern when examining the moral economy of the shelter business, in which unscrupulous and exploitative market practices pointed time and again to the government's failure to provide its people with meaningful civil defense. The shift from private gendered ideas of survival to public models of community protection illustrate the complex role that consumer citizenship played in the growth politics of the Cold War. The shelter business and its appeal to male breadwinners was part of what Meg Jacobs identifies as economic citizenship in the twentieth century, in which a fledgling industry is linked to political interests in an effort to encourage "state-building from the bottom up." In the idealized marketplace of civil defense, "policymakers acted on behalf of the 'consuming public'" to foster and sustain participation in the Cold War.[89] Yet as Lizabeth Cohen observes, grassroots consumer activism may have had a notable impact on drawing federal interest to a matter that politicians might prefer to leave in the hands of the market. This was the case in the growing cultural rejection of home shelters.[90]

Even within the OCD, private shelter companies working with trade associations were no longer seen as the "solution" to public engagement with civil defense.[91] At the same time, the New Frontier's media-savvy advisors began promoting a shift from private to community shelters. In late 1961, during a Thanksgiving meeting at the Kennedy family compound in Hyannisport, Schlesinger, who had steadily been compiling examples of negative shelter coverage, pushed the president to reconfigure his position, stating that the question of "shelter ownership has turned ugly."[92] Schlesinger advised him to stop publicly endorsing do-it-yourself shelters; if civil defense had to be discussed, it should be framed as community welfare. By the summer of 1962, as tensions escalated over Cuba, the marketing of do-it-yourself survival appeared to be increasingly unsustainable.

The FTC's new, stricter guidelines on shelter advertising and the president's diminishing support for home shelters had an immediate impact on the industry. In 1961, OCD-sponsored public shelter exhibits had been commonplace at state fairs, shopping malls, and veterans centers. In November of that year, families visiting Prince George Mall in Washington, DC, were greeted by a "recording of air raid sirens and exploding bombs" and a looped tape of an "anguished male voice" shouting, "My wife, my children . . . if I'd only listened to civil defense . . . I'd be in that shelter now." By the following summer, such public exhibitions had mostly vanished, replaced by presentations that focused on locating and identifying public safety zones.[93]

Private shelter contractors caught operating outside the new FTC guidelines now faced harsh legal repercussions. The Orlando-based firm Survival Shelters was forced to cease operations in March 1962 after local residents reported that the company had used the OCD's civil defense emblem in its promotional materials without authorization.[94] According to OCD officials, the company's sales pamphlets were "designed to give the impression that the Government had approved of the product" and as such "must be taken out of circulation immediately."[95] By then, however, residents of Orlando had already lost confidence in local civil defense efforts.

By the fall of 1962, reports of suede-shoe salesmen were drowning out positive coverage of reputable shelter firms. Civil defense critics filled the pages of the *New Republic, Newsweek,* the *Nation,* and *Commonweal* with anecdotes about profiteering—for instance, about "gullible homeowners" who were paying $850 for shelters that had cost $180 wholesale.[96] Such articles cast shelter salesmen in the role of "racketeers"; anxious fathers were presented as "neurotic men" tricked into making a purchase that offered no actual family safety.[97] In the months preceding the Cuban missile crisis, media critics returned again and again to the image of a tricked father who had purchased a faulty shelter, frequently in conjunction with stories like this one in *Consumer Reports,* which described an OCD officer inspecting a $5,000-dollar shelter and deeming it a "potential tomb."[98] Such articles fueled the perception that shelter owners were not responsible male consumers but dupes taking part in an activity that was at best "ludicrous" and at worst "immoral."[99]

Tales of homeowners deceived by shelter salesmen were not just media sensationalism. Similar accounts filled public correspondence to the White House and the OCD during 1961 and 1962. Not surprisingly, fathers who had bought shelters from sales representatives claiming to speak on behalf of the federal government were quick to register their complaints. Arthur L. Doolittle of Long Island, New York, wrote directly to President Kennedy following his experience with the Port Jefferson–based firm U.S. Fallout Shelter, Inc. He told the president that he had contacted the company after seeing an "advertisement in the local newspaper, *Newsday*, about a shelter for $495 which was civil defense approved." A sales representative promptly appeared at his home, claiming to "speak on behalf of the government." This salesman told the family that the $495 shelter model was unsuitable, due to a "high roentgen count from living so close to New York City." Their best option, he declared, was to convert the home cellar into an underground shelter—a service that the company could provide at a cost of $2,200. When Doolittle told the salesman he could not afford it, the representative appealed to his paternal responsibilities: "[T]heir argument was that, as a husband, the safety of my wife and children should come first." Convinced by the sales pitch, Doolittle agreed to pay $1,250 for a shelter to be built in his cellar, and he took out an FHA loan for the construction. "We are a family of patriots," he wrote. "[W]e went ahead with the shelter, and we felt we were acting as good Americans." The job, however, was never completed. After workers installed the frame, the company's owners came by to inspect it and "stat[ed] that it was not built correctly and they would fix it.... Needless to say no one came around to fix it." When Doolittle tried to contact the company, he was informed that it had "disconnected its phone line." In his letter, he said that both the Better Business Bureau and the OCD officer for Long Island had been unable to help him.[100]

By 1962, the message of civil defense, with its affirmation of individualism and self-reliance, was yielding to the uncomfortable suspicion that the shelter industry was exploiting the fears of a nation. The narratives of people such as James Cline, who had decided to sell shelters from a sense of national service, were quickly forgotten, replaced with stories such as an anecdote in the *Saturday Evening Post* about shelter salesmen posing as civil defense officials to make a quick sale.[101] Rather than giving families agency at a time of increasing international tension, the home-shelter market was highlighting the vulnerabilities of the nuclear age. As the industry declined, issues of class became increasingly visible. Publications such as *Ebony* and *Jet* derided family shelters as a "white suburban craze," and protesters from organizations such as SANE and Women Strike for Peace filled their literature with discussions of the "open sacrifice of the inner city, in favor of the white suburbs."[102] In the *New York Times*, Arthur Krock called civil defense a policy for the "'fortunate'—fortunate in having the money to build private shelters so elaborately designed, or in areas sufficiently remote from a blast area to survive."[103] Columnist James Reston argued that the home-shelter market offered survival to "citizens of rich states like New York, but not the citizens in Mississippi." For many journalists and intellectuals, the true moral horror of civil defense resided in the eager commercialism of the home-shelter market, which "skirted the brink of war" while ostensibly providing protection—but only for people who were lucky enough to own a home.[104]

Just as quickly as they had appeared, shelter salesmen vanished. Businesses with brand-new shelter divisions rapidly closed them down, and their owners often complained in local papers about a year of lost revenue.[105] The housing market went through a similar sudden transition; the family fallout shelter disappeared almost overnight from real-estate advertisements and promotions. Homeowners were doing more than simply rejecting the presence of shelters in their suburban houses. Rather, they were engaging with and negotiating their own positions within the political economy of nuclear survival. Their public correspondence, rich in tales of failed construction projects, pleas for federal assistance, and accounts of cheated customers, charts the limitations of economic citizenship modeled on male consumerism. During the Cold War, private commercial interests faltered at the moment of sales interaction, when the public refused to purchase survival. Instead of recasting men as defenders of the nation, the interaction between fathers and salesmen highlighted the confluence of fears of nuclear annihilation.

By October 1962, the month of the Cuban missile crisis, shelter owners were themselves attracting a substantial level of criticism, especially as reports spread of fathers who were stockpiling their shelters with weapons and ammunition and embracing a survivalist mentality. As protests against civil defense policies erupted on college campuses across the United States, the family fallout shelter came to symbolize, in the words of the journalist Walter Lippmann, the "evil of each family for himself and the devil take the hindmost."[106] The home-shelter market folded, and companies that had opened survival divisions quietly returned to their original purposes. Even the Cuba crisis, a week of intense public engagement with civil defense, could not reverse the industry's fortunes. The loss of presidential backing, coupled with an increasing focus on community survival, equaled consumer rejection, indifference, and faltering sales. By the start of 1963, six hundred shelter companies nationwide had filed for bankruptcy.[107] The market for the family shelter was dead.

SALESMEN AND SURVIVAL

In 1963, the Chicago-based comedy troupe, Second City (some of whose founding members went on to perform on *Saturday Night Live*), had a popular routine they called "The Fallout Shelter Salesmen." The performance followed the antics of a fictional company, Acme Fallout Shelters, and its owner's attempts to train three aspiring salesmen. As the skit developed, it became clear that one was much more adept at selling survival than the others were. Not only was he happy to offer a "money-back guarantee" to any family whose shelter did not survive a direct nuclear blast, but he was also "willing to throw in a free machine gun" to help keep those "pesky" neighbors away. The routine was a "guaranteed crowd pleaser" in Chicago's underground comedy clubs and later in New York City.[108] Clearly, by 1963, the family fallout shelter had become something of a national joke.

Whether he was a nationwide talking point or the object of countercultural satire, the fallout shelter salesman occupied a unique place in the cultural and political imaginations of Cold War Americans. The two-year rise and fall of the home-shelter business supports arguments that the bomb-shelter craze of the early 1960s was, to an extent, a passing fad. Yet the history of fallout shelter sales is far more than a simple narrative of failed expectations, inflated sales rhetoric, and unscrupulous business practices. From New York to California, salesmen and their customers were engaging with the federal politics and policies of nuclear survival. Why, in the end, did the public reject the home fallout shelter? The historian Kenneth D. Rose identifies a "complex" mixture of "fatalism, apathy and skepticism."[109] Yet it is important to remember that shelter salesmen were central and active players in the confused struggle to domesticate, privatize, and normalize nuclear warfare.

CHAPTER FIVE

Survival and Violence at the Shelter Doorway

> What you are about to watch is a nightmare. It is not meant to be prophetic. It need not happen. It's the fervent and urgent prayer of all men of good will that it never shall happen. But in this place, in this moment, it does happen. This is the Twilight Zone.
> —"The Shelter," *The Twilight Zone*, September 29, 1961

> After all what could be more American than a father defending his homestead with a shotgun in a lawless world?
> —Spencer R. Weart, *Nuclear Fear: A History of Images*, 1988

At 10 P.M. on a Friday night in late September 1961, CBS broadcast what would become a critically acclaimed and controversial episode of *The Twilight Zone*.[1] First aired at the height of the Berlin crisis, "The Shelter" opens on a peaceful suburban dinner party at the home of a neighborhood doctor, Bill Stockton. It's Bill's birthday, and Jerry Harlowe, his best friend, honors him as "a man of care and devotion" dedicated to the well-being of the community. His only fault, Jerry jokes, is the "hammering at all times of night" that emanates from his home and the "nocturnal visits" from construction companies that keep his neighbors awake.[2] Bill Stockton, it turns out, has been building his family a fallout shelter, and his friends are teasing him about.

Suddenly, the dinner party is interrupted by a radio bulletin: the United States is under Yellow Alert, and citizens should retreat to their private fallout shelters immediately. The assembled guests realize that a nuclear attack is imminent, and Stockton is the only person in the neighborhood with a fallout shelter. But rather than ushering all of his guests into the bunker, Bill and his family seal themselves off alone, leaving the others outside. Jerry pleads, "Bill, we've got to use your shelter! I've got to keep my family alive! And we won't use any of your stuff. Don't you understand? We will bring our own!"

Bill responds, "I'm sorry, Jerry. As God is my witness—I'm sorry. But I built this for *my* family."

"What about *mine*?" Jerry retorts. "What do *we* do? Just rock on the front porch until we get burned to cinders?"

The neighborhood descends into anarchy. Residents quickly form a mob and prepare to force their way into Bill's shelter. At the precise moment they break open the door, a second bulletin calmly announces that the impending attack was a false alarm. Appalled at their behavior, the neighbors offer to reimburse Bill for the damage to his property. His reply brings the episode to a close: "The damages! The damages I'm talking about are the pieces of ourselves that we've pulled apart tonight. . . . We were spared the bomb tonight; I wonder if we weren't destroyed even without it?"

The Twilight Zone's head writer and narrator, Rod Serling, was well known for his caustic social commentary. In "The Shelter" he cast his mordant gaze on the questionable morality of privatized survival. Jettisoning a model of masculinity prefaced on emotional maturity and reasoned judgment, the fathers portrayed in this episode embrace a model of Cold War masculinity without physical or moral restraints. In a sharp departure from the mainstream political styling of civil defense, which framed shelter fathers as responsible, community-minded citizens, *The Twilight Zone* reveals them as barbaric.[3]

The episode highlighted Serling's brilliant ability to draw out and reflect on the fraught personal conversations that were unfolding in real time in American living rooms during the fall of 1961. For most contemporary viewers, the experience of watching "The Shelter" was disturbing and unpleasant. Clearly, it had struck a nerve.[4] Within two days, CBS received roughly 1,500 response letters from the public,

Serling more than 1,300.⁵ For William Abee of Belmont, North Carolina, Serling's vision of middle-class male violence felt horribly prescient. Writing to Terry Sanford, the governor of North Carolina, he said, "You will see how quickly I am swamped with those people that thought that they didn't need a shelter. It will be like it was in Twilight Zone last night. . . . That can happen to us [who] have these shelters and that is one reason I am asking you now if you don't believe there should be some sort of pressure put on the people if they don't willingly build [them] . . . so that rush on us that have [them] won't happen as bad as it can now."⁶

Abee's letter offers direct insight into the burgeoning gun-thy-neighbor debate around home fallout shelters. While the historian Kenneth D. Rose has conducted important work exploring the rise of shelter violence, the implications of shelter hatch ethics for our understanding of Cold War masculinity has yet to be discussed. Distinctively masculine in tone, this debate reframed the shelter owner into a symbol of national disunity: a father who must be willing to resort to violence to ensure his family's survival. As shows such as *The Twilight Zone* cemented this figure in the national psyche, notions of violence, both real and imagined, entered the narrative of male shelter ownership and had a profound impact on the language of national security. The discourse of patriarchal authority, already inherent in the political language of civil defense, became militant, survivalist, and deeply troubling.

As K. A. Cuordileone notes, Cold War political culture was shaped by an almost "obsessive urge to reinstall the man as the head of the household."⁷ On an everyday level, this became a local drama of survival: a play that was never performed but routinely anticipated. In other words, the family bunker became a complex space of imagined community conflict. This is not to say that Cold War fathers suddenly embraced an antisocial ethos en masse. Nevertheless, they did grapple with the painful knowledge that any survival measures they took would favor the few over the many. OCDM archives record accounts of town hall gatherings that descended into chaos as neighbors threatened each other over access to private shelter space, parents trying to explain to their children why there was no space in the shelter for their classmates, sermons focusing on the ethical implications of denying strangers access to shelter space, survivalists retreating into the wilderness to build secret shelters, and a father worrying because his daughter had spotted a handgun hidden among the canned goods in their family shelter. Meanwhile, government officials were desperately trying to manage public perceptions that, if a nuclear war broke out, neighbors would become their enemies.

A REVIVAL FOR SURVIVAL: THE POLITICS OF SHELTER VIOLENCE

As Kennedy and his team debated how best to manage America's nuclear strategy, policymakers working in the unglamorous halls of the OCD continued their efforts to convince the public that private shelter construction was a sensible choice. During the early months of 1961, Edward Lynman, the agency's deputy assistant for civic affairs, and William F. Heimlich, its deputy director for public affairs, attempted to shift the federal narrative of civil defense away from the scare tactics of the 1950s toward a more soft-sell approach.[8] By the fall, however, they were facing a new problem. Not only were accounts of unscrupulous shelter salesmen generating internal concern, but media coverage of private civil defense efforts was highlighting a worrying number of neighborhood disputes about access to private shelter spaces. Despite Heimlich's and Lynman's best efforts, discussions of fallout shelters were beginning to coalesce around the moralistic, quasi-religious notion that fathers should forcefully defend their families and their shelters from unwanted, unprepared outsiders.

This shift in perception was due, in part, to the OCD's difficulties in managing the political optics of the family shelter. Although the Cold War historian Dee Garrison argues that the Kennedy administration sought, during this era, to "create civil defense hype," the Public Affairs Office of the OCD in fact spent much of 1961 trying to soften the image of the shelter father.[9] Indeed, upon arrival in Battle Creek, in 1960, Franklin B. Ellis, Hoegh's successor as director, was promptly handed a series of briefing reports that outlined how the message of home survival had evolved since 1958. In them, Lynman outlined the issues currently besetting the OCD and charted the role that the Public Affairs Office might play in the coming years.[10] "Think of us as your sales department," he told Ellis. "[O]ur job is to get civil defense turned around in the public mind, so that it appears as a positive, important, dynamic, rather than a negative concept." He advised making the fallout shelter father a respectable figure— "to clothe civil defense in the same mantle of popular respect and national necessity that our military defense traditionally wears."[11] "Scare tactics" and inciting "public frenzy" had to be avoided; instead, the OCD needed to present fathers as citizens who were "building a family shelter not as an isolated gesture of self-protection" but as a "respectable act" worthy of imitation.[12] In closing, Lynman asked Ellis to "give us a chance to advise you before policies affecting the public are formed. We may be able to suggest ways in which they can be made more saleable."[13]

Although Lynman is rarely mentioned in historical accounts of Cold War civil defense, he was a key figure in OCD plans to market the shelter owner as a sensible neighbor rather than a community oddball. His public relations goals were an acknowledgment that fallout shelters were still a hard sell for many Americans. Moreover, as his briefing papers make clear, the government was becoming concerned about the way in which certain citizens were implementing home survival. "[I]t is vital," he urged, "that . . . shelter owner[s] appear commonplace, . . . not neighborhood crackpots."[14] Nonetheless, by mid-1961, despite Lynman's best efforts as well as increased executive support and congressional funding, the OCD was losing the public relations war.[15] To an extent, the declining popularity of civil defense can be linked to the agency's inability to resolve the central public relations problem that Lynman had identified: namely, how to make shelter fathers seem normal, not hostile.[16] Between the Berlin and Cuban crises, public assumptions about shelter builders had morphed drastically from Lynman's ideal into the alarming image of bunker-building fathers as violent, militant, and antisocial.

One of the OCD's early obstacles in this battle came from within, in the form of the agency's newly appointed director. In early 1961, while Lynman and Heimlich were working to soften public perceptions of shelter owners, Ellis was trying to make his own mark on the political landscape of civil defense. Although he served in the position for only four months, his "blunt, brash and intensely religious" instincts pushed him into a series of mismanaged attempts to control and curtail critical media coverage of civil defense.[17] On Ellis's watch, the gun-thy-neighbor debate mutated into an uncontrollable, quasi-religious confrontation. Sorensen saw him as "a man of ambition" who understood all too clearly that the OCD had the potential to become a significant federal agency within an expanding national security state.[18] He aggressively pushed for an expanded OCD presence in Congress, claiming that "the lack of federal leadership has to come to an end."[19] Yet even though Ellis excelled at making "civil defense a national talking point," he struggled to manage the way in which local communities were receiving his self-proclaimed "revival for survival."[20] He also had difficulty with media relations. Early in his tenure, he seemed to be succeeding in that regard, securing support from the *Los Angeles Times*, the *Washington Post*, and the *New York Times*. But as time passed, he became more combative with the media and thus foiled Lynman's and Heimlich's public relations efforts.[21] As a result, he inadvertently intensified public perceptions of the OCD's incompetence just as the national conversation was moving away from the technological feasibility of shelter construction toward the inherently antisocial nature of privatized survival.[22]

Alarmed by this turmoil, Kennedy quickly fired Ellis from his position as OCD director. Given this brief tenure, questions remain about how much influence he really had on the emergence of the gun-thy-neighbor debate and subsequent family conversations about survival. To an extent, his political mismanagement of the civil defense message occurred in concert with growing local awareness that do-it-yourself survival was, by nature, selective. Nevertheless, whereas Val Peterson worried that home shelters offered little protection and Leo

Hoegh saw them as products to be marketed to the middle class, Ellis elevated them to a moral and religious imperative.[23]

To this point, framing shelter construction as a moral necessity was a trope that federal literature had tended to avoid. Typically, it was presented as a domestic opportunity for men, part of their role as responsible fathers and citizens. The distinction between *moral* and *responsible* might seem slight, but the social ramifications were important. A responsible homeowner such as Art Carlson built a shelter to protect himself and his family, thus embracing what was deemed a sensible and rational model of behavior for consumers, citizens, and Cold Warriors. But the call to build shelters for reasons of moral duty unleashed complex questions about the social hierarchy of community survival. Is the survival of an individual family more important than that of the wider community? How does one respond to neighbors who, by forcing themselves into a private shelter, put the family at risk? The moral shelter father has made an ethical distinction that creates a fence around himself and his family, a barrier against those who remain outside. By building a private shelter, he theoretically rejects the public.

In practice, the distinction between moral and responsible shelter fathers was far from clear, but the symbolic resonance of self-survival played an important role in countering the OCD's efforts to normalize civil defense. The issue became even more complicated when religion entered the equation. Ellis, a devout Presbyterian and a former deacon, repeatedly described home-shelter construction as "the Christian thing to do," and his public remarks show a keen awareness of ongoing debates among denominations and church leaders over the theological and moral implications of nuclear warfare.[24] In speeches at a series of civil defense conferences held in May and June 1961, he idealized fathers' actions at home in religious terms: "[A]s we build strong defense at home and strengthen our hands, we must recognize that our civilization is based on a morality of the Christian ethic. The people will learn that nuclear war cannot destroy our American freedom."[25]

The overtly masculine tone in Ellis's evocation of fathers' Christian duty grounded the ethos of privatized survival in a language of religious and familial obligation, linking the moral duty of family defense to the survival of the nation and, in turn, the survival of Christianity. During their tenures as director, both Hoegh and Peterson had worked closely with local religious organizations to spread the gospel of do-it-yourself survival. But Ellis went much further, explicitly framing male homeowners as modern-day Noahs, who, through prudence and careful preparation, would save their families. The public evidently latched onto that notion; the Noah comparison is a surprisingly common feature in letters written to the OCD and elsewhere in 1961. "Noah didn't wait for the rain to build the ark," declared a concerned citizen in a letter to the *Orlando Sentinel*.[26] Many of these writers were eager to remind readers that Noah, the pioneer of protection, had heeded the warning while others mocked or remained ignorant. "Noah's neighbor subjected him to a great deal of abuse as he built his ark," commented an irate shelter owner. "[T]here were probably cracks like 'the water on his knees has reached his brain' but he persevered and civilization was saved."[27] "Now, I know what Noah must have felt," commented John Newhouse, a sportswriter for the *Wisconsin State Journal*. "[S]ome tell me 'that's an aggressive act! You're tempting Providence and we'll all drown in a flood.' . . . [O]thers tell me, 'what're you going to do when I'm drowning and swim up to your ark? Beat me away with a club?'" Yet for Newhouse, a sense of moral uncertainty remained. "We do not know that we are doing the right thing," he concluded, "but we know that we were tired of doing nothing, and know we're at least doing something."[28]

Many of these suburban Noahs did not speak of their actions in violent terms but described instead a struggle to understand why their choice to construct shelters had made them feel like outliers. In letters written directly to Ellis, a number said that they wanted their "sacrifice" to be visible.[29] "I have been laughed at," said Clive Baldwin in a letter to his local OCD office, "but remember they laughed at Noah too."[30] Typically, these shelter owners noted that they were just waiting to be proven right. "Once the rain starts," a shelter builder wrote, "they'll see I never buried my head. . . . [T]he ones who survive, in my view, will be those who faced the reality that they are engaged in a struggle for survival and who are willing to take whatever steps are necessary."[31] Writing from Missouri, Kyle Hank told his local OCDM office, "Those who built shelters, those who see the signs and take on the moral imperative to protect, . . . these people, their sons, their daughters! will rebuild this great nation."[32]

Historians rightly argue that religion in U.S. foreign policy, especially during the Cold War, inspired "several competing visions of America's proper role in the post-war world."[33] While these observations are generally applied to international affairs, they also describe the complex formation of masculine identity around the family fallout shelter. Here, the process of becoming a shelter father was defined by a step toward community alienation, as the survival of the family was prioritized over the well-being of the collective. Ellis's conflation of civil defense with a loosely defined moral-religious imperative had inadvertently tied the act of shelter construction to the question of whether it was right for a father to place the survival of his family above all else. This public misstep was exactly what the critics of civil defense had been waiting for—among them, Carey McWilliams, the editor of the *Nation*. As part of his continuing effort to "wage war against the flurry of misinformation" coming from the OCD, McWilliams exploited Ellis's religiosity as evidence that the federal message of nuclear survival was becoming dangerously divorced from reality, and he pointed out a clear link between the dangers of private survival and its "influence upon the mass of citizens."[34] His article "The Hazards of Civil Defense," which satirizes Ellis's Christian "revival of survival" rhetoric, was published alongside a cartoon in which a suburban father sits in a machine-gun emplacement mounted on the top of his home shelter as his neighbor looks nervously over the fence. McWilliams's conflation of religious zealotry, alienation, and middle-class white violence was a crucial shift in the way in which the press began presenting the family fallout shelter to the public, explicitly connecting the "irrational behavior" of the state to the violence and immorality of its citizens.[35]

Between July and December 1961, the Kennedy administration publicly and privately distanced itself from Ellis's message. According to Sorensen, Kennedy finally lost all patience with the OCD director when Ellis informed him that he "intended to travel to the Vatican in hopes of obtaining the endorsement of the Pope for the installation of shelters in every Church-owned basement."[36] The president quickly dismissed him from his post, denied his request for a cabinet position, and refused to sanction his trip to the Vatican; then Kennedy shifted the bulk of the responsibility for civil defense to the Department of Defense.[37] OCD headquarters were moved to Washington, DC, allowing for greater executive control over the agency's message and rhetoric. Ellis stayed on at the agency for a few months as a special assistant to Steuart Pittman before being given a federal judgeship in Louisiana, which kept him at a safe distance from civil defense policy and commentary.

Despite Kennedy's quick actions to remove Ellis, debates about the morality of the family shelter persisted. Among the staff of the Public Affairs Office, the director's overt religiosity had been more than an "embarrassment"; it had intensified the very problem that Lynman and Heimlich were trying to curtail.[38] By August, the phrase "gun-thy-neighbor" had made its first media appearance, in the title of an article in *Time*'s religion section. The article consisted of a series of interviews with self-proclaimed "shelter hardliners" who were reveling in their survivalist mentality, which included an absolute refusal to allow neighbors access to their private bunkers. The authenticity of *Time*'s interviewees is still in question, but the article nonetheless did its intended work: it highlighted a rising cultural perception that do-it-yourself survival was making fathers violent. Throughout the article, citizens' interpretation of civil defense doctrine, often generalized and loosely defined, was framed as being far more extreme than lawmakers had anticipated. One Chicago suburbanite reportedly said, "[W]hen I get my shelter finished, I'm going to mount a machine gun at the hatch to keep neighbors out if the bomb falls. I'm deadly serious about this. If the stupid American public will not do what they have to do to save themselves, I'm not going to run the risk of not being able to use the shelter I've taken the trouble to provide to save my own family."³⁹ Charles Davis of Austin, Texas, had stocked his shelter with four rifles and a handgun, claiming, "[T]his isn't to keep radiation out. It's to keep people out." If his neighbor were to get access to the shelter first, Davis was ready: "I've got a .38 tear gas gun, and if I fire six or seven tear gas bullets into the shelter they'll either come out or the gas will get them."⁴⁰ According to the *Time* reporter, "[T]his kind of tough talk had echoes all over the U.S., as the headlines spread uneasiness and the shelter business booms."⁴¹

In *Dr. Strangelove's America,* the historian Margot Henriksen argues that the *Time* article marked the moment when the bombshelter craze exploded across the United States and civil defense finally garnered "national prominence and feverish interest."⁴² The article essentially reworked McWilliams's early coverage of civil defense, contextualizing the narratives of violent fathers alongside interviews with religious leaders about the ethics of shelter defense. The featured ministers included two Lutherans, an Episcopalian, a Methodist, a Catholic, and a Baptist, and all disagreed with the notion of armed shelter defense, though they were less certain about the question of freely allowing strangers access to private shelters. The dean of a Baptist seminary, drawing upon notions of active fatherhood, said, "[I]f you allow a tramp to take the place of your children in your shelter you are in error. A Christian has the obligation to ensure the safety of those dependent on him." In contrast, the Methodist minister challenged the root of the debate itself: "[T]he immorality takes place much earlier than when the people are in their shelters. It occurs when people think they can protect themselves from all-out nuclear war."⁴³ *Time*, which was still an arm of Henry Luce's pro–civil defense efforts, was more supportive of the private shelter effort than these quotations might suggest.⁴⁴ Ultimately, the article called for public calm as a way to counter the perceptions of violent self-interest. It is important to note, however, that while none of the interviewed ministers questioned the notion of shelter construction, they were less sure about which actions were permissible in defense of those refuges.

Reader response to "Gun-Thy-Neighbor" was marked by a sense of moral confusion. One Los Angeles resident joked that "shelter owner Mr. Davis" should be "nominated for Neighbor of the Year"; meanwhile, an Austin resident supported the survivalist mentality, writing that "guns are a man's best friend." A California shelter owner wrote, "[S]ince we have spent our time and money to prepare for something we sincerely hope will never come, we should not hesitate to defend ourselves with guns if necessary against these same people who would be threatening our lives because of their ignorance." In contrast, a young man from Connecticut wrote, "I was planning to get my parents to build a bomb shelter with a removable top that could double as a swimming pool. After reading the article about the Davis family, I decided that it would be better to die from the bomb's fallout than live in a world ridden with people who would gun down their neighbors."[45] Another reader spoke of watching a truck haul a bomb shelter up Sepulveda Boulevard in Los Angeles: "[I]t gives you a jolt, seeing that shelter going down the road. A year ago I'd have snickered. Now I shudder."[46]

The religious tone of the gun-thy-neighbor debate was all the more significant because in these years the United States was still an overwhelmingly church-attending, socially conservative nation.[47] Members of the clergy fell on both sides of the debate, and one of the most influential and controversial was directly inspired by the *Time* article. In his own piece, titled "Ethics at the Shelter Doorway" and published in the *National Catholic Weekly Review* in September 1961, Father L. C. McHugh, a Jesuit preacher and a lecturer at Georgetown University, put forth what he termed the "moralist argument" for fathers' defense of their shelters. McHugh took particular issue with the statements of Reverend Hugh Saussy, a pastor at Holy Innocents Episcopal Church in Atlanta. In the *Time* article, Saussy had suggested that fathers "need little guidance of essential morality at the shelter hatchway." In response, McHugh cited Jesuit ethical doctrines proclaiming that a father's responsibility was first and foremost to his wife and children. In his view, "[I]f others steal your family shelter space before you get there, you may use whatever means necessary to recover your inner sanctuary."⁴⁸ Later, during a CBS television debate, McHugh expanded on his distinctive notions about shelter morality:

> Apart from what the legal ordinances are in their town I would see no serious objection to a man having this type of defense. I'd equate him to the man on the prairie schooner going to California and likely to run into rampant Indians on the range. He would be foolish if he didn't have a shotgun, a revolver or a rifle, would he not? He wouldn't have considered he was doing his duty to his family in those desperate circumstances. Perhaps the father of the family could make an analogy out of this for himself? But I wouldn't want to decide that for the individual. I say let him take the general principles and apply them as best he can to his own circumstances.⁴⁹

McHugh's moralist argument reached the ears of Kennedy's inner circle. Schlesinger recalled Attorney General Robert Kennedy's mention of McHugh during civil defense discussions with the president in Hyannisport at Thanksgiving. According to Schlesinger, Robert declared ironically, "[T]here's no problem here—we can just station Father McHugh with a machine gun at every shelter."⁵⁰ Dismayed by this growing survivalist sentiment, President Kennedy focused one of his Fireside Chats on civil defense morality, urging the public to "concentrate more on keeping enemy bombers and missiles from our shores, and . . . less on keeping neighbors away from our shelters."⁵¹

By late 1961, despite the OCD's attempts to curtail critical coverage of civil defense, reports of community conflict over the issue were appearing with increasing frequency in national and regional newspapers. By October 1961, syndicated columnists such as James Reston, Stewart Alsop, and Peter Braestrup were publishing pieces about the gun-thy-neighbor debate.⁵² Sensing that the subject could be an "editorial goldmine," magazines such as *Redbook, Commonwealth*, the *New Republic*, and *Newsweek* worked themselves into a "moral froth" over the question of shelter violence.⁵³ Their articles, though varying in tone, transformed the home fallout shelter controversy into *the* human-interest story of Cold War America. Reporters were dispatched across the United States to find and interview shelter owners, and a narrative involving "violent and anti-social behavior" began to emerge.⁵⁴

One such account, written by the long-time nuclear activist Norman Cousins and published in a two-part editorial in the *Saturday Review*, described a town hall meeting in Hartford, Connecticut, that had descended into chaos when a man identified only as John threatened to shoot his neighbor and her baby if they attempted to get into his fallout shelter without his express permission.[55] The following exchange took place:

"John, you and your family have been our closest friends for ten years. Do you mean to say that if the city was bombed and my baby and I were caught in the open, and we were hurt and came to your shelter you would turn us away?"

John "nodded in the affirmative."

"But suppose we wouldn't go away and kept trying to get in. Would you shoot us?"

John said that, yes, he would: "I've got to look after my family."[56]

Cousins's account was important for two reasons. First, it directly stated that the violent actions of shelter owners were a product of the government's do-it-yourself mentality.[57] In this, the author was not alone: articles by Margaret Mead in *Redbook*, Linus Pauling in *Dissent*, Walter Lippmann in the *New Republic*, and I. F. Stone in the *Weekly* all adopted a similar stance, attacking Kennedy and his team for inspiring a "lunacy of civil defense" that was leading to fathers' "moral degeneration" and "violent behavior."[58] Second, while the authenticity of Cousins's account is difficult to verify, the format of the conversation between John and his neighbor, which was printed as a dialogue separated from the rest of the article, was striking and effective. By choosing to structure his article in this way, Cousins made John's survivalist mentality and his violent will to protect his family the focus of the reader's attention and the center of his critique of federal civil defense. The approach ingrained the image of survivalist fathers into the public imagination of America and beyond. Even the Soviet newspaper *Pravda* took a few swipes at survivalist shelter fathers: "[I]f only we could open the eyes of these moles armed with machines guns.... But moles, as we know, are unseeing creatures, and a mole of bourgeois origins, moreover, suffers from class blindness."[59]

"NEIGHBOR OF THE YEAR": SURVIVALISTS IN THE STREETS

In the national arena, the public relations battle for the family fallout shelter was quickly lost. However, the OCD was always at its most influential on the local and regional stage, where civil defense policymakers struck deals with state senators, gained the support of governors, and ensured that local businessmen had a stake in the evolving consumer market of nuclear survival. So a question remains: how accurate was the media interpretation of the survivalist mentality?

There is no doubt that, behind the gun-thy-neighbor headlines, uneasy conversations were taking place in living rooms and across dinner tables. "Building the thing was tough enough," noted Evan Peterson, a South Carolina engineer who had constructed a home shelter, but his concerns went beyond his family. In a letter to his local OCDM office, he complained that, despite petitioning the agency for a year, it still had not built a community shelter in his hometown of Aiken, located thirty miles away from the Savannah River nuclear site.

> I worry about what those poor souls without safety will do . . . [and] I would like to know what the plans for around here are. Could you verify? Or tell me who to ask? I live in a town of about 2000, my shelter can fit 5–6 at a squeeze. I know you have a lot [going] on but I live 30 miles form a manufacturing site . . . [and] most don't have a shelter to go [to]. I have met a choice group of professional "buck passers," and I mean choice! I see now the responsible thing was for me to do this as a civic task and avoid the home. As an engineer I can build a shelter for around here, just need materials, men and a permit. If I get turned down again then I guess it's time to load up a rifle and wait for it to go bad—AND ON YOUR HEAD BE IT.[60]

For Peterson, violence was inevitable in the absence of appropriate state action, but it was also unwelcome. His letter and other contemporary accounts demonstrate that the militancy of the shelter father existed on a spectrum; and as the Cold War progressed, many families, even survivalist ones, came to understand the politics of private survival as morally and socially bankrupt.

Reflecting on her childhood, the historian Doris Kearns Goodwin noted that, for her, the "Cold War was not an abstraction." Rather, "[t]he air-raid drills in school, the call for bomb shelters, and exposure to the deliberately unsettling horror of civil-defense" were formative experiences.[61] This was also true for shelter fathers. According to the historian Robert Jacobs, "survival of self" during the era acted as a proxy for the "survival of the nation." It was framed and defined by "popular images of tenacious cowboy survivors, . . . personal heroism, national survival, individual savagery, and human impotence" that had "little to do with actual human survival of a nuclear war."[62] In its literature and language, the OCD had bombarded Americans with cultural representations of heroic neo-frontiersman surviving nuclear war, but many of the letters that men sent to the agency reveal a pervasive uneasiness about shelter defense. Writing to President Kennedy in October 1961, Simon Murphy emphasized both his patriotism and his anxiety about the welfare of his fellow citizens:

> I'm reading the local newspapers [and] I find . . . out that this the civil defense organization is out of funds. Well Mr. President, let me tell you this! This caused me concern. I voted for you . . . my whole family did! But as a father you must see what will happen. If you tell them [citizens] strongly to build they will and many lives that might perish will survive. If a rush happens I am ready. But I have known these people for years. Could the Federal Government give us some assistance in money so that we might do an adequate job in providing protection for all?[63]

Although national media representations of the gun-thy-neighbor debate often treated violent shelter owners as stand-ins for a wider critique of civil defense policies, Murphy's letter attends to the personal dimensions of the debate—appealing to the president as a fellow parent, imploring him to stop this "foreign policy madness" so that neighbors can avoid using violence against people they have known for years.[64]

In his study of America's affinity for violence, Richard Slotkin argues that regeneration, whether national, cultural, or local, is often created through physical acts of violence.[65] "After all," as Spencer

Weart writes, "what is more American, than a father wielding a shotgun in a lawless world?"[66] In the discourse of national security, citizens were pioneers defending their homesteads, yet the actual words of fathers did not always line up with stereotypical ideals of heroic male action. As one shelter owner, Joe Tone, asked in a letter to the OCD, "[S]hooting a neighbor, in front of my kids, what kind of father does that make me?"[67] An article in the *Valley Times* of Los Angeles asked the same question:

> If neighbors ever discussed the fallout shelter situation seriously, there'd be a definite falling out among them, according to a *Valley Times* TODAY poll. Non-shelter owners feel it would be the civil and decent thing to share your shelter with neighbors.... Shelter owners think it would be foolish and possible suicide.... To set their true views, non-shelter owners were asked what they'd do if they were the shelter owners.... Paul A. Carson, 8661 Encino Ave., Northridge, agreed, "If there is room I would let my neighbors in. After me they'd come first."[68]

Again and again, letters to the OCD and the media allude to the moral ambiguity of fatherhood and shelter defense. Frequently, the writers framed their concerns around the question of why, in a shelter, a handgun should be as necessary as canned food and an emergency radio. Guns are not always mentioned directly in correspondence or media accounts, but appear obliquely—in the words of one man, as a "secret everyone knows about" (see figure 10).[69] Simon Murphy, for instance, never overtly stated that he had decided to stock his shelter with firearms; he simply hinted that he would be "ready" when "the rush happen[ed]."[70] Some writers, however, were more direct. "Everyone knows," said a teacher named James Banville in a letter requesting federal funds to construct a shelter near his school, "that those with shelters have them armed with guns." Likewise, Frank Deviale told the OCDM, "Shelters are a step towards war.... [T]hey are a step towards pitch[ed] battle in my street!"[71]

Historians have long acknowledged the pivotal role that religious figures and organizations played in both disseminating OCD attitudes and mobilizing the anti-nuclear movement. When it came to

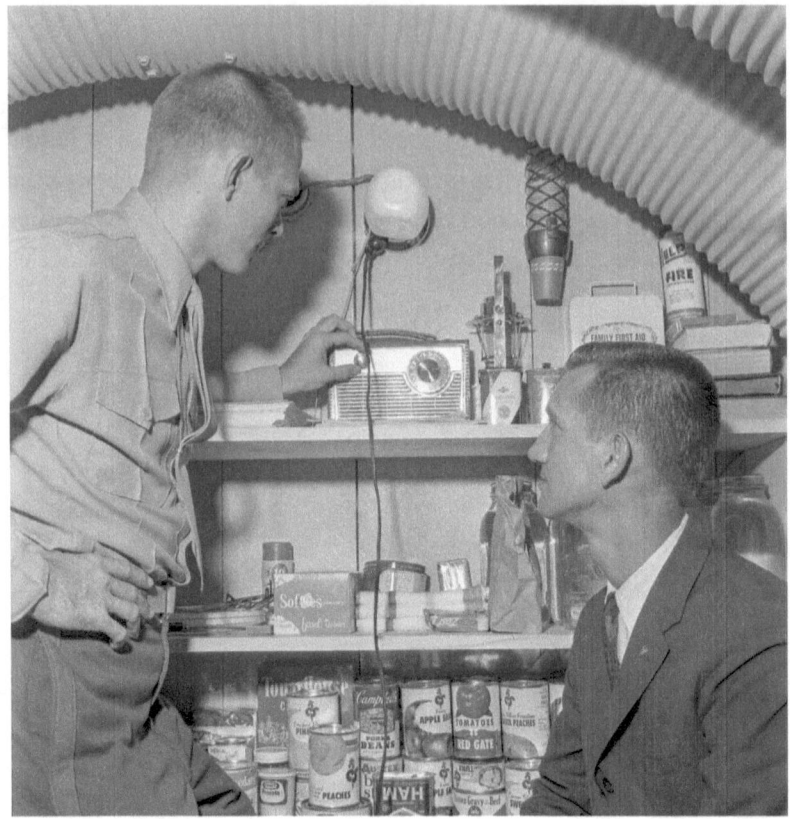

FIGURE 10. Two men in a demonstration fallout shelter at the state fair, 1960. Courtesy of Richland Library, Columbia, South Carolina.

family shelters, however, even staunchly pro-government clergymen were conflicted. In a *Washington Post* article, the well-known Southern Baptist evangelist Billy Graham noted that, as a father "I feel a primary responsibility for my family," yet "I don't believe I myself could stay in a shelter while my neighbor had no protection." Graham was not alone. Across the United States, church leaders took a range of stances that further complicated the idea of survivalist fathers. In the same *Post* article, James H. Parrot, an executive officer for the Disciples of Christ, made it clear that he could not speak for his entire denomination but admitted that he personally understood the dilemma: "Inherent in every one of us is the fear of destruction and this is a sort of protective identity tied to our love of family and friends. I personally have no place to build a shelter. So far I haven't thought about it as the sort of thing I wanted to do. The value of a shelter would be lost, if it were not used as planned. Yet I cannot see excluding my people in a time of general tragedy."[72] In contrast, Paul R. Woudenberg of Californian Heights Methodist Church in Long Beach took a far more critical view of the question of private survival:

> Bomb shelters have certainly brought to the surface some rather basic feelings of survival which cut sharply through the veneers of neighborliness which some folks profess. . . . The immorality of the shelter issue really lies in the president's delusion that there is any worthwhile or effective answer to atomic war. This is no time for us to act like moles. If the human race is to draw to a close, let us face our Lord with a clear record that we did our best to bring sanity into a time of madness.[73]

Some church groups tried to strike a balance between the notion of survival as a Christian duty and the need to avoid violence. In Montgomery County, Maryland, members of Christ Episcopal Church called a meeting in October 1961 to discuss if a shelter was needed in the parish. The meeting had been convened by the head of the church's women's group, Louise Hazell, who believed that "all this talk about men shooting some outsider who might try and get into their shelter is getting very silly." Flipping the survivalist ethos on its head, she suggested a different way for her friends and neighbors to think about shelters: "[I]t's like a lifeboat. A lifeboat picks up as many survivors of a shipwreck as possible." Pastor John Anschutz agreed, reminding attendees not to "forget that the first Christians were driven underground—into the catacombs—but when they came out, they kept the world alive. It's our Christian duty to survive nuclear war."[74] Hazell then posited that the "natural inclination of any community is towards the togetherness, not the separation. . . . [W]e owe it you, our young people."[75]

Faith-based gatherings were important forums for concerned community members, and, interestingly, accounts of groups seeking practical solutions far outweigh those describing confrontations among neighbors. In New York City, Orthodox Jewish congregations and the Rabbinical Council of America agreed on a resolution calling for shelters to be included in any new building permits for synagogues. These spaces were intended to give "all residents of an area a haven from nuclear attack" and would be "open to all persons regardless of creed or affiliation." Rabbi Charles Weinberg, the president of the Rabbinical Council, noted that the dual-purpose shelter could also be used as a social center or meeting hall.[76]

Time and again, local momentum was on the side of collective rather than individual action. Yet rumors persisted that shelter owners were violent forces in the community, and fears that the streets would become battlegrounds fed a growing sense that these men were, by nature, irrational actors. At many community meetings, speakers worried that shelter owners would take any excuse to act violently. Fearing that she might be accidentally shot, a concerned mother named Lucie Davis wrote to the OCD suggesting that such people were "spooked by phantom missiles."[77] Letters often stereotyped survivalist fathers as suspicious figures, nervously peering over their picket fences at passersby while waiting for the bomb to drop. Few of these letters offered any empirical evidence but merely echoed the national press in characterizing shelter fathers as irrational, secretive, and antisocial. As a West Texas woman named Chloe Shepard wrote, the assumption reflected "common sense about the type of person around here who might do something so stupid."[78] In a letter to the *Arizona Sun*, another worried citizen declared, "I know they hide their entrances [and] I'd rather not stumble across it and they start taking pot shots!"[79] In an October 1961 letter, Mrs. Robert Rowe of Plainview, New York, expanded on this perceived male irrationality:

Dear Mr. Kennedy,

I sincerely hope this letter finds you and your wife well. I guess you don't probably read agony columns. Most men don't. But almost every woman in this country does and identifies herself with the writers. Look and see what you find. I think you'll find it interesting. How to deal with this shelter business, and him buying guns for something we won't come back from. There are many other ways of reaching people and making this a group effort. The P.T.A is organized nationally, as are the hospitals. If we women take charge we can make this a community effort, and avoid the nastiness this seems to be turning into.[80]

It is impossible to know exactly how many shelter owners actually stocked their bunkers with firearms, given that local gun laws varied, not all shelters were finished, not all shelter owners wrote public letters, and even those who did write may not have mentioned weapons. Nonetheless, the stereotype of the paranoid shelter owner was powerful enough on its own to delegitimize the government's vision of logical, patriotic, do-it-yourself survival. Stories of fathers stocking shelters appeared often in regional newspapers during the fall of 1961. In a series of articles published in the *Denver Post* between October and December, the family shelter and fears of violent survivalist men were framed as part of a crisis evolving in the city's middle-class suburbs. One of these articles, titled "Moral Dilemma at the Shelter Door," filled an entire front page and featured a photograph of a local father standing at his shelter door with a rifle in hand. The article attempted to provide readers with answers to "tangled questions of right and wrong faced by men who prepare to meet the fallout danger." Suburbanites, both with and without shelters, were asked if they would be willing to use force to protect their families and defend their shelters. The "choice of horror," the article claimed, "haunts the suburbs leaving confusion and fatalism [in its wake.]" Residents worried that a "morality of wolves" might take over their communities: "Will it be every man for himself at the fallout shelter? . . . [S]ome men have already made up their minds to kill their neighbors to save themselves and every man who builds a fallout shelter must contemplate the possibility."[81]

As a critique of civil defense, the article did not offer any real insight into the state of the national shelter program, though it succeeded in fueling citizens' fears. So how accurate was its depiction of the local situation? Close analysis of the public correspondence sent to Colorado's regional OCD office reveals that public reactions were often contradictory and far more complex than the *Denver Post* articles suggested. Citizens certainly did express concern about the potential for community hostility, and many sought to assuage their anxiety by requesting more public shelters in order to avoid unwanted pressure on private ones.[82] "I built a shelter because I am worried about my own [family]. But I can't let my block know. Just in case there's trouble," wrote a Denver resident named Bobby Hightower. "[W]hy the hell isn't the government doing something about it?"[83] Kenneth Dills, a shelter father from the Denver suburbs, told the OCD that the local conversation about civil defense had changed his perception of his community: "[T]his whole business has us worried about our neighbors. . . . [T]he neighborhood just feels different now."[84] Other residents drew attention to the high personal cost of building shelters; one wrote, "[I]f the government would possibly make individual fall-out shelters fully deductible for tax purposes, it would ease things round here."[85] Olin J. Farnsworth, a local shelter builder, questioned the role that suburban citizens were expected to play, wondering if "people living near larger cities [should] be <u>required</u> to build shelters" for evacuees or if it was "the duty of apartment dwellers to ensure they had adequate protection in their own building."[86]

Correspondence levels in Colorado were replicated in OCD offices around the nation. The number of letters increased sharply in October 1961 and remained steady until another sharp increase occurred during the October 1962 Cuban missile crisis.[87] Most letter writers were not requesting help in fending off unwanted neighbors but seeking practical advice on converting basement spaces into shelters. In other words, the media portrait of shelter fathers as violent survivalists seems to have been inaccurate. Even at the height of the gun-thy-neighbor controversy, questions about the shelter-building process and complaints about a lack of federal investment in community defense projects remained the primary topics of inquiry. In a letter to the president, William Lemon asked "whether or not there is a filter available which cleans out radioactive material from the air."[88] Another letter writer, Mark Falk, asked the same question and then requested "information on how to obtain a [shelter] building permit" from his local housing authority.[89] "Frankly," another writer named Craig Fuller told the OCDM, "I am ready to build [a shelter] or have one built, per your recommendation, but to date, after contacting people and companies in Denver, Colorado, that claim to be builders I have been unable to find one that knows enough about it."[90] Evidently, public conversation—with governmental bodies, at least—still centered around the mundane practicalities of do-it-yourself survival.

Although it is tempting to conclude that many narratives about violent shelter owners were press exaggerations, the fact remains that a small yet persistent number of citizens wrote to the OCD in 1961 and 1962 to say that "all this talk about shelters" was making them uncomfortable.[91] Their correspondence clearly reveals the pressures and burdens that civil defense was placing on male householders. Letter writers frequently demanded federal action on public civil defense efforts and asked that shelters be built in public spaces to ease the tension between those who owned them and those who did not. These letters make it clear that OCD officials were failing to offer a persuasive counter-narrative to press reports of survivalist fathers. As a result, the agency was unable to sustain its local authority.

When civil defense supporters asked their local OCD officers to "ease tension," their requests often met with indecision and inaction.[92] The historian Alice George notes a distinct governmental paralysis on civil defense matters in the months before the Cuban missile crisis, a period when "most Americans lacked the will or resources to run and hide . . . [and] therefore . . . sought answers, however tenuous, in their own communities."[93] That paralysis was evident in regional OCD offices, especially during the gun-thy-neighbor controversy. Agency records reveal that official replies to public concerns about violent shelter owners were, for the most part, rote and passive. Correspondents frequently received a form letter stating, "[F]allout shelters are insurance for the civilian population in the event of a miscalculation. Fallout shelters that meet most of the standards set by the Office of Civil Defense could save most survivors from the blast and heat of nuclear attack. You apparently are sufficiently aware of the need for safety for your family and yourself. One possible solution is to encourage your local government to provide shelters in existing public buildings."[94] The tone was alarmingly neutral, given that the organization's primary mission was to mobilize the American public and retain their support for civil defense policies. In 1962, Gabriel Kolko, a Harvard professor and a SANE activist, wrote that federal neutrality over the gun-thy-neighbor issue had damaged what little faith remained in the OCD at the local level.[95] In his view, the agency was "passive" in both design and function, staffed with officials who were "not [likely] to complain when shelterless neighbors removed their armed neighbors' shelter filters or slipped a plastic bag over the air intake."[96] In Colorado, federal neutrality was amplified by logistical problems that beset local OCD offices throughout 1961 and 1962, when they were "swamped" and "overwhelmed" by public inquiries.[97]

A telling example of how thoroughly OCD had lost control over public perceptions of family shelters appeared in a federally funded study into public attitudes about civil defense, commissioned in late 1961 and presented to Pittman and the National Security Council in early 1962. According to the study, 70 percent of Americans thought that "bombs and missiles would rain down on their own communities," and almost 60 percent "believed that family shelter owners would have to fight to keep their neighbors out if war began." Even more damaging to the OCD's reputation: 30 percent of the public, when faced with the prospect of surviving while friends and families did not, said they would "prefer to die" rather than retreat to and defend their prepared shelters. Clearly, public understandings of civil defense had shifted away from seeing family shelters as a "responsible consumer choice" to believing that they inspired violent antisocial behavior.[98]

Throughout these years, regional civil defense officials struggled with organizational and fiscal shortcomings, some of which related to local ordinances, geography, or politics. In New York City, the OCD was heavily engaged with issues related to Governor Rockefeller's ambitious fallout shelter legislation; in Florida, agents were focused on events in Cuba and building shelters in public schools; midwestern offices were dealing with anxiety about evacuees from the East Coast; California offices were preoccupied with how the Los Angeles highway system might fare under the strain of mass evacuation. Nevertheless, as the historian Kenneth D. Rose writes, while "regional interest often put a slightly different spin on the discussion, to a remarkable degree the basic concerns that were expressed were similar throughout the country."[99] One common concern was how the act of private shelter construction seemed to be inspiring militant behavior in fathers.[100]

Moreover, both the press and the public were concerned about the behavior of several local civil defense leaders who appeared to be skirting the protocols of the Department of Defense.[101] In Douglas County, Colorado, one OCD official advised residents to arm themselves and prepare to defend their private shelters.[102] In Las Vegas, another regional official, J. Carlton Adair, called for the creation of a "five-thousand man militia" ready to repel refugees from California, who would otherwise "pour like locusts" into the region and "pick the valley clean of food, medical supplies and other goods."[103] In California, Keith Dwyer, the civil defense coordinator for Riverside County, advised all local residents to keep pistols in their shelters, lest refugees from Nevada descend on them. During a speech to a group of police reservists, he brandished "a pistol about his head" and said, "[G]et one of these and learn how to use it."[104] These accounts were picked up by the national press and still appear in historical accounts of the era.[105]

The reports of regional civil defense leaders to regional offices, even though they were often brief one-sentence summaries, add a layer of complexity to such headline-capturing actions. For instance, a regional civil defense director in Charlotte, North Carolina, complained that citizens "jammed his phone lines whenever they heard a strange a noise and subsequently requested educational pamphlets on the Conelrad emergency radio station that he . . . pass[ed] out to ease pressures on his staff."[106] Passing out literature had been common since the 1950s. As Laura McEnaney writes, "any adult active in the

PTA, social clubs or local civic groups would likely encounter home protection literature through such affiliation" because civil defense officials openly targeting their mailing lists.[107] By the early 1960s, however, links between such organizations and the OCD were becoming fraught, not least because civil defense coordinators were often civic leaders who served on various town or city boards. One OCD official wrote that a local PTA meeting in Rochester, New York, had ended in disarray as parents and the school board clashed about plans to construct a public shelter in the city's new high school. Some people at the meeting worried about the "negative psychological impact shelters and civil defense drills might have on their children," while others believed that the school board needed to take more responsibility for educating the public and the community on civil defense matters. Many of the protesters at school meetings around the nation were associated with the grassroots organization Women Strike for Peace. Echoing articles in the press, these parents routinely made reference to the militant behavior of shelter owners as proof that the whole notion of home defense was troubling and that individuals' violence was linked to the irrationality of civil defense as a societal practice.[108]

Government policy quickly adjusted to these new attitudes. Throughout the gun-thy-neighbor debate, Schlesinger had been collecting and cataloguing media responses to private shelter policies.[109] Schlesinger had considerable influence on Kennedy: the historian Robert Dallek credits him with helping the president construct "a distinctive liberal outlook," and scholar of the Cold War K. A. Cuordileone calls him the "chief architect of the New Frontier's liberal identity, . . . [one] crafted from the beginning with an unusually sharp eye on history."[110] While Schlesinger's influence on the evolution of civil defense policy has yet to be fully documented, by 1962 he had assumed a more active role in drafting Kennedy's statements on issues of national security. His voice was undoubtedly an important one during the administration's shelter debates, when he encouraged the president to shift from an emphasis on individual paternal duty toward a focus on community safety. While preserving the president's distinctively masculine tone, Schlesinger realigned his position on nuclear security to fit into the postwar liberal consensus—in this case, advocating that shelters be presented to the public as a form of community welfare.

As I have mentioned, early discussions about moving away from private shelters took place at the president's family compound in Hyannisport during Thanksgiving weekend in 1961. Attendees included Schlesinger, Pittman, the joint chiefs of staff, and numerous other officials, who had convened to consider the administration's position on national security.[111] Pittman recalled a tense day during which Kennedy systematically reviewed his past statements regarding civil defense and asked McNamara "read him a short part" from his speech to Congress in May. The White House's science advisor, Jerome B. Wiesner, who had long-standing reservations about civil defense, told the president in a prepared statement that any fallout shelter programs "would be obsolete in five years" and that it therefore "made no sense whatsoever" to increase civil defense funding.[112] According to Pittman, Kennedy "didn't say anything" in response to Wiesner's argument. In their memoirs, both Pittman and Schlesinger mention that Robert Kennedy arrived halfway through the meeting, "heavily perspiring after [playing] touch football outside," and declared that the executive branch should avoid making sudden changes until regional and local civil defense offices were "up to speed."[113] At the behest of Schlesinger, McNamara, and Pittman, the president decided to extend federal funding of civil defense by an additional $700 million, which would provide grants for "non-profit health, educational, and welfare institutions that would construct public shelters big enough to house at least fifty people of up to $25 per shelter space."[114] In addition, Kennedy confirmed that the national shelter survey, designed to identify and stock potential public shelter spaces, would continue, and he officially sanctioned the use of fallout shelter signs on public buildings throughout the United States.

According to the historian David Monteyne, the shift in federal discourse around shelters was part of a larger Democratic shift in civil defense policy.[115] During Eisenhower's Republican administration, family shelters and the gospel of self-help had satisfied liberal anxieties about the military control of federal agencies and tamped down conservative fears that a massive federal investment in civil defense and new housing developments would pave the way for an expensive, militarized New Deal.[116] The psychiatrist Charles Fritz, a member of the National Academy of Science's Disaster Research Group, summarized the Democrats' shift in discourse when he said that policymakers "must stop thinking of American society as if it were simply a collection of individuals and families who are individually responsible for the defense of the homeland. The realistic unit of administration and management in a nuclear attack is the nation as a whole."[117] This new vision of community action allowed the administration to retain its competitive Cold Warrior masculine identity while responding usefully to growing public hostility to private civil defense. The New Frontiersmen could still pride themselves on being "liberals with balls": active statesmen who would not be satisfied with "the safe mediocrity and timid executive leadership of the past."[118]

From policy strategizing within the Kennedy administration, to regional town hall debates, to local PTA meetings, discussions of male violence and the family fallout shelter reshaped U.S. perceptions of national security between 1961 and 1963. On the national level, the gun-thy-neighbor debate revealed the persistent inability of the OCD's Public Affairs Office to bridge the gap between responsible mainstream shelter owner and neighborhood crackpot. On the local level, the debate manifested as community anxiety about violence and disunity. Largely as a result of these combined concerns, OCD authority weakened dramatically. In 1963, the agency was folded into the Office of Emergency Preparedness, a move that marked the end of federal efforts to privatize nuclear survival. For the American public, however, the gun-thy-neighbor debate was a unique moment in their nation's history, when the people themselves actively engaged with the wider policies and practices of nuclear survival. The shelter controversy itself created a unique Cold War space in which foreign policy's pursuit of a masculine persona had a significant impact on the domestic landscape. Survivalist masculinity made the fallout shelter one of the most compelling social problems of the nuclear age.

CONCLUSION
Take to the Hills

> Can the American man—after years of protective conditioning—vie with the barbarian who has lived by his wits, his initiative and his brawn? Will he retain the will to fight for his country?'
>
> —Hanson W. Baldwin, "Our Fighting Men Have Gone Soft," *Saturday Evening Post,* August 8, 1959

Writing for the *Calgary Herald* in 2015, the journalist Lisa Kadane reflected on how the pressures of the nuclear age had affected her father. Thinking back on a childhood spent in Evergreen, a small town located in the foothills west of Denver, she recalled how her dad had prepared the family for the possibility of nuclear war:

> It would have been basic survival—nothing fancy. A single bare bulb in the center of the ceiling illuminated an old mattress wedged into a corner, a year's supply of freeze-dried food stacked in boxes along a wall, and a short-wave radio poised to deliver breaking news of Armageddon and its aftermath. My dad had even purchased an air-filtration system from the Office of Civil Defense (which was evidently profiting from its fallout expertise). There were games, candles, back issues of *National Geographic*, a chemical toilet and, according to my dad, lots of wine. There was also, unbeknownst to me, a gun—as a survivalist, Dad's greatest fear wasn't radioactive fallout, it was the prospect of having to harm or kill someone while defending our hideout.

Kadane grew up in the shadow of nuclear war: talk of "arms races," "missile gaps," and "mutually assured destruction" was common at the dinner table. In her essay, she recalled a particularly unpleasant conversation with her father, which took place after she visited him in the family bunker to ask if there would there be enough room there for her third-grade best friend, Pam Gordon, if the bomb dropped. Her father said no. "For him, the threat of nuclear war was every day," and the construction of a shelter lay at the heart of his "quaint belief" that if he "encased a room in concrete he could somehow save us all from a nuclear apocalypse."[1] For the Kadane family, the mere presence of a fallout shelter in their home made the Cold War personal and fraught.

During a brief but intense period of U.S. history, from 1958 to 1963, the threat of a direct nuclear confrontation with the Soviet Union had an enormous effect on ideas of fatherhood and masculinity. As Kadane's essay highlights, the family fallout shelter brought the politics of the nuclear age directly into the homes of millions of Americans. The cultural ideal in which fathers would build shelters to protect their families originated in the political discourse of the national security state as civil defense policymakers desperately sought a palatable solution for citizens' anxiety. Elected officials, security bureaucrats, and defense experts infused the military priorities of the nuclear state with the domestic consumer culture of postwar America, framing ordinary suburban fathers as the true custodians of the family and the nation. Rather than devoting the necessary resources to the construction of vast urban shelter complexes intended to safeguard the greatest number of Americans, the decision-making class set out to convince ordinary families to take Cold War survival into their own hands. Directing their policies toward middle-class suburbanites, policymakers asked these citizens to realign their lives and family relationships in accordance with doctrines of civil defense and the priorities of the national security state—as if, in the missile age, these fathers had the capacity to protect themselves and their families from the worst-possible manmade disaster.

Implanting this civil defense doctrine required an almost unprecedented level of state penetration into the private sphere. Yet as the ideal of shelter fatherhood permeated society, a widening gap emerged between the political underpinnings of domestic civil defense and the ways in which citizens received and implemented the doctrine of domestic survival. U.S. citizens were not passive actors in the history of civil defense but remained in active dialogue with the nuclear state, interpreting and reinterpreting government policy and responding to initiatives in ways that often ran counter to those envisioned by the nation's elite. Rather than fostering a singular politicized vision of Cold War fatherhood, civil defense doctrine revealed interlinking visions of paternalism rooted in the narratives of domestic, militarized, and survivalist forms of masculinity. As the public records make clear, the idea that every family should construct their own shelter and train themselves in its use was one of the great paradoxes of the national security state, and fallout shelter fatherhood inspired a wide range of reactions, ranging from acceptance, to protest, to militancy. Understanding it is essential to understanding the Cold War's gender history, in part because the doctrine of the civil defense father shows how the nation's decision-making class set out to reshape ideas of fatherhood in order to maintain American global authority.

So why did the federal project of domestic civil defense fail to inspire mass civic participation?[2] It is striking that very few private fallout shelters were actually constructed during these years. Although the National Archives and the Kennedy and Eisenhower libraries are filled with thousands of letters from citizens with questions or comments about shelters, only a small number of homeowners actually took the necessary steps to convert their homes and basements into bunkers. Estimates of that number vary, but according to one government report only about 4 percent of the population owned a private shelter during the week of the Cuban missile crisis.[3] Considering that more than 50 million pieces of OCDM propaganda were distributed in the 1950s alone and that President Kennedy's July 1961 televised call for shelter building had an audience of 25 million viewers, it is remarkable that so few Americans took survival into their own hands.

Scholars have argued that public disengagement with home survival was tied to an increasing level of skepticism about the effectiveness of civil defense during a nuclear attack. By 1958, they note, the U.S. public had learned about the true horror and destructive capabilities of nuclear weapons, meaning that even at its peak the OCDM's promulgation of do-it-yourself survival was viewed cynically by politicians, the public, and the press. While I agree in part with this conclusion, I also believe we need to learn more about the local drama of civil defense and how shelter-owning fathers were perceived by their individual communities. More than any other postwar defense institution, OCD bureaucracy relied on public education campaigns to make the home shelter seem to be a normal addition to everyday life. Yet civil defense planners were persistently frustrated by the actions of the people whom they, in theory, were sworn to protect. As the fallout shelter became *the* human-interest story of Cold War America, ordinary fathers, according to national and local press reports, were becoming increasingly militant and antisocial, rejecting community survival and their nation and retreating, gun in hand, to their private bunkers. In fact, letters written to the president and to the OCD illustrate that most fathers were confused and worried about the prospect of do-it-yourself survival rather than actively survivalist. Nonetheless, as the gun-thy-neighbor debate provoked intense headlines and debates, civil defense officials lost control of their political narrative, and the civil defense ideal of shelter owner as ideal Cold Warrior ruptured.

During the Eisenhower presidency, the home fallout shelter was a political compromise that balanced the imperatives of the nuclear state with the protection of the American population. Grounding the policies of civil defense in a persuasive language of gender and domesticity, the administration set out to divert the responsibility of nuclear survival away from the state and toward the family. Thanks to limited funding and a lack of congressional support for government shelter construction, civil defense became one of the most extensive propaganda campaigns of Cold War America. Under Eisenhower, a subtle yet salient form of militarized fatherhood was central to the message of do-it-yourself survival. Framed as suburban America's quintessential home-improvement exercise, the act of constructing a family fallout shelter brought Cold War military logic into the suburban home.

Eisenhower had been happy to allow civil defense to fade into relative obscurity, but his successor embraced it as a key presidential and personal responsibility. Although the intellectual underpinnings of civil defense remained mostly unchanged, Kennedy shifted the family fallout shelter into the forefront of his foreign policy rhetoric. Yet even as he declared that it was the sober duty of every man to take what steps he could to protect his family, he struggled to implement a policy of shelter loans, and he and his advisors became increasingly aware of the practical and political costs of sheltering the nation. Among citizens, local realities took on outsized importance—as in Colorado, where concerns about finance, the construction process, and building permits took center stage in a region heavily dependent on the military-industrial complex.

As shelter-salesmen's records show, the OCD was unable to translate Kennedy's rhetoric of do-it-yourself survival into an appealing idea for its target audience. Indeed, one of the most striking aspects of the home-shelter market was the consumer backlash it engendered among the American public. Male participation in civil defense was predicated on buying, constructing, and maintaining a family fallout shelter. Yet growing public concerns about exploitation by politicians and businessmen fed into national perceptions that shelter owners were the neurotic consumers of Cold War America, duped by suede-shoe salesmen into buying a product of limited value. In other words, suburban Americans persistently refused to participate in the government's notion of heroic masculinity.

With the explosion of the gun-thy-neighbor debate, the fallout shelter father became a source of embarrassment among members of the nation's decision-making class. In his drafted but never publicly delivered "Fireside Chat on Civil Defense," Kennedy openly reflected on how public perceptions of shelter owners had changed: "[W]e are not going to enter a time of divisive and degrading arguments about a shelter owner's right to kill his neighbors. We are not going to permit unscrupulous men to racketeer on people's anxieties over nuclear war." In Kennedy's speech, the shelter father was no longer defined by his adherence to a state-constructed narrative of heroic domestic masculinity but by irrationality and violence. Possessing a shelter, declared the president, did not give such self-proclaimed "super patriots" the right "to tyrannize [over] their fellow Americans."[4] But federal authority over the political message of nuclear survival had waned. By the end of the era, the act of building a backyard shelter was becoming increasingly untenable within U.S. political culture.

Since the 1960s, the American decision-making class has worked hard to keep discussions of private shelters off the political agenda. Nonetheless, the image of fathers preparing their families for doomsday isolation remains powerful. The formation of the Minutemen, for instance, illustrates the way in which the militant, antisocial nature of shelter fatherhood stayed alive among some Americans from 1963 to 1968. Branded by the FBI as a "civilian militia," the Minutemen were members of a small, militant, anti-Communist group that took to the hills of California, Nebraska, and Kansas, stockpiling weapons, food, and medical supplies in "secret family shelters."[5] Members saw these shelters as a special zones of family resistance that needed to be camouflaged and defended at all costs.

The Minutemen were far-right political extremists, more adept at generating headlines than attracting members, whose impact and influence faded into obscurity in the aftermath of the Cuban missile crisis.[6] Yet their origins, formation, early rhetoric, and media popularity during the mid-1960s demonstrate how drastically the image of shelter fathers had changed since the 1950s. Calling themselves the "fathers" of their rural communities, the Minutemen were a loose collective of doomsday preppers, who, during the nuclear crisis years, mobilized around the belief that nuclear war and a Communist takeover were only days away.[7] According to the group's leader, the soft-spoken but charismatic Robert DePugh, it was the "duty" of every father to train both himself and his family for the end of the world. "[I]t is easy to see why most Americans have shied away from the government's civil defense program. It is the American tradition to fight, . . . not to abandon their homes and flee helter-skelter to nowhere."⁸ For DePugh and his followers, the family shelter was "not merely a hole to hide in" but the nation's last line of defense and the "center of resistance for an underground army."⁹

After listening to President Kennedy's Berlin Address in July 1961, DePugh established the fledgling organization, charging $2 per month in membership fees and placing classified ads in local papers and key magazines under the provocative headline "Wanted Patriots."¹⁰ Calling on every man to "buy his own rifle, . . . stockpile supplies, build shelters and prepare for the battle," the ads invited men across America to embrace a rugged individualism, and to "pledge yourself" and "your rifle" to the cause.¹¹ Though the Minutemen claimed that they had 12,000 active members on their books in 1961, their actual numbers, according to the FBI, never totaled more than a few hundred.¹² Still, they attracted attention. At a time when the evolving gun-thy-neighbor debate dominated the press, the Minutemen's choice to reject all community obligations to look after their own appeared to many to be the logical conclusion of a federal policy of privatized survival. Not only were the Minutemen survivalist and irrational, but they were also a source of embarrassment for the nation's political elite.

In November 1962, DePugh, to raise the movement's profile, fired off a mortar full of recruitment pamphlets on the lawn next to the Washington Monument. Soon thereafter, a series of high-profile interviews with him and other Minutemen leaders appeared in *Time*, *Playboy*, the *Nation*, *Newsweek*, and *Life*.¹³ Characterizing the movement as a band of "oddballs" and "kooks," the coverage in *Life* and elsewhere framed the group as extremists within popular discussions of the ethics and morality of nuclear survivalism.¹⁴ "These so-called patriots," Peter W. Salschi wrote in the *Nation*, "are the true supporters of the unequal policy of privatized survival civil defense."¹⁵ In his view, they were the logical end of a policy of nuclear survival that privileged the few over the collective.

The Minutemen are a fascinating example of how radically the image of do-it-yourself survival had changed. DePugh was frequently described in the popular press as a "paranoid figure" who was forcing his family and friends to become guerrilla fighters.[16] "We must stop wondering if and when World War III will start," he told a *Kansas Star* reporter in 1968. "[W]e are up to our ears in it."[17] Rather than supporting the priorities of the national security state, these shelter fathers had to be monitored by federal authorities to ensure national security. Like other doomsday groups that have since arisen in the United States, the Minutemen were symbols of paranoia, fear, and violence. The group eventually faded from public view after several of its leaders were arrested for trafficking guns across state boundaries, but they and others like them remain a powerful statement on the nation's civil defense efforts.

As nuclear tension eased in the mid-1960s, the family fallout shelter faded from the national conversation. After passage of the Partial Test Ban Treaty in 1963, federal discussions of private shelters were reduced to a bare minimum, and the OCD was absorbed into the Federal Emergency Management Agency. Now, instead of promoting family bunkers, government officials pointed out that storm cellars and tornado shelters could double as private bomb shelters. In the 1980s, as President Ronald Reagan took the United States to the nuclear brink and back, civil defense conversations briefly revived, only to be shelved once again under a barrage of scorn at the notion that the country could withstand a nuclear assault.[18] Yet the fallout shelter father and the notion of do-it-yourself survival remain fascinating icons for a nation preparing for nuclear annihilation. Within the larger political history of a decision-making class trying to manage public perceptions of nuclear war, they form a complex domestic tale of fathers and families debating, engaging, accepting, and at times rejecting the politics of the Cold War nuclear state. Clearly, the actions of the nuclear state exerted a profound and unexpected influence on what it meant to be a father in the United States.

NOTES

INTRODUCTION: FATHERHOOD AND THE FAMILY FALLOUT SHELTER

1. John F. Kennedy, "Report to the American People on the Berlin Crisis," July 25, 1961, John F. Kennedy Speech Files, 1961–63, Theodore C. Sorensen Personal Papers, John F. Kennedy Presidential Library, Boston (henceforth cited as JFKL), 4.

2. "Family in the Shelter, Snug, Equipped and Well Organized," *Life*, September 15, 1961, 105.

3. The Detroit-based company Kelsey Hayes was one of the most successful and prominent shelter manufacturers of the 1960s. After signing a lucrative contract with Sears, Roebuck, the company turned out an average of 5,000 shelters a month in the Detroit region alone and was featured in articles in *Life*, *Time*, and *Newsweek*. Part of Kelsey Hayes's success was due to its being labeled a "federal[ly] sanctioned shelters company." A Kelsey Hayes shelter was designed to meet civil defense specifications; could be acquired with an interest-free, FHA-insured loan; and was inspected by an official civil defense engineer (see chapter 3).

4. The steps involved in constructing the shelter are detailed in the photo caption ("Family in the Shelter," 104).

5. Ibid., 105.

6. Ibid., 106.

7. For background information about *Life*'s fallout shelter article, see the memoir by the magazine's managing editor, Edward K. Thompson: *A Love Affair with "Life" & "Smithsonian"* (Columbia: University of Missouri Press, 1995), 253.

8. "Family in the Shelter," 105.

9. Ibid.

10. "Gun-Thy-Neighbor," *Time*, August 18, 1961, 58.

11. Ibid.

12. Norman Cousins, "Shelter, Survival and Common Sense," *Saturday Review*, October 21, 1961, 26.

13. "Civil Defense: Who'd Survive?," *Newsweek*, August 7, 1961, 23.

14. Paul Boyer, *By the Bomb's Early Light: American Thought and Culture at the Dawn of the Atomic Age* (Chapel Hill: University of North Carolina Press, 1985); Spencer R. Weart, *Nuclear Fear: A History of Images* (Cambridge: Harvard University Press, 1988); Robert A. Jacobs, *The Dragon's Tail: Americans Face the Atomic Age* (Amherst: University of Massachusetts Press, 2010); Guy Oakes, *Imaginary War: Civil Defense and American Cold War Culture* (Oxford: Oxford University Press, 1994).

15. For a recent survey of U.S. and U.K. nuclear scholarship, see Jonathan Hogg, *British Nuclear Culture: Official and Unofficial Narratives* (London: Bloomsbury, 2016). My study has been influenced by several important works on U.S. nuclear history: Lawrence Freedman, *The Evolution of Nuclear Strategy*, 3rd ed. (New York: Palgrave, 2003); Matthew Jones, *After Hiroshima: The United States, Race and Nuclear Weapons* (Cambridge: Cambridge University Press, 2010); Francis J. Gavin, *Nuclear Statecraft: History of Strategy in America's Atomic Age* (Ithaca, NY: Cornell University Press, 2012); Marcus Trachtenberg, *The Cold War and After: History, Theory, and Logic of International Politics* (Princeton, NJ: Princeton University Press, 2012); Shane Maddock, *Nuclear Apartheid: The Question for American Atomic Supremacy from WWII to Present* (Chapel Hill: University of North Carolina Press, 2014); Matthew Connelly, Matt Fay, Guilia Ferrini, Micki Kaufman, Will Leonard, Harrison Monsky, Ryan Musto, Taunton Paine, Nicholas Standish, and Lydia Walker, "'General, I Have Fought Just as Many Nuclear Wars as You Have': Forecasts, Future Scenarios, and the Politics of Armageddon," *American Historical Review* 117, no. 5 (2012): 1431–60; Gar Alperovitz, *Atomic Diplomacy: Hiroshima and Potsdam* (London: Secker and Warburg, 1966); Fabienne Collignon, *Rocket States: Atomic Weaponry and the Cultural Imagination* (London: Bloomsbury, 2014); Fred Kaplan, *The Wizards of Armageddon* (New York: Touchstone, 1983); and Tracy C. Davis, *Stages of Emergency: Cold War Nuclear Civil Defense* (Durham, NC: Duke University Press, 2007).

16. Although previous scholars have noted Kennedy's concerns about toughness and the distinctively masculine tone of his political rhetoric, Dean provocatively situates a specific class-based masculine ideology at the heart of 1960s-era foreign policy decisions. His study depicts Kennedy and his New Frontiersmen as quintessential Cold War statesmen with remarkably similar patterns of socialization. The New Frontiersman all attended elite male prep schools, served in elite military units during World War II, were educated at Ivy League universities,

and embarked on prestigious government careers. They instilled their collective experience of 1950s life—their elite masculine ideology—into the center of the U.S. foreign policy establishment. Kennedy and his advisors shared and exploited cultural perceptions that equated a crisis in American masculinity at home with the decline of American power abroad. Characteristic of this elite masculinity was their almost uniform adherence to the doctrine that male toughness, defined in terms of strength and weakness, was inextricably bound to the legitimacy of political leadership. See Robert Dean, *Imperial Brotherhood: Gender and the Making of Cold War Foreign Policy* (Amherst: University of Massachusetts Press, 2001), 4.

17. For excellent summaries of how studies of gender have come to inform our understanding of U.S. foreign policy, see Judy Tzu Wu, "Gendering America Foreign Relations," in *Explaining the History of American Foreign Relations*, 3rd ed., ed. Frank Costigliola and Michael J. Hogan (Cambridge: Cambridge University Press, 2016), 271–84; and Kristin Hoganson, "What's Gender Got to Do with It? Gender History as Foreign Relations History," in *Explaining the History of American Foreign Relations*, 2nd ed., ed. Michael J. Hogan and Thomas G. Peterson (Cambridge: Cambridge University Press, 2004), 304–22. This book was also influenced by the following works: Joan Scott, "Gender: A Useful Category of Historical Analysis," *American Historical Review* 91, no. 5 (1986): 1053–74; Emily S. Rosenberg, "Gender," *Journal of American History* 77, no. 1 (1990): 116–245; Glen Jeansonne, *Women of the Far Right: The Mothers' Movement and World War II* (Chicago: Chicago University Press, 1996); Frank Costigliola, *France and the United States: The Cold War Alliance Since World War II* (New York: Macmillan, 1992); Frank Costigliola, "'Unceasing Pressure for Penetration': Gender, Pathology, and Emotion in George Kennan's Formulation of the Cold War," *Journal of American History* 83, no. 4 (1997): 1309–39; Kristin Hoganson, *Fighting for American Manhood: How Gender Politics Provoked the Spanish-American and Philippine American Wars* (New Haven, CT: Yale University Press, 1998); Michael Mart, "Tough Guys and American Cold War Policy: Images of Israel, 1948–1960," *Diplomatic History* 20, no. 3 (1996): 357–80; Gail Bederman, *Manliness and Civilization: A Cultural History of Gender and Race in the United States, 1880–1917* (Chicago: Chicago University Press, 1995); John D'Emilio, *Sexual Politics, Sexual Communities: The Making of a Homosexual Minority in the United States, 1940–1970*, 2nd ed. (Chicago: Chicago University Press, 1998); Geoffrey S. Smith, "National Security and Personal Isolation: Sex, Gender, and Disease in the Cold War United States," *International History Review* 14, no. 2 (1992): 303–37; and Allan Bérubé, *Coming Out Under Fire: The History of Gay Men and Women in World War II* (New York: Columbia University Press, 2012).

18. K. A. Cuordileone, *Manhood and American Political Culture in Cold War*

America (New York: Routledge, 2005), 32. See also Dean, *Imperial Brotherhood*; Aaron Belkin, *Bring Me Men: Military Masculinity and the Benign Façade of American Empire, 1898–2001* (New York: Columbia University Press, 1981); and Elaine Tyler May, *Homeward Bound: American Families in the Cold War Era* (New York: Basic Books, 1988).

19. Hogg, *British Nuclear Culture*, 10.

20. Sarah Alisabeth Fox, *Downwind: A People's History of the Nuclear West* (Lincoln: University of Nebraska Press, 2014).

21. Kenneth D. Rose, *One Nation Underground* (New York: New York University Press, 2001).

22. For more on the family fallout shelter, see David Monteyne, *Fallout Shelter: Designing for Civil Defense in the Cold War* (Minneapolis: University of Minnesota Press, 2011); Thomas J. Kerr, *Civil Defense in the U.S.: Bandaid for a Holocaust?* (Boulder, CO: Westview Press, 1983), 128–31; and Sarah A. Litchman, "Do-It-Yourself Security: Safety, Gender, and the Home Fallout Shelter in Cold War America," *Journal of Design History* 19, no. 1 (2006): 39–55.

23. Dean, *Imperial Brotherhood*, 4.

24. Much of the burgeoning scholarship on American manhood focuses on narratives of crisis and tends to look at specifically two eras, the 1890s and the 1950s. In *Manliness and Civilization: A Cultural History of Gender and Race in the United States* (Chicago: University of Chicago Press, 1995), Gail Bederman argues that the crisis was derived from the tensions between manhood and the ideology of civilization. In *Manhood in America: A Cultural History* (Oxford: Oxford University Press, 1995), Michael Kimmel focuses on moments of crisis in terms of three competing visions of masculinity: the self-made man, the patriarch, and the heroic artisan battling for cultural dominance. Kimmel and Bederman have set the tone for subsequent scholarship: Steven Cohen, *Masked Men* (Bloomington: Indiana University Press, 1997); James Gilbert, *Men in the Middle* (Chicago: University of Chicago Press, 2005); and Cuordileone, *Manhood and American Political Culture*.

25. Guy Oakes, *Imaginary War: Civil Defense and Cold War Culture* (Oxford: Oxford University Press, 1994), 31.

26. Ibid., 14.

27. Laura McEnaney, *Civil Defense Begins at Home: Militarization Meets Everyday Life in the Fifties* (Princeton, NJ: Princeton University Press, 2000), 68.

28. Ibid., 6.

29. A note on terminology: I have divided national civil defense efforts between the FCDA, which existed from 1950 to 1958, and the OCDM, which existed from 1958 to 1963. These two bodies were superseded by the Office of Civil Defense (OCD) in 1961, but the OCDM continued to operate on a regional level,

often at the forefront of local civil defense initiatives. See Andrew Grossman, *Neither Dead nor Red: Civil Defense and American Political Development During the Early Cold War* (London: Routledge, 2001), 12.

30. Ibid., 158.

31. McEnaney, *Civil Defense Begins at Home*, 68.

32. Grandma's Pantry was an early civil defense policy that encouraged women to keep their homes stocked with canned goods in case of a sudden nuclear attack. It exploited nostalgia about maternal domestic roles and thus reinforced conceptions of the paternal-maternal role divide in the fallout shelter family and in civil defense.

33. May, *Homeward Bound*, 102.

34. Paul Larsen, "Self Help and Mutual Aid in Civil Defense," speech to members of the aviation industry, Beverly Hills, CA, July 14, 1950, OCDM RG304, no. 12, box 40, National Archives II, College Park, MD (hereafter cited as NAII).

35. U.S. Civil Defense Administration, "The National Pattern of Civil Defense: Civil Defense and You" (Washington, DC: Government Printing Office, 1953).

36. The national civil defense pattern was also discussed in public addresses; see, for instance, Katherine Graham Howard, "A New Stronghold of Nation Security—Civil Defense," Katherine Graham Howard Papers, box 10, NAII. Also see chapter 1.

37. Michael Sherry, *In the Shadow of War: The United States* (New Haven, CT: Yale University Press), 193.

38. Oakes, *Imaginary War*, 6.

39. Jacobs, *The Dragon's Tail*, 62.

40. I. F. Stone, "Almost as Safe as Ivory Soap Is Pure?," *Weekly*, September 25, 1961, 2.

41. McEnaney, *Civil Defense Begins at Home*, 89.

42. Ibid.

43. James Gilbert, *Men in the Middle: Searching for Masculinity in the 1950s* (Chicago: University of Chicago Press, 2005); Margot Canaday, *Straight State: Citizenship in Twentieth-Century America* (Princeton, NJ: Princeton University Press, 2009); Bill Osgerby, *Playboys in Paradise: Masculinity, Youth and Leisure-Style in Modern America* (Oxford: Berg, 2001); Michael Davidson, *Guys Like Us: Citing Masculinity in Cold War Poetics* (Chicago: University of Chicago Press, 2003); Cuordileone, *Manhood and American Political Culture*.

44. Graham Dawson, *Soldier Heroes: British Adventure, Empire, and the Imagining of Masculinities* (New York: Routledge, 1994), 1. Dawson's work offers a useful discussion on the role of narrative in gender construction.

45. Key members of the Kennedy and Eisenhower administrations operated

on this premise of male toughness, and they were, at different stages during the nuclear crisis years, charged with presenting and formulating the doctrine of civil defense self-help to the American public. Thus, the family fallout shelter added a uniquely domestic and local dimension to the gender politics of the national security state (see chapters 1 and 2).

46. Ralph LaRossa, *The Modernization of Fatherhood: A Social and Political History* (Chicago: University of Chicago Press, 1997), 34.

47. See Lawrence R. Samuel, *American Fatherhood: A Cultural History* (London: Rowman and Littlefield, 2015); E. Anthony Rotundo, *American Manhood: Transformations in Masculinity from the Revolution to the Modern Era* (New York: Basic Books, 1993); Joseph H. Pleck, "American Fathering in Historical Perspective," in *Changing Men: New Directions on Men and Masculinity*, ed. Michael S. Kimmel (Newbury Park, CA: Sage, 1987), 83–97; Charlie Lewis, *Becoming a Father* (Milton Keynes, UK: Open University Press, 1986); and John Nash, "Historical and Social Changes in the Perception of the Role of the Father," in *The Role of the Father in Child Development*, ed. Michael E. Lamb (New York: Wiley, 1989), 272–306.

48. Robert L. Griswold, *Fatherhood in America* (New York: Basic Books, 1993), 206–7.

49. R. W. Connell, *Masculinities* (Cambridge: Polity, 1995); Michael Kimmel, *The History of Men: Essays on American and British Masculinities* (Albany: State University of New York Press, 2006).

50. McEnaney, *Civil Defense Begins at Home*, 77.

51. Ibid.

52. The term *domestic masculinity* first appeared in Steven Gelber, "Do-It-Yourself: Constructing, Repairing, and Maintaining Domestic Masculinity," *America Quarterly* 49, no. 1 (1997): 66–112. Since then it has been mentioned in the scholarship of Joanne Hollows, Eric J. Arnold, and James W. Gentry.

53. U.S. Department of Commerce, "The Do-It-Yourself Market," in *Mass Leisure* (New York: Free Press, 1958), 274.

54. "Gun-Thy-Neighbor," 58.

55. Margot Henriksen, *Dr. Strangelove's America: Society and Culture in the Atomic Age* (Berkeley: University of California Press, 1997), 189.

56. The notion of bomb-shelter hysteria is so common that it often appears in the chapter titles of Cold War studies. See, for example, Kaplan, "Shelter Mania," in *The Wizards of Armageddon*, 307.

CHAPTER ONE: THE LOG CABIN OF THE NUCLEAR AGE

1. Edward Hazel, letter to the Office of Civil and Defense Mobilization, October 5, 1961, Office of Civil and Defense Mobilization, Central Files, 1961–68, Record of the Defense Preparedness Agency, Shelters and Vulnerability Reduction, September–October, RG397, box 24, NAII.

2. Hazel's letter is somewhat of an outlier in this regard. The majority of public letters expressed frustration over shelter construction. Discussions of burst water pipes, collapsed ceilings, and confusing internal measurements are common features (see chapter 3).

3. Hazel, letter to OCDM.

4. See Yanek Mieczkowski, *Eisenhower's Sputnik Moment: The Race for Space and World Prestige* (Ithaca, NY: Cornell University Press, 2013).

5. George Reedy, *The Twilight of the Presidency* (New York: Market Paperbacks, 1970), 62.

6. Andrew Hartman, *Education and the Cold War: The Battle for the American School* (New York: Palgrave, 2008), 176.

7. Mieczkowski, *Eisenhower's Sputnik Moment*, 16.

8. Ibid., 3.

9. Michael Sherry, *In the Shadow of War: The United States* (New Haven, CT: Yale University Press), 181.

10. The phrase "every home a fortress" was first articulated by Leo Hoegh, "Address of Leo A. Hoegh," January 21, 1958, OCDM Central Files, Official Files, box 195, folder OF 20 1957, Dwight D. Eisenhower Library (hereafter DDEL).

11. National Civil Defense Advisory Council, agenda for meetings, May 28–29, 1958, Records Relating to Civil Defense Advisory Council, RG396, entry 1044, box 1, NAII.

12. The persistent underfunding of civil defense is detailed in Laura McEnaney, *Civil Defense Begins at Home: Militarization Meets Everyday Life in the Fifties* (Princeton, NJ: Princeton University Press, 2000), 43. For an example of how civil defense was discussed in Congress, see "Federal Civil Defense Act of 1950: Hearing before a Subcommittee of the Committee on Armed Services," 81st Cong., 2nd sess., December 7, 1950, 80–81; and Subcommittee of the Committee on Armed Services, "Hearing on the Operation and Politics of Civil Defense Program," 84th Cong., 1st sess., February 22, 1955, 46–47.

13. On defense budgets, the New Look, and civil defense, see Thomas J. Kerr, *Civil Defense in the U.S.: Bandaid for a Holocaust?* (New York: Westview, 1983).

14. Leo Hoegh, handwritten note attached to a draft speech, May 1959, Leo

Hoegh Papers, Campaign Material, folder 4, box 6, Special Collections Department, University of Iowa Libraries, accessed NAII.

15. Stephen E. Ambrose, *Eisenhower: Soldier and President* (New York: Touchstone, 1983), 453.

16. John Lewis Gaddis, *Strategies of Containment: A Critical Appraisal of Post-War American National Security Policy* (Oxford: Oxford University Press, 1982), 183; and Sherry, *In the Shadow of War*, 215.

17. White House Office of Staff Research, "Reaction to the Soviet Satellite: A Preliminary Evaluation," October 11, 1957, Dwight D. Eisenhower Papers, National Security Council series, box 35, NAII.

18. Stewart Alsop, "Debate on the Satellite," October 25, 1957, Record of the Office of Emergency Preparedness, Public Affairs Office Subject, 1960–61, box 2, RG396, NAII.

19. K. A. Cuordileone, *Manhood and American Political Culture in Cold War America* (New York: Routledge, 2005), 179.

20. John D. Morris, "Johnson Outlines Broad Agenda for Senate Inquiry on Missiles," *New York Times*, November 23, 1957, 7.

21. Paul Dickson, *Sputnik: The Shock of the Century* (New York: Bloomsbury, 2009), 112.

22. Katherine Graham Howard, "The Responsibility of Women in Civil Defense," speech to the New England Conference of Federated Women's Clubs, Bretton Woods, NH, September 17, 1953, Katherine Graham Howard Papers, box 4, DDEL. Please note that Howard's papers are kept at both DDEL and NAII.

23. Office of Special Assistant for National Security Affairs, "The Civil Defense Program," June 30, 1955, in *Foreign Relations of the United States, 1955–1957*, vol. 19, *National Security Policy* (Washington, DC: Government Printing Office, 1990), 6.

24. Federal Civil Defense Administration, *Annual Report* (Washington, DC: Government Printing Office, 1954), 13–16.

25. Ibid., 130–34.

26. Office of Special Assistant for National Security Affairs, "A Federal Shelter Program for Civil Defense," March 20, 1957, National Security Council Policy Papers Subseries, box 21, NAII.

27. Katherine Graham Howard, "Civil Defense Both at Home and Abroad," speech to the Massachusetts Society of Colonial Dames of America, Boston, March 31, 1955, Katherine Graham Howard Papers, box 5, DDEL.

28. Office of Civil Defense and Mobilization, "The Story Nobody Wants to Hear," March 1955, Office of Civil Defense and Mobilization General Files, RG397, box 377, NAII.

29. Federal Civil Defense Administration, *Annual Report* (Washington, DC: Government Printing Office, 1954).

30. On Rockefeller's support of civil defense, see chapter 2. Also see David Krugler, *This Is Only a Test: How Washington Prepared for Nuclear War* (London: Palgrave, 2006).

31. Dwight D. Eisenhower, letter to Henry Luce, July 6, 1960, Henry Luce Papers, box 21, folder "Dwight D. Eisenhower," Library of Congress, Manuscripts Division (hereafter LCMD).

32. On how Eisenhower tried to deal with SANE and CND, see Andrew Rojeck, *Silencing the Opposition: Antinuclear Movements and the Media in the Cold War* (Champaign: University of Illinois Press, 1999).

33. Kerr, *Civil Defense in the U.S.*, 20.

34. Ralph E. Lapp, "Civil Defense Aces New Peril," *Bulletin of the Atomic Scientists* 9 (1954): 351.

35. Ralph Lapp, "An Interview with Governor Val Peterson," *Bulletin of the Atomic Scientists* 10 (1954): 375–77.

36. Peterson's personal papers are a fascinating source. It is clear from internal correspondence that he toed the party line and found it difficult to act without direction from Eisenhower's administration. Time and again he requested a "strong statement" from Eisenhower in support of the FCDA, but he was frequently turned down. See FCDA Central Files, RG397, Val Peterson Papers, folder "White House 1957," NAII.

37. House Committee on Government Operations, "Civil Defense for National Survival," 84th Cong., 2nd sess., June 25, 1956, 79.

38. For more on Operation Alert, see McEnaney, *Civil Defense Begins at Home*, 50.

39. David Krugler, *This Is Only a Test*, 55.

40. Guy Oakes, *The Imaginary War: Civil Defense and American Cold War Culture* (New York: Oxford University Press, 1994).

41. House Committee on Government Operations, "Civil Defense for National Survival," 79.

42. On the planning of Operation Alert 1955, see Dwight D. Eisenhower Administration, White House Central Files, Confidential Files, box 16, folder CD 1, DDEL.

43. Kenneth D. Rose, *One Nation Underground* (New York: New York University Press, 2001), 27.

44. As Oakes notes, attempts to control press coverage of Operation Alert had limited success (*The Imaginary War*, 96). See also "Civil Defense: So Much to

Be Done," *Newsweek,* June 27, 1955, 21–22; "Civil Defense Best Defense? Prayers," *Time,* June 27, 1959, 17–18; and Robert Manson, "When Ike 'Fled' Washington," *U.S. News & World Report,* June 25, 1955, 66–69.

45. Richard Dyke, *Mr. Atomic Energy: Congressman Chet Holifield and Atomic Energy Affairs, 1945–1974* (London: Praeger, 1986), 193.

46. The records for the next section are from House Subcommittee for Civil Defense, summary report, Records of the Office of Emergency Preparedness, Regional Office Administration File 1961, RG396, file 1 "Holifield Committee," NAII. This file is an exact copy of the original 1956 report, reprinted for the Kennedy administration.

47. House Committee on Government Operations, "Civil Defense for National Survival," 5–6.

48. House Subcommittee for Civil Defense, summary report, 57.

49. Ibid., 35.

50. The $20 billion price tag was an educated guess. Holifield was "sensitive" to the fact that the overly expensive shelter system proposed by Rockefeller and Gaither in 1958 would not make him popular in Congress. See McEnaney, *Civil Defense Begins at Home,* 58.

51. According to a 1989 interview with Holifield, he proposed a federal shelter system to emphasis the futility, not the viability, of shelters. See Dee Garrison, "Our Skirts Gave Them Courage," *Not June Cleaver Women and Gender in Post War America 1945–1960,* ed. Joanne Meyerowitz (Philadelphia: Temple University Press, 1994), 223.

52. Harry Yosphe, *Our Missing Shield: The U.S. Civil Defense Program in Historical Perspective* (Washington, DC: Federal Emergency Management Agency, 1981), 164–68.

53. National Civil Defense Advisory Council, agenda for meetings, May 28–29, 1957.

54. Dwight D. Eisenhower Administration, memo of discussions at the 343rd meeting of the National Security Council, November 7, 1958, Dwight D. Eisenhower Papers, National Security Council series, box 10, folder "343rd Meetings of NSC November 7, 1958," NAII; Yosphe, *Our Missing Shield,* 27.

55. Dwight D. Eisenhower Administration, memo of discussions at the 293rd and 294th Meetings of the National Security Council, August 16–17, 1956, Dwight D. Eisenhower Papers, National Security Council series, box 8, folder "293rd and 294th Meetings of NSC August 16 & 17, 1956," DDEL.

56. See Gaddis, *Strategies of Containment;* and Francis J. Gavin, *Nuclear*

Statecraft: History of Strategy in America's Atomic Age (Ithaca, NY: Cornell University Press, 2012).

57. "Report to the President by the Security Resources Panel Science Advisory Committee on Deterrence and Survival in the Nuclear Age," November 7, 1957, in *Foreign Relations of the United States, 1955–1957,* vol. 19, *National Security Policy* (Washington, DC: Government Printing Office, 1990), 245–56.

58. Science Advisory Committee, Technological Capabilities Panel, "Meeting the Threat of Surprise Attack," February 14, 1955, in *Foreign Relations of the United States, 1955–1957,* vol. 19, *National Security Policy* (Washington, DC: Government Printing Office, 1990), 609.

59. Fred Kaplan, *The Wizards of Armageddon* (New York: Simon and Schuster, 1983), 155.

60. Federal Civil Defense Administration, memo of a conversation, May 29, 1957, in *Foreign Relations of the United States, 1955–1957,* vol. 26, *Central South Eastern Europe* (Washington, DC: Government Printing Office, 1957), 290.

61. Kaplan, *Wizards of Armageddon,* 138.

62. Science Advisory Committee, Security Resources Panel, "Deterrence and Survival in the Nuclear Age," November 7, 1957, National Security Council Staff Papers, 1948–61, Disaster File, box 36, folder "Mobilization (10)," DDEL, 2. The report was declassified and published.

63. Eisenhower Administration, memo of discussion at the 343rd meeting of the National Security Council, 2.

64. See Lawrence R. Samuel, *American Fatherhood: A Cultural History* (London: Rowman and Littlefield, 2015); E. Anthony Rotundo, *American Manhood: Transformations in Masculinity from the Revolution to the Modern Era* (New York: Basic Books, 1993); Joseph H. Pleck, "American Fathering in Historical Perspective," in *Changing Men: New Directions on Men and Masculinity,* ed. Michael Kimmel (Newbury Park, CA: Sage, 1987), 407–18; Charlie Lewis, *Becoming a Father* (Milton Keynes, UK: Open University Press, 1986); John Nash, "Historical and Social Changes in the Perception of the Role of the Father," in *The Role of the Father in Child Development,* ed. Michael E. Lamb (New York: Wiley, 1989), 211–28; Robert L. Griswold, *Fatherhood in America* (New York: Basic Books, 1993), 206–7; R. W. Connell, *Masculinities* (Cambridge: Polity Press, 1995); Michael Kimmel, *The History of Men: Essays on American and British Masculinities* (Albany: State University of New York Press, 2006).

65. Cuordileone, *Manhood and American Political Culture.*

66. National Civil Defense Advisory Council, agenda for meetings, May 28–29, 1957.

67. McEnaney, *Civil Defense Begins at Home*, 60.

68. Edward Lyman, letter to John Kirby, July 5, 1957, Public Affairs Office, Records of the Office for Emergency Preparedness, RG396, box 2, NAII.

69. Leo Hoegh, letter to William Heimlich, August 9, 1958, Office of Civil Defense and Mobilization, Operational Headquarters Central Files, 1958–60, RG396, box 1, NAII.

70. William Heimlich, letter to Leo Hoegh, August 10, 1958, Office of Civil Defense and Mobilization, Operational Headquarters Central Files, 1958–60, RG396, box 1, NAII.

71. Although the FCDA existed until the body became reorganized into the OCDM on July 1, 1958, I have referred, throughout this chapter, to civil defense as primarily driven by the OCDM because the personnel change and direction were distinctive under Hoegh. The OCDM existed for only three years (1958–61) before Kennedy moved civil defense into the purview of the Department of Defense. Hoegh was sworn in as the administrator of the FCDA on July 19, 1957, and was named director of the OCDM on July 1, 1958.

72. McEnaney, *Civil Defense Begins at Home*, 66.

73. The Public Affairs Office of the OCDM kept details about its consultations with external agencies on the public presentation of civil defense. Among them were many newspaper clippings of civil defense–related advertisements. See Public Affairs Office Subject 1958–60, RG397, boxes 1–6, NAII.

74. House Military Operations Subcommittee, *New Civil Defense Program: Ninth Report by the Committee on Government Operations* (Washington, DC: Government Printing Office, 1961), 44.

75. Evidence for the soft selling of shelters appears in a series of local newspaper articles published between 1960 and 1962. See Edward Lyman, "Briefing on Civil Defense," May 4, 1958, Records of the Office of Emergency Preparedness, Public Affairs Office Subject, 1960–61, RG396, box 2, 4 NAII. This collection will be discussed in chapter 3.

76. William Heimlich, letter to Edward Lyman, April 29, 1958, Records of the Office of Emergency Preparedness, Public Affairs Office Subject, 1960–61, RG396, box 1, NAII.

77. On the history of advertisement in civil defense, see "An Approach to Advertising Council Support of Civil Defense Objectives," June 29, 1954, White House Central Files, box 658, DDEL, 1; Edward Lyman, letter to Murray Snyder, August 1, 1956, White House Central Files, box 658, DDEL; Edward Lyman, memo,

July 12, 1957, Records of the Office of Emergency Preparedness, Public Affairs Office Subject, 1960–61, RG396, box 2, NAII.

78. Criticism of this approach can be found in Herbert Jolovitz, memo to Stephen Young, "Considerations on Civil Defense for the Office of the President," Presidential Campaign Files, Position and Briefing Papers, 1960, series 14, box 1, 1, John F. Kennedy Library (hereafter JFKL).

79. Katherine Graham Howard, "A New Stronghold for National Security— Civil Defense," speech to the Region 1 Women's Advisory Committee, Cambridge, MA, April 24, 1957, Katherine Graham Howard Papers, box 10, DDEL.

80. Office of Civil Defense and Mobilization, information and publicity, June 3, 1959, Records of the Defense Preparedness Agency, RG397, box 12, NAII.

81. Office of Civil Defense and Mobilization, "A Federal Shelter Program for Civil Defense," March 20, 1957, National Security Council Policy Papers, subseries, RG397, box 21, NAII.

82. Dwight D. Eisenhower Administration, memo of discussions at the 471st meeting of the Nation Security Council, December 22, 1960, in *Foreign Relations of the United States 1958–1960*, vol. 3, *Arms Control and Disarmament* (Washington, DC: Government Printing Office, 1958), 516–28.

83. Ibid., 520.

84. Ibid., 521.

85. See Marion Boggs, "Measures for the Passive Defense of the Population with Particular Regard to Fallout Shelter"; Executive Secretary of OCDM, memo to National Security Council, "U.S. Policy on Continental Defense," July 14, 1960; National Security Council Action 2300-e; Deputy Executive Secretary of OCDM, memos to National Security Council, "Measures for the Passive Defense of the Population, with Particular Regard to Fallout Shelter," December 7–8, 1960, all in *Foreign Relations of the United States, 1958–1960*, vol. 3, *Arms Control and Disarmament* (Washington, DC: Government Printing Office, 1990).

86. McEnaney, *Civil Defense Begins at Home*, 147.

87. Dwight D. Eisenhower Administration, memo of discussions at the 351st meeting of the Nation Security Council, January 22, 1958, *Foreign Relations of the United States, 1958–1960*, vol. 3, *Arms Control and Disarmament* (Washington, DC: Government Printing Office, 1996), 354.

88. Edward Lyman, memo, July 12, 1957, Records of the Office of Emergency Preparedness, Public Affairs Office Subject, 1960–61, RG396, box 2, NAII.

89. "The Hidden Revolution," *CBS News*, March 18, 1959.

90. House Subcommittee, *Civil Defense* (Washington, DC: Government Printing Office, 1960), xiv–554.

91. McEnaney, *Civil Defense Begins at Home*, 71.

92. Ibid., 88–123; Sarah A. Litchman, "Do-It-Yourself Security: Safety, Gender and the Home Fallout Shelter in Cold War America," *Journal of Design History* 19, no. 1 (2006): 39.

93. Office of Civil and Defense Mobilization, "Shelter, Commercial Prospects," July 6, 1960, Records of the Office of Civil and Defense Mobilization, Mobilization and Manpower Region 7, Subject Files Leo Hoegh, box 4, NAII.

94. Hoegh, "Address of Leo A. Hoegh," 5.

95. Jacki Wilson, "Surviving the Bomb," *New York Times*, October 15, 1961, 224.

96. "Family in the Shelter, Snug, Equipped and Well Organized," *Life*, September 15, 1961, 105. See Gail Bederman, *Manliness and Civilization: A Cultural History of Gender and Race in the United States, 1880–1917* (Chicago: Chicago University Press, 1995); Elaine Tyler Mays, *Homeward Bound: American Families in the Cold War Era* (New York: Basic Books, 1988); Steve Cohan, *Masked Men: Masculinity and the Movies in the Fifties* (Indianapolis: Indiana University Press, 1997); Cuordileone, *Manhood and American Political Culture*; James Gilbert, *Man in the Middle: Searching for Masculinity in the 1950s* (Chicago: University of Chicago Press, 2005); and Aaron Belkin, *Bring Me Men: Military Masculinity and the Façade of American Empire, 1898–2011* (New York: Columbia University Press, 2012).

97. Office of Civil Defense and Mobilization, report 7/9, Records of the Office of Emergency Preparedness, OCDM Regional Publication, RG397, box A1–1002, NAII.

98. Office of Civil Defense and Mobilization, report on LYN shelter report at the New York State Fair, December 1960, Records of the Office of Emergency Preparedness, OCDM Publications 1950–60, RG396, box 2, NAII.

99. J. R. Sanchez, letter to Val Peterson, May 5, 1960, Records of the Office of Emergency Preparedness, OCDM Publications, 1950–60, RG396, box 2, NAII, 1.

100. Records of the Office of Emergency Preparedness, OCDM Publications, 1950–60, RG396, box 2, NAII.

101. "You Can Build a Low-Cost Shelter Quickly," *Popular Mechanics* 32 (December 1961): 85–89. *Popular Mechanics* provided guidelines on outdoor and indoor shelter construction in addition to tips on how to maintain shelter air filters and antennas. See "Outdoor Antenna for Fallout Shelter," *Popular Mechanics* 32 (February 1962): 204.

102. McEnaney, *Civil Defense Begins at Home*, 67.

103. David Monteyne, *Fallout Shelter: Designing for Civil Defense in the Cold War* (Minneapolis: University of Minnesota Press, 2011).

104. Alfred Balk, "Anyone for Survival?," *Saturday Evening Post*, March 27, 1965, 75.

105. See Norman Cousins Records, SANE Subject Files, box 15, Swarthmore College Peace Collection (hereafter SCPC).

106. Advertising alert, August 12, 1960, Federal Trade Commission Papers, box 3, JFKL.

107. Margaret Mead, "Are Shelters the Answer?," *New York Times Magazine*, November 26, 1961, 125; Sam Recchia, "The Paradox of Civil Defense," *Commonweal* 27 (March 1962): 15–37; I. F. Stone, "Civil Defense Right Wing Madness," *Weekly*, September 20, 1961, 45–50; Linus Pauling, "Shelter Muddle," *Dissent* 34 (October 1961): 5–7; Norman Cousins, "Shelters and Survival: A Report on Civil Defense," *New Republic* (November 1961): 140.

108. Office for Civil Defense and Mobilization, "Briefing for the Director on National Organizations and Civic Affairs," Records of the Office of Emergency Preparedness, Public Affairs Office Subject, 1960–61, RG396, box 1, 4, NAII.

109. Cuordileone, *Manhood and American Political Culture*, 153.

110. On the gendered nature of do-it-yourself, see Carlyon Goldstein, *Do-It-Yourself: Home Improvement in the 20th Century America* (Princeton, NJ: Princeton Architectural Press, 1998), 67–82. Penny Sparke notes that feminine domesticity and the gendered division of labor during the 1950s were still predicated on "Darwinian ideas" of differences between men and women (*As Long as It's Pink: The Sexual Politics of Taste* [Ontario: Pandora Press, 1995], 169).

111. Office of Civil Defense and Mobilization, "Individual and Family Preparedness a1 of *The National Plan for Civil Defense and Defense Mobilization*," October 1958, Subject Series, Alpha Subseries, box 8, NAII.

112. Jack A. Vernon, "Project Hideaway: A Pilot Feasibility Study of Fallout Shelters for Families," December 21, 1959, Office of Emergency Preparedness, Nuclear Attack Research Papers, 1956–62, RG396, entry 1019, NAII.

113. "Project Hideaway," *New York Times*, August 16, 1959, 20.

114. "The Brown Family," *Retrospect*, episode 10 (March 5, 1959).

115. Ibid.

116. Office of Civil Defense and Mobilization, memo of discussions of possible nonmilitary defense legislative proposals, Records of Advisory Council, Draft Staff Papers, box 1, NAII.

117. Dwight D. Eisenhower, letter to Freeman Gosden, October 15, 1957, Post-Presidential Papers, Special Names Series, box 4, folder "Gosden, Freeman," DDEL.

118. "Caddyshack: Eisenhower's Fallout Shelter Dilemma," *Conelrad Adjacent*, http://conelrad.blogspot.com.

119. "Shelter Value Uncertain to Eisenhower," *Los Angeles Times*, October 19, 1961, 31.

120. Hazel, letter to OCDM.

CHAPTER TWO: THE FALLOUT SHELTER FATHER ON THE NEW FRONTIER

1. John F. Kennedy, report to the American people on the Berlin crisis [Berlin Address], July 25, 1961, John F. Kennedy Speech Files, 1961–63, Theodore C. Sorensen Personal Papers, JFKL, 4.

2. Ibid.

3. For regional OCD staff, the morning of July 26 was exceptionally busy and stressful. Reports reveal a sharp and quickly overwhelming number of requests for information, and especially for copies of *Family Fallout Shelter*, a 1960 construction manual. See Office of Civil Defense, office record, NAII.

4. Alice L. George, *Awaiting Armageddon: How Americans Faced the Cuban Missile Crisis* (Chapel Hill: University of North Carolina Press, 2003), 59.

5. Frank Fields, letter to the Office of Civil Defense, November 10, 1961, Public Affairs Office Record, box 1, file "Correspondence Cards," NAII.

6. Subsequent chapters will detail the financial implications of shelter construction; suffice it to say here that letters and correspondent cards frequently mentioned them. For example, Fred Hunt wrote to his local paper about the argument he had had with his wife over whether buying or financing a shelter might preclude getting a new television. Such commodity balancing between survival and luxury informed many actions of shelter salesmen. See Fred Hunt, letter to the editor, *Sarasota News*, October 5, 1961, 56.

7. Theodore C. Sorensen, memo to John F. Kennedy, November 23, 1961, Theodore C. Sorensen Personal Papers, box 30, file "Civil Defense," JFKL, 1.

8. See Laura McEnaney, *Civil Defense Begins at Home: Militarization Meets Everyday Life in the Fifties* (Princeton, NJ: Princeton University Press, 2000), chap. 5.

9. Richard Crawford, "'Cold War Fallout': Big Boom in Building of Home Shelters," *San Diego Union*, August 13, 1961, 12.

10. On Kennedy's decision to treat civil defense as an insurance policy, see Robert Dallek, *John F. Kennedy: An Unfinished Life 1917–1936* (Oxford: Oxford University Press, 2013), 405; and Ernst R. May and Phillip D. Zelikow, eds., *The Kennedy Tapes: Inside the White House during the Cuban Missile Crisis* (Cambridge, MA: Harvard University Press, 1997), 265.

11. Herbert Jolovitz, "Considerations on Civil Defense for the Office of the President," January 7, 1961, Presidential Campaign Files, Position and Briefing Papers, 1960, series 14, box 1, JFKL, 2, 1.

12. Ibid., 2.

13. Unknown author, memo to McGeorge Bundy, February 6, 1961, John F.

Kennedy Papers, National Security Files, Civil Defense: General, January–March 1961, series 5, box 295, JFKL, 1.

14. Kennedy historians do not often consider early discussions of civil defense, including JFK's and his father Joseph's support of the FDCA throughout the 1950s. For studies of Kennedy's civil defense policy beginning with the May 1961 congressional address, see Kenneth D. Rose, *One Nation Underground* (New York: New York University Press, 2001); Tracy C. Davis, *Stages of Emergency: Cold War Nuclear Defense* (Durham, NC: Duke University Press, 2007); Dee Garrison, *Bracing for Armageddon: Why Civil Defense Never Worked* (Oxford: Oxford University Press, 2006).

15. See K. A. Cuordileone, *Manhood and American Political Culture in the Cold War*, (New York: Routledge, 2005), 167–220.

16. Franklin B. Ellis, "Briefing for the Director on National Organizations and Civic Affairs," March 15, 1959, Records of the Office of Emergency Preparedness, Public Affairs Office Subject, 1960–61, RG396, box 1, NAII, 4.

17. Ibid.

18. See McEnaney, *Civil Defense Begins at Home*, chap. 5.

19. William Heimlich, memo to Frank Ellis, April 29, 1961, Records of the Office of Emergency Preparedness, Public Affairs Office Subject, 1960–61, RG396, box 1, NAII, 3.

20. U.S. House of Representatives, "Civil Defense Program: Hearing Before a Subcommittee of the Committee for Armed Services," 84th Congress, 1st sess. (Washington, DC: Government Printing Office, May 20, 1955), 707.

21. Irving Lester Janis, *Air War and Emotional Stress: Psychological Studies of Bombing and Civilian Defense* (New York: McGraw-Hill, 1991), 202–3.

22. See U.S. Bureau of the Census, *U.S. Census of Housing, 1960*, vol. 1, *States and Small Areas* (Washington, DC: Government Printing Office, 1963), part 1.

23. Charles A. Haskins, memo to McGeorge Bundy, February 21, 1961, National Security Files, series 5, box 295, JFKL.

24. Bundy viewed Stimson, whom he called "the Colonel," as "an exemplary man" and a "stoic servant of the state," whose foreign policy service and "liberal internationalism" made him a "heroic model" to be both admired and imitated. Stimson's portrait hung in Bundy's office during his tenure in the White House; and among those who joined what became known as the foreign policy establishment, his "rugged integrity, force, and courage" became the benchmark for how they should act in times of crisis. See Robert Dean, *Imperial Brotherhood: Gender and the Making of Cold War Foreign Policy* (Amherst: University of Massachusetts Press, 2001), 10–16.

25. Andrew Preston, *The War Council: McGeorge Bundy, the NSC, and Vietnam* (Cambridge, MA: Harvard University Press, 2006), 59.

26. See chap. 1; also see FCDA, *Civil Defense for National Security* (Washington, DC: Government Printing Office, 1948), 186.

27. McGeorge Bundy, *Danger and Survival* (New York: Random House, 1988), 355, 356.

28. Carl Kaysen, "Second Oral History Interview with Theodore C. Sorensen," April 6, 1964, John F. Kennedy Oral History Collection, JFKL, 7. Sorensen's answers were lengthy: he mentioned the threat from Rockefeller in the 1964 election and feared an "inconsistentcy with his general stance."

29. McGeorge Bundy, memo to Marcus Raskin, May 6, 1961, National Security Files, box 295, folder 2, JFKL.

30. For a complete discussion of civil defense and FHA loans, see John F. Kennedy Papers, National Security Files, Civil Defense: General, January–March 1961, JFKL.

31. Bundy reviewed the findings of numerous reports, studies, proposals before providing Kennedy with a condensed summary of his options. The Gaither report (circulated as National Security Council, "Report to the President by the Security Resources Panel Science Advisory Committee on Deterrence and Survival in the Nuclear Age," November 7, 1957, reprinted in *Foreign Relations of the United States, 1955–1957*, vol. 19, *National Security Policy* [Washington, DC: Government Printing Office, 1990]) stated that a national shelter program costing $25 billion to construct and a future $10 billion in equipment and supplies might save "fifty million American lives" while allowing "our own air defense to use nuclear warheads with greater freedom" (35–45). Two subsequent studies, the Rockefeller report (1957) (Science Advisory Committee, Security Resources Panel, "Deterrence and Survival in the Nuclear Age," November 7, 1957, National Security Council Staff Papers, 1948–61, Disaster File, box 36, folder "Mobilization [10]," DDEL, 2), (which was declassified and published), and the RAND Corporation's commissioned *Report on a Study of Non-Military Defense* (1958), Report R-322-RC, *The Rand Corporation* (July 1958) both written in the wake of Sputnik, verified the initial appraisal of the nationwide shelter program, noting that the costs might range between $20 billion and $150 billion, depending on the scale. Eisenhower understandably balked at these costs, seeing grave social and geopolitical implications in what he called the "fortress America" concept (see Guy Oakes, *Imaginary War: Civil Defense and Cold War Culture* [Oxford: Oxford University Press, 1994], 31).

32. On Kaysen and Raskin, see Frank Kaplan, *The Wizards of Armageddon* (New York: Touchstone, 1983).

33. Marcus Raskin, "Civil Defense and Berlin," July 7, 1961, National Security Files, box 295, folder 3, JFKL.

34. Carl Kaysen, "The Vulnerability of the United States to Enemy Attack," *World Politics* 6, no. 2 (January 1954): 190–208.

35. Marcus Raskin, memo to McGeorge Bundy, May 19, 1961, National Security Files, box 295, folder 2, JFKL.

36. See Cuordileone, *Manhood and American Political Culture*, 167–220.

37. See Kenneth T. Jackson, *Crabgrass Frontier: The Suburbanization of the United States* (Oxford: Oxford University Press, 1985), 222.

38. Carl Kaysen, "First Oral History Interview," November 7, 1966, John F. Kennedy Oral History Collection, JFKL.

39. Policymakers discussed potential resolutions related to large-scale home construction projects, the identification of public spaces as makeshift shelter sites, the diplomatic utility of civil defense, and the need to carefully consider if civil defense should be under civilian or military control.

40. Theodore C. Sorensen, *Kennedy* (New York: Harper and Row, 1965), 613–14.

41. Kaplan, *The Wizards of Armageddon*, 309.

42. Raskin was building on the work of Willard Libby; see Thomas Keer, *Civil Defense in the United States: Band-Aid for the Holocaust* (Boulder, CO: Westview Press, 1983), 90–91.

43. Gary Wills, *The Kennedy Imprisonment: A Meditation on Power* (New York: Simon and Schuster, 1981), 179.

44. On the quest to solve the problems of civil defense, see David Monteyne, *Architecture, Landscape, and American Culture: Fallout Shelter: Designing for Civil Defense in the Cold War* (Minneapolis: University of Minnesota Press, 2011), 35–77. See also Gerald E. Klonglan, George M. Beal, and Joe M. Bohlen, *Adoption of Public Fallout Shelters: A 1964 National Study* (Ames: Iowa State University, 1964), 186–91.

45. Marcus Raskin, *Essays of a Citizen: From National Security to State to Democracy* (New York: Routledge, 1991), 60. On the Stanford report, see Tracy C. Davis, *Stages of Emergency: Cold War Nuclear Defense* (Durham, NC: Duke University Press, 2007), 421.

46. Raskin, *Essays of a Citizen*, 60, 61.

47. Raskin, memo to Bundy, May 19, 1961.

48. Sorensen, memo to Kennedy, November 23, 1961, 1.

49. John F. Kennedy, "Special Message to Congress on Urgent National Needs," May 25, 1961, John F. Kennedy Papers, Speech Files, series 3, JFKL, 6.

50. Ibid.

51. Ibid.

52. FHA loans were mortgages used for purchasing or refinancing one- to four-unit, owner-occupied, residential properties, condominiums, and manufactured homes. Home loans were not funded directly by the agency, but the FHA guaranteed that they will be repaid if the borrower defaults. For full details, including the changing regulations in 1961–62, see U.S. House of Representatives, *Hearings Before a Subcommittee of the Committee on Government Operations*, part 2, *Appendixes*, 87th Cong., 2nd sess. (Washington, DC: Government Printing Office, 1962), 366.

53. Newspapers often published details of the FHA regulations; see U.S. Department of Housing and Urban Development, *Aids for Fallout Shelters* (Washington, DC: Government Printing Office, 1967).

54. Details of approved shelter loans were recorded in U.S. House of Representatives, *Annual Report of the Activities of the Joint Committee on Defense Production* (Washington, DC: Government Printing Office, 1961), 370.

55. *Hearings Before a Subcommittee of the Committee on Government Operations*, 366.

56. Office of Civil Defense, information bulletin, October 1961, 2:1.

57. *Janesville Daily Gazette*, October 11, 1961, 11; *Albuquerque Journal*, November, 1961, 35; *Post Standard*, October 22, 1961, 17; *Miami News Florida*, September 24, 1961, 25.

58. "Shelter Loans Now Available," *Herald Press*, October 12, 1961, 29.

59. *Baytown Sun*, October 15, 1961, 12; *Sarasota News*, November 3, 1961, 13; *Nashua Telegram*, October 4, 1961, 42; "Home Shelter Loan," *Beckley Post Herald*, November 14, 1961, 16.

60. *Las Vegas Daily*, October 13, 1961, 12.

61. "Baldwin Couple Likes Neighbors," *Pittsburgh Press*, October 1, 1961, 56.

62. Ibid.

63. *Chicago Defender*, November 3, 1961, 12; "Shelters on Sale," *Pittsburgh Courier*, October 4, 1961, 45.

64. Norman Cousins, "On Shelter," August 15, 1961, Records of SANE, Norman Cousins Subject Files, box 15, SCPC.

65. See, for instance, Office of Civil Defense, Records of the Defense Preparedness Agency, Subject File: Correspondence Cards, boxes 1 and 2, NAII.

66. During the 1950s, the FCDA and the OCDM used an extensive network of religious movements to transmit the message of civil defense to local communities. See Office of Civil Defense, Public Affairs Office, boxes 765–74, NAII.

67. Percy Hamner, letter to the Office of Civil Defense, November 21, 1961, Records of the Defense Preparedness Agency, Shelters and Vulnerability Reduction, Central Files, 1961–68, RG396, NAII, 1.

68. Lawrence Hank, letter to the Office of Civil Defense, October 3, 1961, Records of the Defense Preparedness Agency, Shelters and Vulnerability Reduction, Central Files, 1961–68, RG396, NAII, 2.

69. Vincent Intondi, *African Americans Against the Bomb: Nuclear Weapons, Colonialism, and the Black Freedom Movement* (Stanford, CA: Stanford University Press, 2015).

70. Initially, the FHA did not require all shelters to be inspected before it processed loans. But after internal discussion and with a growing awareness of unethical practices, FHA and Federal Trade Commission (FTC) officials decided in December 1961 to work together to regulate all products sold and loans processed. This ruling required that each shelter be inspected. See Federal Trade Commission, ruling, December 1961, in *Annual Report*, Federal Trade Commission Papers, box 1, series 1, JFKL; and *Hearings Before a Subcommittee of the Committee on Government Operations, House*, 366.

71. "FHA Home Shelter Offer," *Sarasota News*, November 13, 1961, 34.

72. "FHA Offers Shelter," *Eugene Guard*, October 12, 1961, 8.

73. Unknown author, letter to the Office of Civil Defense, December 4, 1961, Records of the Defense Preparedness Agency, Shelters and Vulnerability Reduction, Central Files, 1961–68, NAII, 2.

74. James Scott, letter to the Office of Civil Defense, December 12, 1961, Records of the Defense Preparedness Agency, Shelters and Vulnerability Reduction, Central Files, 1961–68, NAII, 2.

75. Robert Scott, Jr., letter to the editor, *Arizona Republic*, September 10, 1961, 26.

76. "Shelters for All?," *Tucson Daily Citizen*, June 18, 1962, 15.

77. "Shelters the New Fab," *Morning Call*, November 10, 1961, 13.

78. Ibid., 13.

79. "The New Craze," *San Francisco Chronicle*, November 12, 1961, 29.

80. "Let Us Talk about Shelter," *Beckley Post Herald*, July 15, 1962, 40.

81. "Civil Defense Spotlight," *Morning Call*, November 14, 1961, 16.

82. For more on Khrushchev's bullish behavior, see Dallek, *An Unfinished Life*, 403–14.

83. Jennifer Lynn Walton writes that attempts to "make a powerful first impression had fallen short" and that Vienna had a formative effect upon the policy decision and the renewed rhetorical "emphasis on responsibility patriarchy" in the following months ("Moral Masculinity," in *The Vienna Summit and Its*

Import in International History, ed. Gunter Bischof, Stefan Karner, and Barbara Stelzl-Marx [Cambridge, MA: Lexington Books, 2003], 320–29).

84. Dallek, *An Unfinished Life,* 403, 405.

85. See Kenneth D. Rose, *One Nation Underground* (New York: New York University Press, 2001), 32.

86. Dallek, *An Unfinished Life,* 412.

87. Marcus Trachtenberg, *A Constructed Peace: The Making of the European Settlement, 1945–1963* (Princeton, NJ: Princeton University Press), 322.

88. Eugene Rostow, memo to Chester Bowles, June 16, 1961, National Security Files, Countries Series: Germany, box 81, JFKL.

89. Dean Acheson, memo to John F. Kennedy, April 3, 1961, National Security Files, Countries Series: Germany, box 81, JFKL.

90. National Security Council, memo for the record, National Security Council meeting 486, June 29, 1961, National Security Files, box 313, JFKL.

91. Kaplan, *The Wizards of Armageddon,* 309.

92. Richard Reeves, *President Kennedy: Profile of Power* (New York: Simon and Schuster, 1994), 232.

93. Robert McNamara, memo to John F. Kennedy, September 18, 1961, National Security Files, Countries Series: Germany, box 81, JFKL.

94. John F. Kennedy, memo to Robert McNamara, September 18, 1961, National Security Files, Countries Series: Germany, box 61, Germany, JFKL.

95. Lawrence Freedman, *Kennedy's Wars: Berlin, Cuba, Laos, and Vietnam* (Oxford: Oxford University Press, 2000), 66.

96. Arthur Schlesinger, memo to John F. Kennedy, July 7, 1961, National Security Files, Country Series: Germany, box 81, JFKL.

97. In "Theodore Sorensen," Michael Brenes considers the partnership between Sorensen and Kennedy and argues that Sorensen's liberal ideology failed to translate into policy action (*A Companion to John F. Kennedy,* ed. Marcus J. Selverstone [Oxford: Wiley Blackwell, 2014], 115–32).

98. Theodore C. Sorensen, memo to John F. Kennedy, July 17, 1961, Theodore C. Sorensen Personal Papers, Classified Subject Files: Berlin, box 42, folder 1, JFKL.

99. McGeorge Bundy, memo to Theodore C. Sorensen, July 5, 1961, Theodore C. Sorensen Personal Papers, Classified Subject Files: Berlin, box 42, folder 1, JFKL.

100. Theodore C. Sorensen, "Drafts: Berlin Speech," July 24–25, 1961, Theodore C. Sorensen Personal Papers, box 60, JFKL.

101. Kennedy, Berlin Address, 4.

102. "CD—The Weak Spot," *Newsweek,* July 31, 1961, 14.

103. Rose, *One Nation Underground,* 37.

104. Stephen M. Young, "Civil Defense: Billion Dollar Boondoggle," *Progressive* 24 (December 1960): 18–20.

105. "CD Successes," *Washington Post*, August 2, 1961, 12.

106. Marcus Raskin, memo to McGeorge Bundy, October 10, 1961, National Security Files, Civil Defense Records, box 295, folder 3, JFKL.

107. Kaplan, *The Wizards of Armageddon*, 309.

108. Adam Yarmolinsky, interview no. 1, March 26, 1964, John F. Kennedy Oral History Collection, JFKL, 38–39.

109. Adam Yarmolinsky, clipping, Adam Yarmolinsky Personal Papers, Subject File: Civil Defense, box WHo.9a, JFKL.

110. Rose, *One Nation Underground*, 32.

111. Adam Yarmolinsky, "First Oral History with Adam Yarmolinsky," March 1, 1964, John F. Kennedy Oral History Collection, JFKL, 38–39.

112. Arthur Schlesinger, *A Thousand Days: John F. Kennedy in the White House* (New York: Houghton Mifflin Harcourt, 1965), 391.

113. Edward K. Thompson, *A Love Affair with "Life" & "Smithsonian"* (Columbia: University of Missouri Press, 1995), 253.

114. Marcus Raskin, memo to McGeorge Bundy, October 17, 1961, National Security Files, box 295, folder 3 "Civil Defense," JFKL.

115. Kaplan, *The Wizards of Armageddon*, 309.

116. The original draft of *Fallout Protection and You* is in Adam Yarmolinsky Personal Papers, Subject File "Civil Defense," box WHo.9a, JFKL.

117. John Kenneth Galbraith, memo to John F. Kennedy, November 9, 1961, National Security Files, Civil Defense, October 28–November 17, 1961, box 295, folder 7, JFKL.

118. *Fallout Protection and You*, 65.

119. Frederick G. Dutton, memo to McGeorge Bundy, October 28, 1961, National Security Files, Civil Defense, October 28–November 17, 1961, box 295, folder 7, JFKL.

120. Galbraith, memo to Kennedy, November 9, 1961, 2.

121. Arthur Schlesinger, memo to John F. Kennedy, November 22, 1961, National Security Files, Civil Defense, October 28–November 17, 1961, box 295, folder 7, JFKL, 3.

122. Marcus Raskin, memo to McGeorge Bundy, November 7, 1961, National Security Files, Civil Defense, October 28–November 17, 1961, box 295, folder 7, JFKL.

123. See Kaplan, *The Wizards of Armageddon*, 309.

124. Pittman recalled how, "after several tortured months, we did what we could've done almost immediately, which was to take the material that had already been written by OCDM, revise it somewhat, and put it out in the name of the

Defense Department.... [I]t was really a ridiculous episode." ("First Oral History Interview with Steuart L. Pittman," September 18, 1970, John F. Kennedy Oral History Collection, JFKL, 6.)

125. "First Interview with Carl Kaysen," June 11, 1966, John F. Kennedy Oral History Collection, JFKL, 12.

126. Sorensen, memo to John F. Kennedy, November 11, 1961, Theodore C. Sorensen Personal Papers, Subject Files: Civil Defense, 1961–64, box 30, JFKL.

127. This annotated copy of *Fallout Protection and You* is in Arthur Schlesinger Personal Papers, Classified Subject Files: Civil Defense, box WH29, folder 2, JKFL.

128. Carl Kaysen, memo to John F. Kennedy, undated, National Security Files, Civil Defense, October 28–November 17, 1961, box 295, folder 7, JFKL.

129. Draft statements for *Fallout Protection*, Arthur Schlesinger Personal Papers, Classified Subject Files: Civil Defense, box W04, folder 3, JFKL, 2.

130. Carl Kaysen, memo to Marcus Raskin, November 15, 1961, National Security Files, Civil Defense, October 28–November 17, 1961, box 295, folder 8, JFKL.

131. Department of Defense, *Fallout Protection: What to Know and Do about Nuclear Attack* (Washington, DC: Government Printing Office, 1961), 46.

CHAPTER THREE: FATHERHOOD IN THE TARGET ZONE

1. Marcus Raskin, memo to Carl Kaysen, November 15, 1961, National Security Files, Civil Defense: General, box 295, folder 3, JFKL.

2. Marcus Raskin, memo to McGeorge Bundy, October 17, 1961, National Security Files, Civil Defense: General, box 295, folder 3, JFKL.

3. Arthur Chase, letter to John F. Kennedy, February 6, 1962, Office of Civil Defense, Central Files, 1958–60, Records of the Defense Preparedness Agency, Shelters and Vulnerability Reduction, February, RG397, box 24, NAII.

4. Laura McEnaney, *Civil Defense Begins at Home: Militarization Meets Everyday Life in the Fifties* (Princeton, NJ: Princeton University Press, 2000).

5. This point is supported by Jeffrey Engel, ed., *Local Consequences of the Global Cold War* (Stanford, CA: Stanford University Press, 2008).

6. Sarah Alisabeth Fox, *Downwind: A People's History of the Nuclear West* (Lincoln: University of Nebraska Press, 2014), 14.

7. For recent regional histories of the nuclear age, see ibid.; Kate Brown, *Plutopia: Nuclear Families, Atomic Cities, and the Great Soviet and American Plutonium Disasters* (Oxford: Oxford University Press, 2015); Gretchen Heefner, *The Missile Next Door: The Minutemen in the American Heartland* (Cambridge, MA: Harvard

University Press, 2012); and Lindsey A. Freeman, *This Atom Bomb in Me* (Stanford, CA: Stanford University Press, 2019).

8. It was not until 1966 that an operational network of radar detectors could track a Soviet missile from launch pad to detonation. On NORAD's technology, see Eric Schlosser, *Command and Control: The Story of Nuclear Weapons and the Illusion of Safety* (New York: Penguin, 2014).

9. On the historical importance of Colorado, see Courtenay W. Daum, Robert Duffy, and John Straayer, eds., *State of Change: Colorado Politics in the Twenty-First Century* (Boulder: University Press of Colorado, 2011), intro. Also see Rebecca Solnit, *Savage Dreams: A Journey into the Hidden Wars of the American West*, 20th anniversary ed. (Berkeley: University of California Press, 2014).

10. Edward Soja, *Postmodern Geographies: The Reassertion of Space in Critical Social Theory* (New York: Verso, 1989), 14.

11. See Stephanie A. Malin, *The Price of Nuclear Power: Uranium Communities and Environmental Justice* (New Brunswick, NJ: Rutgers University Press, 2015); and B. N. Webber, "Geology and Ore Resources of the Uranium-Canadium Depositional Province of the Colorado Plateau Region," Report RMO-437 (Washington, DC: Atomic Energy Commission, 1947), 279. The report classified by the AEC in 1959.

12. Kristen Iversen, *Full Body Burden: Growing Up in the Shadow of a Secret Nuclear Facility* (New York: Random House, 2012), 13.

13. Schlosser, *Command and Control*, 253–54.

14. For example, on June 20, 1958, the *Greeley Daily Tribune* ran an article detailing a new workers' contract ratified between the Rocky Flats Union and the AEC. On November 19, 1953, the paper covered the commission of Rock Flats, which it said would bring "between 3,000 and 1,200 workers" to produce a "highly secretive product." Horace Greely, "New Power to AEC," *Greeley Daily Tribune*, June 20, 1958, 7 and Horace Greely, "New Atomic Jobs," *Greeley Daily Tribune*, November 19, 1953, 4.

15. U.S. Department of Defense, *Appropriations* (Washington, DC: Government Printing Office, 1965), 786.

16. B. Burwell, "Construction, Operation, and Maintenance Report of Uranium Sludge Plants Operated by United States Vanadium Corporation in the Colorado Area" (Denver: Vanadium Corporation of America, 1946), 231. The report was declassified by the U.S. Department of Energy in 2000 and is available in RG434-00-051, National Archives, Denver.

17. Duane A Smith, *The Trail of Gold and Silver: Mining in Colorado, 1859–2009* (Boulder: University Press of Colorado, 2009), 154.

18. U.S. Bureau of the Census, "U.S. Demography, 1790 to Present [1960]," http://www.socialexplorer.com.

19. Charles A. Graham and Robert Perkin, "Denver: Reluctant Capital," in *Rocky Mountain Cities*, ed. Ray B. West (New York: Norton, 1949), 313.

20. Dawn Bunyak, Thomas H. Simmons, and R. Laurie Simmons, *Denver Area Post-World War II Suburbs* (Washington, DC: U.S. Department of Transportation, Federal Highway Administration, 2011), 3.

21. Carl Abbott, "The Metropolitan Region: Western Cities in the New Urban Era," in *The Twentieth-Century West. Albuquerque, New Mexico*, ed. Gerald D. Nash and Richard W. Etulain (Santa Fe: University of New Mexico Press, 1989), 125.

22. Henry J. Frank, letter to OCDM, May 13, 1958, Office of Civil Defense, Central Files, 1958-60, Records of the Defense Preparedness Agency, Shelters and Vulnerability Reduction, May-June, RG397, box 24, NAII, 1.

23. Ibid., 1, 2.

24. Jeremy Knox, letter to the Office of Defense and Mobilization, March 16, 1961, Office of Civil Defense, Central Files, 1961-68, Records of the Defense Preparedness Agency, Shelters and Vulnerability Reduction, March, RG397, box 29, NAII.

25. Stewart Parks, letter to OCDM, September 30, 1961, Office of Civil Defense, Central Files, 1961-68, Records of the Defense Preparedness Agency, Shelters and Vulnerability Reduction, RG397, box 12, NAII.

26. Location-specific civil defense literature was part of OCDM's efforts to "target and convince community leaders" (agribusiness, industrialists, local law enforcement officers, religious leaders and teachers) to participate in civil defense and thus ensure "sustained and motivated" public support for its polices. See William Heimlich memo, to Leo Hoegh "re Armstrong Circle Theatre," April 13, 1960, Records of the Office of Emergency Preparedness, Public Affairs Office Subject 1960-61, RG396, box 1, NAII.

27. Leo Hoegh, remarks on Mobilization and Manpower Region 7, Records of the Office of Defense and Mobilization, Subject Files: Leo Hoegh, box 4, NAII.

28. Office of Civil Defense and Mobilization, region 7 report on major exhibit for state and county fairs, July 19, 1961, Records of the Office of Emergency Preparedness, Regional Office Administration Files, 1961, box 1030, NAII.

29. Minutes of annual meeting, Chicago, August 9-12, 1955, Records of the Office of Emergency Preparedness, Central Files, 1960-61, RG396, box 23, NAII.

30. See a collection of index cards, Western History Subject Index, Colorado Civil Defense Agency, Denver Public Library Digital Collections http://digital.denverlibrary.org/cdm/whsi/.

31. Fabienne Collignon, *Rocket States: Atomic Weaponry and the Cultural Imagination* (London: Bloomsbury, 2014), 24.

32. Brent M. Rogers, "The Urbanization of the American West: The Processes and People in the Rise of Instant Cities and Their Evolution into the Twenty-First Century" in *The World of the American West*, ed. Gordon Morris Bakken (New York: Routledge, 2011), 284

33. Bunyak, Simmons, and Simmons, *Denver Area Post-World War II Suburbs*, 125.

34. *Food for Thought* Colorado Civil Defense Agency (1956).

35. In 2006 the Centre for Historic Perseveration Research and Office of Archaeology produced a report entitled *Database of the Annual Denver Area Parade of Homes 1953–1963* from which the follow data is taken. https://www.historycolorado.org/sites/default/files/media/documents/2018/si_postwwii_dbparadeofhomes.pdf.

36. "Parade of Homes," *Denver Post*, October 30, 1955, 20A.

37. In 1960, the Structural Clay Products Institute published a booklet with plans for basement and above-ground shelters, noting they could be put to other uses during peacetime and also serve during natural disasters (13).

38. Charlie Lewis, *Becoming a Father* (Milton Keynes, UK: Open University Press, 1986); John Nash, "Historical and Social Changes in the Perception of the Role of the Father," in *The Role of the Father in Child Development*, ed. Michael E. Lamb (New York: Wiley, 1989), 15.

39. Robert L. Griswold, *Fatherhood in America* (New York: Basic Books, 1993), 206–7.

40. Kenneth T. Jackson, *Crabgrass Frontier: The Suburbanization of the United States* (Oxford: Oxford University Press, 1985).

41. Kevin M. Kruse, *White Flight and the Making of Modern Conservatism* (Princeton, NJ: Princeton University Press, 2005).

42. Richard Weingroff, *Federal-Aid Highway Act of 1956: Creating the Interstate System Public Roads* (Washington, DC: U.S. Department of Transportation, Federal Highway Administration, 1956).

43. Martin Richards, letter to OCDM, October 18, 1958, Office of Civil Defense, Central Files, 1958–60, Records of the Defense Preparedness Agency, Shelters and Vulnerability Reduction, October, RG397, box 24, NAII.

44. Database of the annual Denver area Parade of Homes, 1953–63, Center for Historic Preservation Office of Archaeology and Historic Preservation, Colorado Historical Society, 29.

45. *Denver Post*, August 24, 1959, 14; "Civil Defense Comes Home," *Rocky Mountain News*, August 24, 1959, 6.

46. "Homes on Display," *Denver Post*, August 24, 1959, 14.

47. "Shelter Is a New Topic of Discussion," *Denver Post*, August 23, 1959, 6E; Lloyd Gorrell, *Arvada Comes of Age: A History of Arvada, Colorado, during the Period 1942–1976* (Arvada: Arvada Historical Society, 2002), 215; Inter-County Regional Planning Commission, "Community Shelter Planning: Denver Region" (Denver: Inter-County Regional Planning Commission, June 15, 1965), 7.

48. Database of the annual Denver area Parade of Homes 1953–63, 35.

49. David Monteyne, *Fallout Shelter: Designing for Civil Defense in the Cold War* (Minneapolis: University of Minnesota Press, 2011).

50. "Fallout Shelter Feature of Home in 1960 'Parade,'" *Colorado Springs Gazette-Telegraph*, July 3, 1960, 12.

51. Ibid.

52. John Parker, letter to L. T. Vickers, July 25, 1960, Office of Civil Defense, Central Files, 1958–60, Records of the Defense Preparedness Agency, Shelters and Vulnerability Reduction, July–August, RG397, box 25, NAII.

53. Ibid.

54. Thomas J. Noel and William J. Hansen, *The Park Hill Neighborhood* (Denver: Historic Guides Denver, 2002), 23.

55. William Simonds, letter to OCDM, October 7, 1961, Office of Civil Defense, Central Files, 1961–62, Records of the Defense Preparedness Agency, Shelters and Vulnerability Reduction, October, RG397, box 28, NAII.

56. Mark Jenkins, letter OCDM, October 9, 1961, Office of Civil Defense, Central Files, 1961–62, Records of the Defense Preparedness Agency, Shelters and Vulnerability Reduction, October, RG397, box 28, NAII.

57. Jenkins, letter to OCDM, October 9, 1961.

58. "Fallout Shelter Feature of Home in 1960 'Parade,'" 12

59. Ralph LaRossa, *Of War and Men: World War II in the Lives of Fathers and Their Families* (Chicago: University of Chicago Press, 2011).

60. Luke Gardner, letter to the Federal Housing Authority, November 10, 1962, Office of Civil Defense, Public Affairs Office, Records of the Defense Preparedness Agency, Subject File: Correspondence Cards, NAII.

61. Frank Vivian, clipping, 1962, Office of Emergency Preparedness, Records of Central Staff Offices, 1962, RG397.2.4, box 16, NAII, 3.

62. Jason Murphy, letter to OCDM, October 7, 1962, Office of Emergency Preparedness, Records of Central Staff Offices, 1962, RG397.2.4, box 16, NAII, 1.

63. Charlie Coates, letter to OCDM, October 6, 1962, Office of Emergency Preparedness, Records of Central Staff Offices, 1962, RG397.2.4, box 16, NAII 2, 4.

64. "Request for interview," November 10, 1961, Office of Civil Defense, Public

Affairs Office, Records of the Defense Preparedness Agency, Subject File: Correspondence Cards, NAII, 2.

65. Alice George, *Awaiting Armageddon: How Americans Faced the Cuban Missile Crisis* (Durham: University of North Carolina Press, 2013), 61.

66. "Request for booklet 'Fallout Protection: What to Know and Do about Nuclear Attack,'" November 10, 1962, Office of Civil Defense, Public Affairs Office, Records of the Defense Preparedness Agency, Subject File: Correspondence Cards, NAII, 1.

67. OCDM officials stamped each letter with the date and time of receipt and reply. See Office of Civil Defense, Central Files, 1961–68, Records of the Defense Preparedness Agency, Shelters and Vulnerability Files, NAII.

68. *Greeley Daily Tribune,* November 20, 1961, 26.

69. Ibid., 26.

70. Jack Lynn, letter to OCDM, October 7, 1961, Office of Civil Defense, Central Files, 1961–68, Records of the Defense Preparedness Agency, Shelters and Vulnerability Reduction, September–October, RG397, box 24, NAII, 3.

71. Beatriz Colomina, *Cold War Hothouses: Inventing Postwar Culture from Cockpit to Playboy* (Princeton, NJ: Princeton University Press, 2004), 17.

72. James Haynes, letter to the Office of Civil Defense, April 5, 1961, Office of Civil Defense, Central Files, 1961–68, Records of the Defense Preparedness Agency, Shelters and Vulnerability Reduction, April, RG397, box 24, NAII.

73. Frank Miles, letter to the Office of Civil Defense, October, 7, 1961, Office of Civil Defense, Central Files, 1961–68, Records of the Defense Preparedness Agency, Shelters and Vulnerability Reduction, September–October, RG397, box 24, NAII, 3.

74. Michael Ellis, letter to John F. Kennedy, November 1, 1961, Office of Civil Defense, Central Files, 1961–68, Records of the Defense Preparedness Agency, Shelters and Vulnerability Reduction, November, RG397, box 26, NAII, 1.

75. David Brown, clipping, Office of Emergency Preparedness, Records of Central Staff Offices, 1960, RG397.2.4, box 12, NAII, 3.

76. Henry Taylor, letter to OCDM, March 19, 1961, Office of Civil Defense, Central Files, 1961–68, Records of the Defense Preparedness Agency, Shelters and Vulnerability Reduction, January–March, RG397, box 25, NAII; Jack Booker, letter to OCDM, undated, Office of Civil Defense, Central Files, 1961–68, Records of the Defense Preparedness Agency, Shelters and Vulnerability Reduction, January–March, RG397, box 25, NAII.

77. Carl Hendel, letter to OCDM, October 15, 1961, Office of Civil Defense, Central Files, 1961–68, Records of the Defense Preparedness Agency, Shelters and Vulnerability Reduction, September–October, RG397, box 26, NAII, 3.

78. William Rowan, letter to OCDM, November 18, 1961, Office of Civil Defense, Central Files, 1961–68, Records of the Defense Preparedness Agency, Shelters and Vulnerability Reduction, November, RG397, box 24, NAII, 1, 3.

79. OCDM, quoted in Arthur I. Waskow, "The Shelter Society: A Report of a Peace Research Institute Conference on Potential Implications of a National Civil Defense Program," January 13–14, 1962, Margaret Mead Papers, box 1, 104, LCMD.

80. Newspaper clippings about Kirt MacBride's experiment, Records of the Office of Emergency Preparedness, Public Affairs Office Subject 1960–61, RG396, box 2, NAII, 1, 2, 1.

81. James Sauer, letter to OCDM, February 6, 1962, Office of Civil Defense, Central Files, 1961–68, Records of the Defense Preparedness Agency, Shelters and Vulnerability Reduction, February, RG397, box 24, NAII.

82. See Guy Oakes, *Imaginary War: Civil Defense and Cold War Culture* (Oxford: Oxford University Press, 1994), 26–27.

83. Marvin Taylor, letter to OCDM, November 11, 1961, Office of Civil Defense, Central Files, 1961–68, Records of the Defense Preparedness Agency, Shelters and Vulnerability Reduction, November, RG397, box 24, NAII, 1, 2, 1. Also see Norman Cousins, "Shelter, Survival, and Common Sense," *Saturday Review,* October 21, 1961; Margaret Mead, "Are Shelters the Answer?" *New York Times Magazine,* November 26, 1961; and "Open Letter to President Kennedy," *New York Times,* November 10, 1961.

84. For a regional breakdown, see Office of Civil Defense, Central Files, 1961–68, Central Operational Files, NAII.

85. "Farmers Needed for Success against Air Attack," *Successful Farming* 50 (October 1952): 80–83.

86. American Farm Bureau, "Summary of the Statement of the American Farm Bureau Federation for the Subcommittee on Economic Statistics," November 20, 1959, Records of the Office of Emergency Preparedness, Public Affairs Office Subject 1959–60, RG396, box 12, NAII.

87. Richard E. Bell, *An Agricultural Comparison: The United States and the Soviet Union* (Washington, DC: U.S. Department of Agriculture, Economic Research Service, 1961).

88. Federal Civil Defense Agency, information bulletin, June 12, 1958, Records of the Office of Emergency Preparedness, Subject File: Information Bulletin, box 5, NAII.

89. Carl Vinson, Democrat of Georgia and chairman of the House Armed Services Committee, statements at Leo Hoegh hearing, May 1958, Records of the Office of Emergency Preparedness, Central Files, December 6, RG397, box 7, NAII, 5.

90. Ella Loughran Brown, "What Are You Afraid Of?," letter to the editor of the *Iowa Farm Bureau Spokesman,* April 27, 1957, Records of the Office of Emergency Preparedness, Central Files, April, RG397, box 7, NAII, 4–5.

91. Leo A. Hoegh, "Accomplishments of the Office of Civil Defense Mobilization, 1953–1960," December 27, 1960, Records of the Office of Emergency Preparedness, Central Files, December, RG397, box 3, NAII.

92. Morris Fleming, "Civil Defense News," *Douglas County News,* March 14, 1963, 5.

93. Policymakers had considered the potential problems of this rural civil defense policy. In 1954, during a speech to the National Women's Advisory Council, Barrett Landstreet, the former director of FCDA's evacuation policy and the architect of Operation Alert, noted, "[W]hen you evacuate a tremendous industrial area, with a polyglot of nationalities or religions, or different income levels into a quiet middle-class, mostly agriculture town things happen" ("Evacuation and Dispersal," in "A Report on the 1955 Washington Conference of the National Women's Advisory Committee: Federal Civil Defense," Records of the Office of Emergency Preparedness, Subject Files: Women's Advisory Board, RG396, box 2, NAII.

94. "Memo: Douglas County," July 6, 1961, Office of Civil Defense, Public Affairs Office, Records of the Defense Preparedness Agency, Subject File: Correspondence Cards, NAII.

95. "Denver: Region 7 Annual Review," Office of Civil Defense, Public Affairs Office, Records of the Defense Preparedness Agency, Subject File: Region 7, box 4, NAII, 6.

96. *Denver Post,* October 21, 1961, AA.

97. *Denver Post,* November 3, 1961, AA.

98. Paul Boyer, *By the Bomb's Early Light: American Thought and Culture at the Dawn of the Atomic Age* (Chapel Hill: University of North Carolina Press, 1985).

CHAPTER FOUR: THE STRUGGLE TO SELL SURVIVAL

1. "Civil Defense: Boom to Bust," *Time,* May 18, 1962, 20.

2. "Shelter Boom," *Newsweek,* September 18, 1961, 32.

3. Frank Norton, letter to the Office of Civil Defense, November 5, 1961, Office of Civil Defense, Records of the Defense Preparedness Agency, Correspondence Files, September–November 1961, box 6, NAII. The OCD's reply to Norton is not in the records.

4. Margaret Mead collected clippings of this and other advertisements when researching her article "Are Shelters the Answer?" See Margaret Mead Papers, box I 104, LCMD.

5. Kenneth D. Rose, *One Nation Underground: The Fallout Shelter in American Culture* (New York: New York University Press, 2001), 192.

6. "Civil Defense: Boom to Bust," 20.

7. On consumer culture in the Cold War, see Laura Belmonte, *Selling the American Way: U.S. Propaganda and the Cold War* (Philadelphia: University of Pennsylvanian Press, 2008); Matthew W. Dunne, *A Cold War State of Mind: Brainwashing and Postwar American Society* (Amherst: University of Massachusetts Press, 2013); Thomas Doherty, *Cold War, Cool Medium: Television, McCarthyism, and American Culture* (New York: Columbia University Press, 2003); Lary May, *Recasting America: Culture and Politics in the Age of the Cold War* (Chicago: University of Chicago Press, 1989); Lynn Spigel, *Make Room for TV: Television and the Family Ideal in Post-war America* (Chicago: University of Chicago Press, 1992); and Walter L. Hixson, *Parting the Curtain: Propaganda, Culture and the Cold War, 1945–61* (New York: St. Martin's Press, 1997). On the role that shelters played in the Cold War imagination, see Elaine Tyler May, *Homeward Bound: American Families in the Cold War Era* (New York: Basic Books, 1988); Laura McEnaney, *Civil Defense Beings at Home: Militarization Meets Everyday Life in the Fifties* (Princeton, NJ: University of Princeton Press, 2000); Guy Oakes, *Imaginary War: Civil Defense and American Cold War Culture* (Oxford: Oxford University Press, 1994); Andrew Grossman, *Neither Red nor Dead: Civil Defense and American Political Development* (London: Routledge, 2001); Joseph Masco, *Nuclear Borderlands: The Manhattan Project in Post-Cold War New Mexico* (Princeton, NJ: University of Princeton Press, 2006); and Kenneth D. Rose, *One Nation Underground: Fallout Shelter in American Culture* (New York: New York University Press, 2004).

8. See Lizabeth Cohen, *A Consumers' Republic: The Politics of Mass Consumption in Post War America* (New York: Doubleday Publishing, 2003); and Meg Jacobs, *Pocketbook Politics: Economic Citizenship in Twentieth-Century America* (Princeton, NJ: University of Princeton Press, 2005).

9. "Shelters, Survival and Common Sense," part 4, *Saturday Review*, November 15, 1961, 31.

10. Alfred Balk, "Anyone for Survival?" *Saturday Evening Post*, March 27, 1965, 74.

11. U.S. House Subcommittee on Government Operations, *Civil Defense*, 86th Cong., 2nd sess. (Washington, DC: Government Printing Office, 1961), 20.

12. "Civil Defense: Who'd Survive?," *Newsweek*, August 7, 1961, 48.

13. Lee Services, letter to Office of Civil Defense, October 1, 1960, Office of Emergency Preparedness, Records of Central Staff Offices, 1960, box 12, NAII.

14. The names of trade associations that worked with the OCD were printed on the back covers of civil defense literature. For example, see *Fallout Protection:*

What to Know and Do about Nuclear Attack (Washington, DC: Government Printing Office, December 1961), which lists eight such names.

15. The jointly authored Department of Defense and OCD booklet *Family Shelter Design* (Washington, DC: Government Printing Office, 1961) lists eight shelter designs, each linked to a specific material provided by one of the endorsed trade associations. For example, the Belowground New Construction Clay Masonry Shelter was designed and built with materials from the National Concrete Masonry Association.

16. "Family in the Shelter, Snug, Equipped and Well Organized," *Life*, September 15, 1961, 105. Details on Armco Steel can be found in Public Affairs Office, Subject Files: 1960–61, box 1, NAII.

17. "Shelters on Sale," *Kansas City Star*, March 5, 1962, 13.

18. American Institute of Decorators advertisement, Public Affairs Office, Subject Files: 1958–60, box 2, NAII, 1, 3.

19. Quoted in memo to Steuart Pittman, November 10, 1961, Office of Civil Defense, Central Files, 1961–68, Records of the Defense Preparedness Agency, Accounting and Finance Files, box 1, NAII.

20. "You Can Build a Low-Cost Shelter Quickly," *Popular Mechanics*, December 9, 1961, 85–89. The article provided guidelines on outdoor and indoor shelter construction and instructions on how to maintain shelter air filters and antennas.

21. "Fallout Shelter: A Room with Seven Lives," *Lake Charles American Press*, January 9, 1961, 9

22. Report, May 3, 1961, Office of Civil Defense, Records of the Office of Emergency Preparedness, Regional Publications, box 1, NAII, A1–1002.

23. Mark Finn, letter to Office of Civil Defense, October 9, 1961, Office of Civil Defense, Central Files, 1961–68, Records of the Defense Preparedness Agency, Shelters and Vulnerability Reduction, September–October 1961, box 24, NAII.

24. See, for instance, clipping from *Miami Herald*, September 20, 1961, Public Affairs Office, Subject Files: 1958–60, box 2, NAII.

25. "Civil Defense: The Sheltered Life," *Time*, October 10, 1961, 23.

26. K. A. Cuordileone, *Manhood and American Political Culture in Cold War America* (New York: Routledge, 2005), 153.

27. Robert L. Griswold, *Fatherhood in America* (New York: Basic Books, 1993), 206–7.

28. James Gilbert, *Men in the Middle: Searching for Masculinity in the 1950s* (Chicago: University of Chicago Press, 2003), 220.

29. Griswold, *Fatherhood in America*, 206–7.

30. "Do-It-Yourself Is Big Business," *New York Times*, August 2, 1959, 10.

31. "Leisure Could Mean a Better Civilization," *Life*, December 28, 1959, 62–63.

32. U.S. Department of Commerce, "The Do-It-Yourself Market," in *Mass Leisure*, ed. Eric Larrabee and Rolf Meyerson (New York: McMillian Company, 1958), 274.

33. Robert Coughlan, "A $40 Billion Bill Just for Fun," *Life*, December 28, 1959, 70.

34. Steven M. Gelber, *Hobbies: Leisure and the Culture of Work in America*, rev. ed. (New York: Columbia University Press), 278.

35. "The New Do-It-Yourself Market," *Business Week*, June 14, 1952, 61.

36. Request for interview on shelter sales, November 10, 1961, Office of Civil Defense, Public Affairs Office, Records of the Defense Preparedness Agency, Subject File: Correspondence Cards, box 2, NAII, 2; Request for copy of *Fallout Protection*, October 3, 1962), Office of Civil Defense, Public Affairs Office, Records of the Defense Preparedness Agency, Subject File: Correspondence Cards, box 2, NAII, 1.

37. "Shelter Life," *Pottstown Mercury*, October 14, 1961, 20.

38. For more on Survive-All Shelters, see the Conelrad website, Office of Civil Defense, Records of the Defense Preparedness Agency, Information and Public Files, 1960–61, box 2, NAII.

39. Mark Finn, writing to FTC, October 9, 1961, Federal Trade Commission Papers, series 1, box 3, JFKL.

40. Walter A. Friedman, *Birth of a Salesman: The Transformation of Selling in America* (Princeton, NJ: Princeton University Press, 2009), 13.

41. Prices varied greatly. "Fallout Shelters For Sale—Cheap," *Anniston Star*, April 12, 1962, 24, lists a model costing $150 that included basic materials for self-assembly; *Morning Herald*, July 25, 1962, 33, mentioned luxury models costing more than $10,000.

42. Frank Hopkins, letter to OCDM, November 4, 1961, Office of Civil Defense, Central Files, 1961–68, Records of the Defense Preparedness Agency, Shelters and Vulnerability Reduction, September–October 1961, RG397, box 24, NAII, 1–2.

43. Robert Ambley, letter to OCDM, December 5, 1961, Office of Civil Defense, Central Files, 1961–68, Records of the Defense Preparedness Agency, Shelters and Vulnerability Reduction, November–December 1961, RG397, box 24, NAII. The ad also appeared in the *Cincinnati Enquirer*, July 22, 1962, 48.

44. "Enter the Survival Merchants," *Consumer Reports*, January 3, 1962, 47.

45. Arthur I. Waskow, "The Shelter Society: A Report of a Peace Research Institute Conference on Potential Implications of a National Civil Defense Program," Jan. 13–14, 1962, box I, LCMD, 104.

46. "Enter the Survival Merchants," 47.

47. Steven Heck, letter to Office of Civil Defense, November 10, 1961, Office of Civil Defense, Public Affairs Office, Records of the Defense Preparedness Agency, Subject File: Correspondence Cards, box 1, NAII.

48. Balk, "Anyone for Survival?," 74.

49. "Survival of the Fewest" memo, December 1961, White House Central Files, box 597, JFKL; Norman Cousins, "Shelter, Survival and Common Sense," *Saturday Review,* October 21, 1961, 26.

50. These records are archived among letters from shelter builders; see Office of Civil Defense, Central Files, 1961–68, Records of the Defense Preparedness Agency, Shelters and Vulnerability Reduction, January–March 1961, boxes 12, NAII.

51. See, for example, Michael Kimmel, "Temporary about Myself: White-Collar Conformists and Suburban Playboys, 1945–1960," in *Manhood in America: A Cultural History* (Oxford: Oxford University Press, 2005), 223–58; and Ralph LaRossa, *The Modernization of Fatherhood* (Chicago: University of Chicago Press, 1997).

52. Steven Gelber, "Do-It-Yourself: Constructing, Repairing, and Maintaining Domestic Masculinity," *American Quarterly* 49, no. 1 (1997): 66.

53. D. B. Holt and C. J. Thompson, "Man-of-Action Heroes: The Pursuit of Heroic Masculinity in Everyday Consumption," *Journal of Consumer Research* 31, no. 2 (2004): 425–40.

54. John Boyd, letter to Office of Civil Defense, July 30, 1961, Office of Civil Defense, Central Files, 1961–68, Records of the Defense Preparedness Agency, Shelters and Vulnerability Reduction, July 1961, box 5, NAII.

55. Jake Willis, letter to Office of Civil Defense, November 1, 1961, Office of Civil Defense, Central Files, 1961–68, Records of the Defense Preparedness Agency, Shelters and Vulnerability Reduction, November–December 1961, box 14, NAII.

56. Michelle Pomerleau, letter to Office of Civil Defense, August 5, 1961, Office of Civil Defense, Central Files, 1961–68, Records of the Defense Preparedness Agency, Shelters and Vulnerability Reduction, August 1961, box 14, NAII.

57. Linda Hope, letter to Office of Civil Defense, Office of Civil Defense, Central Files, 1961–68, Records of the Defense Preparedness Agency, Shelters and Vulnerability Reduction, September–August 1961, box 14, NAII.

58. Alice Laurel, letter to Office of Civil Defense, Office of Civil Defense, Central Files, 1961–68, Records of the Defense Preparedness Agency, Shelters and Vulnerability Reduction, September–October 1961, box 15, NAII.

59. Charlie Wilkins, letter to John F. Kennedy, October 3, 1961, Office of Civil Defense, Central Files, 1961–68, Records of the Defense Preparedness Agency, Shelters and Vulnerability Reduction, September–October 1961, box 15, NAII.

60. Archie Bowers, letter to John F. Kennedy, December 5, 1961, Office of Civil Defense, Central Files, 1961–68, Records of the Defense Preparedness Agency, Shelters and Vulnerability Reduction, November–December 1961, box 16, NAII.

61. Balk, "Anyone for Survival?," 74.

62. *Life*, September 15, 1961, 10.

63. Balk, "Anyone for Survival?," 74.

64. Ibid., 75.

65. Ibid., 75

66. "Summary of Studies of Public Attitudes towards Civil Defense," December 2, 1961, Office of Civil Defense, Records of the Defense Preparedness Agency, Subject Files: Information and Public, RG396, box 2, NAII, 14.

67. Steuart Pittman, memo to regional directors, Office of Civil Defense, December 18, 1961, Office of Civil Defense, Central Files, 1961–68, Records of the Defense Preparedness Agency, Shelters and Vulnerability Reduction, November–December 1961, box 6, NAII, 2.

68. Balk, "Anyone for Survival?," 75.

69. Claims that the public was ignoring shelter sales pitches were common in articles discussing the bomb shelter craze. See Walter Karp, "When Bunkers Last in Backyards Bloomed," *American Heritage* (February 1980): 92.

70. Balk, "Anyone for Survival?," 75, 78.

71. Internal memo, Office of Civil Defense, November 4, 1961, Office of Civil Defense, Records of the Office of Emergency Preparedness, 1961–63, Executive Correspondence and Memos, box 1, NAII.

72. "Civil Defense: The Sheltered Life," *Time*, October 20, 1961, 23.

73. "Civil Defense: Boom to Bust," 20.

74. Frank Ringer, letter to Office of Civil Defense, February 13, 1962, Office of Civil Defense, Records of Civil and Defense Mobilization, Correspondence Cards, box 2, NAII.

75. Allan Winkler, *Life under a Cloud: American Anxiety About the Atom* (Oxford: Oxford University Press, 1993), 129.

76. Steuart Pittman, oral history interview, no. 2, March 5, 1983, John F. Kennedy Oral History Collection, JFKL.

77. "Coffins or Shields," *Time*, February 2, 1962.

78. Thomas Hagen, letter to Pierre Salinger, September 15, 1961, ND2 Civil Defense, ND2 Civil Defense, box 5, JFKL, 2.

79. James Reston, "Those Sweet and Kindly Shelter Builders," *New York Times*, November 12, 1961, 3.

80. James Reston, "How to Be Evaporated in Style," *New York Times*, October 15, 1961, 32.

81. William L. Shirer, "Let's Stop the Fallout-Out Shelter Folly!," *Good Housekeeping*, February 1962, 151.

82. Walt Goodman, "The Truth about Fallout Shelter," *Redbook*, 118, no. 3 (March 1962): 24.

83. Thomas Hagen, memo to Pierre Salinger, August 11, 1961, Office of Civil Defense, Central Subject Files, box 595, NAII.

84. Rose, *One Nation Underground*, 192.

85. Paul Rand Dixon, speech to the Chicago Better Business Bureau, November 14, 1961, Federal Trade Commission Papers, Paul Rand Dixon Papers, 1961–63, box 5, JFKL.

86. Federal Trade Commission, advertising alert, August 12, 1961, Federal Trade Commission Papers, series 1, box 3, JFKL.

87. U.S. House of Representatives, Committee on Interstate and Foreign Commerce Committee, congressional hearing, August 22, 1961, Federal Trade Commission Papers, box 5, JFKL.

88. Helen Tangires, *Public Markets and Civic Culture in Nineteenth Century America* (Washington, DC: Johns Hopkins University Press, 2003), 7.

89. Jacobs, *Pocketbook Politics*, 5.

90. Cohen, *A Consumers' Republic*, 12.

91. Office of Civil Defense, draft memo about civil defense booklet, undated, Office of Civil Defense, Classified Subject Files: Civil Defense, box W04, folder 3, NAII, 2.

92. Arthur Schlesinger, Jr., "Reflections on Civil Defense," November 1961, National Security Files, Civil Defense Files, November 1961, box 295, JFKL, 1.

93. Federal Trade Commission, information bulletin, September 22, 1961, Federal Trade Commission Papers, box MF01, JKFL.

94. Federal Trade Commission, information bulletin, August 12, 1962, Federal Trade Commission Papers, box MF01, JKFL.

95. Office of Civil Defense, report on survival shelters, July 1, 1962, Office of Civil Defense, Subject Records of the Office of Defense Mobilization, Mobilization and Manpower Region 7, box 4, NAII.

96. Quote from Margaret Mead, "Are Shelters the Answer?," *New York Times Magazine*, November 26, 1961, 115. "The Paradox of Civil Defense," *Commonweal*, March 23, 1962, 12; I. F. Stone, "Civil Defense Madness," *Weekly*, November 14, 1961, 62; Linus Pauling, "Shelter Muddle," *Dissent*, October 17, 1961, 89; "Shelters and Survival: A Report on Civil Defense," *New Republic*, November 12, 1961, 23.

97. Cousins, "Shelter, Survival and Common Sense," 25.

98. "Enter the Survival Merchants," 47.

99. Mead, "Are Shelters the Answer?," 29.

100. Arthur L. Doolittle, letter to Office of Civil Defense, November 4, 1961, Office of Civil Defense, Central Files, 1961–68, Records of the Defense Preparedness Agency, Shelters and Vulnerability Reduction, November, box 12, NAII, 1–3.

101. Balk, "Anyone for Survival?," 75.

102. Norman Cousins, "On Shelters," August 15, 1961, Records of the National Committee for a Sane Nuclear Policy, Subject Files: Norman Cousins, box 15, SCPC; "To Protect Fallout Shelter," *Jet*, October 12, 1961, 49; "Shelter Craze Hits," *Ebony*, October 12, 1961, 32.

103. Herbert Leiderman and Jack H. Mendelson, "Some Psychiatric Considerations in Planning for Defense Shelters," in *The Fallen Sky: Medical Consequence of Thermonuclear War*, ed. Saul Aranow, Frank R. Ervin, and Victor Sidels (New York: Hill and Wang, 1963), 44.

104. James Reston, "Kennedy's Shelter Policy Re-examined," *New York Times*, November 26, 1961, 23.

105. Federal Trade Commission, information bulletin, January 3, 1963, Federal Trade Commission Papers, box MF01, JKFL.

106. Walter Lippmann, "Mistaken Fallout Shelter Scare," *St. Louis Dispatch*, November 15, 1961, 13.

107. Balk, "Anyone for Survival?," 75.

108. Second City Revue, "Shelter Salesmen," January 1963, videotape, WNEW-TV. For more on Second City, see Stephen E. Kercher, *Revel with a Cause: Liberal Satire in Postwar America* (Chicago: University of Chicago Press, 2010).

109. Rose, *One Nation Underground*, 220.

CHAPTER FIVE: SURVIVAL AND VIOLENCE AT THE SHELTER DOORWAY

1. "The Shelter," *The Twilight Zone* (New York: CBS-TV, September 29, 1961). All subsequent quotations are from this episode.

2. For more on "The Shelter," including Rod Serling's conversation with Frank R. Dunbar of the Los Angeles Shelter Survey Office, see Melvin E. Matthews, Jr., *Duck and Cover: Civil Defense Images in Film and Television from the Cold War* (Jefferson, NC: McFarland, 2012), 138.

3. See Margot A. Henriksen, *Dr. Strangelove's America: Society and Culture in the Atomic Age* (Berkeley: University of California Press, 1997), 189.

4. For more about terms such as *shelter hatch ethics*, *shelter morality*, and

shelter doorway dilemmas, see Walter Karp, "When Shelters in the Backyard Bloom'd," *American Heritage* 31, no. 2 (March 1980): 85.

5. Bob Crane, interview with Rod Serling, *The Bob Crane Show* (Los Angeles: KNX, October 1961). Also see Matthews, *Duck and Cover*, 126. For a selection of these letters, see Office of Civil Defense, Central Files 1961-68, Records of the Defense Preparedness Agency, Shelters and Vulnerability Reduction, September–October 1961, RG397, box 24, NAII.

6. William Abee, letter to Terry Sanford, September 29, 1961, North Carolina Area, Folder: Civil Defense Bulletins, box 27, NAII. Typos have been silently corrected.

7. K. A. Cuordileone, *Manhood and American Political Culture in Cold War America* (New York: Routledge, 2005), 32. See also Robert Dean, *Imperial Brotherhood: Gender and the Making of Cold War Foreign Policy* (Amherst: University of Massachusetts Press, 2001); Gary Wills, *The Kennedy Imprisonment: A Meditation on Power* (New York: Mariner, 1981); Elaine Tyler May, *Homeward Bound: American Families in the Cold War Era* (New York: Basic Books, 1988); Margot Canaday, *Straight State: Citizenship in Twentieth-Century America* (Princeton, NJ: Princeton University Press, 2009); John D'Emilio, *Sexual Politics, Sexual Communities: The Making of a Homosexual Minority in the United States, 1940-1970*, 2nd ed. (Chicago: University of Chicago Press, 1998); and James Gilbert, *Men in the Middle: Searching for Masculinity in the 1950s* (Chicago: University of Chicago Press, 2005).

8. Edward Lynman, memo to William Heimlich, May 3, 1960, Office of Civil Defense, Public Affairs Office, Records of the Office of Emergency Preparedness, Subject: 1960-61, RG396, box 1, NAII, 1.

9. Dee Garrison, *Bracing for Armageddon: Why Civil Defense Never Worked* (Oxford: Oxford University Press, 2006), 153; "Briefing for the Director on National Organizations and Civic Affairs," March 15, 1959, Office of Civil Defense, Records of the Office of Emergency Preparedness, Public Affairs Office Subject, 1960-61, RG396, box 1, NAII, 4.

10. Frank Ellis's directorship was a political reward for mobilizing Democratic support in Louisiana before the 1960 presidential election. During his tenure, he frequently encouraged Kennedy and the New Frontiersmen to take a more active stance in matters of civil defense. See Frank B. Ellis, memo to McGeorge Bundy, January 17, 1962, National Security Files, Office of Emergency Planning, box 28A, JFKL.

11. "Briefing for the Director," March 15, 1959, 4, 5.

12. Evidence of soft selling appears in a number of newspaper articles published in 1960-62; see Office of Civil Defense, Records of the Office of

Emergency Preparedness, Public Affairs Office Subject, 1960–61, RG396, box 2, NAII.

13. "Briefing for the Director," March 15, 1959, 4.

14. Ibid., 3.

15. On congressional funding and the relationship between state and federal construction projects, see unattributed memo to Steuart Pittman, March 7, 1961, John F. Kennedy Papers, National Security Files, Civil Defense: General, January–March 1961, series 5, box 295, JFKL.

16. Kenneth D. Rose, Dee Garrison, and Tracy C. Davis all begin their coverage of Kennedy's civil defense policy by looking at the May congressional address; they do not address the administration's earlier discussion of the Public Affairs Office. See Kenneth D. Rose, *One Nation Underground* (New York: New York University Press, 2001); Dee Garrison, *Bracing for Armageddon: Why Civil Defense Never Worked* (Oxford: Oxford University Press, 2006); Tracy C. Davis, *Stages of Emergency: Cold War Nuclear Civil Defense* (Durham, NC: Duke University Press, 2007).

17. Arthur Schlesinger, Jr., *A Thousand Days: John F. Kennedy in the White House* (Boston: Houghton Mifflin, 1965), 703.

18. Theodore Sorensen, memo to John F. Kennedy, June 13, 1961, Theodore Sorensen Personal Papers, Subject Files: Civil Defense, 1961–64, box 30, JFKL, 2.

19. Franklin B. Ellis, "Report of Budget Fiscal Year, 1961–1962," undated, Office of Civil Defense, Records of the Office of Emergency Preparedness, Subject Files: Executive Office, 1961–62, RG396, box 14, NAII.

20. Garrison, *Bracing for Armageddon*, 111.

21. Initially, Ellis received some positive coverage for his efforts: for example, "the director of the Office of Civil Defense Mobilization has one of the most thankless chores in Washington. The public yawns whenever civil defense is mentioned, and Congress finds the OCDM budget a dandy place to practice economy, trimming off an average of 76% of the requested funds over the last ten years. OCDM directors of the past have sometimes seemed to absorb the public's apathy. But Frank B. Ellis, the energetic new OCDM chief, is determined to overcome the frustrations of his job, even if it means going over President's head" ("Louisiana Haymaker," *Time*, April 4, 1961, 32).

22. Herbert Jolovitz, "Considerations on Civil Defense for the Office of the President," January 7, 1961, Presidential Campaign Files, Position and Briefing Papers, 1960, series 14, box 1, JFKL, 2.

23. Franklin B. Ellis, memo to Frank Ward, April 5, 1961, Office of Civil Defense, Records of the Office of Emergency Preparedness, Executive Correspondence, RG396, box 1, NAII.

24. The OCDM had always seen religious organizations as a potential source of support. In July 1959, Hoegh's interview with *Catholic Weekly*, "Is Your Church Ready Should the Bomb Fall?," 12–13, was included in the agency's monthly bulletin as a prime example of how officials might "encourage your local religious leader no matter the denomination to include civil defense in his weekly sermon" (Office of Civil Defense and Mobilization, information bulletin, February 1960, Office of Civil Defense and Mobilization, Central Files, Leo A. Hoegh Papers, box 12, NAII).

25. "Re: Ellis, Frank Consultations," June 5, 1961, Office of Civil Defense, Records of the Defense Preparedness Agency, Central Operational Files: Publicity, RG396, box 3, NAII, 2.

26. Letter to the editor, *Orlando Sentinel*, October 16, 1961, 4.

27. "Shelters Are the New Talk," *Ottawa Journal*, February 1, 1961, 30.

28. John Newhouse, "Modern Day Noah," *Wisconsin State Journal*, November 26, 1961, 15.

29. Ellis quoted in Walter McDonald, "The Last Word," *Florence Morning News*, October 22, 1961, 4.

30. Clive Baldwin, "Local Talk Turns to Civil Defense," *Morning Call*, December 24, 1961, 27.

31. "Richland Farmer Leads the Way on Fallout Shelter Program," *Florence Morning News*, October 26, 1961, 10.

32. Ibid., 10.

33. See Andrew Preston, *Sword of the Spirit, Shield of Faith: Religion in American War and Diplomacy* (New York: Knopf, 2012), 415; Dianne Kirby, "Truman's Holy Alliance: The President, the Pope, and the Origins of the Cold War," *Borderlines* 4, no. 1 (1997): 1–17; Jon Butler, "Jack-in-the-Box Faith: The Religion Problem in Modern American History," *Journal of American History* 90 (March 2004): 1357–78; and William Inboden, *Religion and American Foreign Policy, 1945–1960: The Soul of Containment* (Cambridge: Cambridge University Press, 2008).

34. Carey McWilliams, "The Hazards of Civil Defense," *Nation*, May 5, 1961, 37.

35. Ibid.

36. Thomas Kerr, *Civil Defense in the United States: Bandaid for a Holocaust?* (Boulder, CO: Westview, 1983), 118–99.

37. David F. Krugler, *This Is Only a Test: How Washington D.C. Prepared for Nuclear War* (London: Palgrave Macmillan, 2006), 170.

38. Edward Lynman, memo to Franklin Eilis, July 12, 1961, Office of Civil Defense, Records of the Office of Emergency Preparedness, Public Affairs Office Subject, 1960–61, RG396, box 2, NAII.

39. "Gun-Thy-Neighbor," *Time*, August 18, 1961, 60.

40. Also see "Civil Defense: Who'd Survive?," *Newsweek*, August 7, 1961, 48.

41. "Gun-Thy-Neighbor," 60.

42. Henriksen, *Dr. Strangelove's America*, 189.

43. "Gun-Thy-Neighbor," 60.

44. See Robert E. Herzstein, *Henry R. Luce, "Time," and the American Crusade in Asia* (Cambridge: Cambridge University Press, 2005), 202–4.

45. Letters to the editor, *Time*, September 6, 1961, 41.

46. "All Out against Fallout," *Time*, April 8, 1961, 13.

47. Some civil defense historians have been criticized for not accounting for the religious nature of anti-shelter sentiment at the local level. See, for example, David W. McFadden's review of Garrison's *Bracing for Armageddon*, in *Peace and Change* 32, no. 4 (2007): 590–93.

48. L. C. McHugh, "Ethics at the Shelter Doorway," *America*, September 30, 1961, 825.

49. Robert A. Jacobs, *The Dragon's Tail: Americans Face the Atomic Age* (Amherst: University of Massachusetts Press, 2010), 75–78.

50. Schlesinger, *A Thousand Days*, 703.

51. John F. Kennedy, "Fireside Chat on Civil Defense," Theodore Sorensen Personal Papers, Subject File: Civil Defense, box 30, JFKL, 1.

52. James Reston, "How to Be Evaporated in Style," *New York Times*, October 15, 1961, 8; Stewart Alsop "The Grim Truth about Civil Defense," *Washington Post*, July 15, 1961, 19–21; Peter Braestrup, "The Shelter Dilemma: Great Confusion Exists over What to Do," *New York Times*, October 22, 1961, 22.

53. Quoted in Kenneth D. Rose, *One Nation Underground* (New York: New York University Press, 2001), 97. Don Oberdorfer, "Survival of the Fewest," *Saturday Evening Post*, March 23, 1963, 17; James T. Rogers, "Report from the Nation: Reaction to Fall-Out Shelters," *New York Times*, November 19, 1961, 23, clipping collected in Office of Emergency Planning, White House Central Files, June 1962, OCD, box 597, NAII.

54. Michael Amrine, "The Issue of Fall-Out," *Newsweek*, November 6, 1961, 19–23.

55. Norman Cousins, "Shelter, Survival, and Common Sense," *Saturday Review*, October 21, 1961, 25.

56. Ibid.

57. Norman Cousins, "Reflections of C. D.," August 3, 1961, Records of the National Committee for a Sane Nuclear Policy, Subject Files: Norman Cousins, box 15, SCPC.

58. Margaret Mead, "Are Shelters the Answer?," *New York Times Magazine*, November 26, 1961, 29; Vincent Wilson, Jr., "Shelter Morality," *Commonweal*, October 27, 1961, 109; I. F. Stone, "Civil Defense Madness," *Weekly*, September 30,

1961, 17 (quotations); Linus Pauling, "Shelter Muddle," *Dissent,* October 6, 1961, 34; Garrett Underhill, "Shelters and Survival: A Report on Civil Defense," *New Republic,* November 15, 1961, 3.

59. Quoted in Rose, *One Nation Underground,* 97.

60. Evan Peterson, letter to the Office of Civil Defense, September 19, 1961, Office of Civil Defense, Central Files, 1961–68, Records of the Defense Preparedness Agency, Shelters and Vulnerability Reduction, September–October 1961, RG397, box 24, NAII, 1.

61. Doris Kearns Goodwin, *Wait Till Next Year* (New York: Simon and Schuster, 1998), 158.

62. Robert Jacobs, *The Dragon's Tail: Americans Face the Atomic Age* (Amherst: University of Massachusetts Press, 2010), 118.

63. Simon Murphy, letter to John F. Kennedy, October 10, 1961, Office of Civil Defense, Central Files, 1961–68, Records of the Defense Preparedness Agency, Shelters and Vulnerability Reduction, September–October, RG397, box 24, NAII, 1.

64. Ibid.

65. Richard Slotkin, *Gunfighter Nation: The Myth of the Frontier in the Twentieth Century* (Norman: University of Oklahoma Press, 1998).

66. Spencer Weart, *Nuclear Fear: A History of Images* (Cambridge, MA: Harvard University Press, 1988), 149.

67. Joe Tone, letter to the Office of Civil Defense, December 16, 1962, Office of Civil Defense, Public Affairs Office, Records of the Defense Preparedness Agency, Subject File: Correspondence Cards, NAII, 2.

68. "On Fallout Shelters," *Valley Times Los Angeles,* October 15, 1961.

69. Elaine Holzschuh, "We Talk Shelters," *Rochester Chronicle New York,* February 17, 1962, 17.

70. Simon Murphy, letter to John F. Kennedy, October 19, 1961, Office of Civil Defense, Central Files, 1961–68, Records of the Defense Preparedness Agency, Shelters and Vulnerability Reduction, September–October 1961, RG397, box 24, NAII, 1.

71. James Banville, letter to John F. Kennedy, September 1, 1961, and Frank Deviale, October 12, 1961, both in Office of Civil Defense, Central Files, 1961–68, Records of the Defense Preparedness Agency, Shelters and Vulnerability Reduction, September–October 1961, RG397, box 24, NAII, 2 and 1, respectively.

72. Louise Hazell, "Church Group Explores Parish Shelters," *Washington Post,* October 19, 1961, 22, 21.

73. Ibid., 22.

74. Ibid.

75. Ibid.

76. George Dugan, "Shelters Urged for Synagogues: Rabbis Want New Edifices to Include Fall-Out Areas," *New York Times,* October 20, 1961, 3.

77. "Missiles," undated, Office of Civil Defense, Public Affairs Office, Records of the Defense Preparedness Agency, Subject File: Correspondence Cards, NAII, 2.

78. Chloe Shepard, letter to John F. Kennedy, October 3, 1961, Office of Civil Defense, Central Files, 1961–68, Records of the Defense Preparedness Agency, Shelters and Vulnerability Reduction, September–October 1961, RG397, box 24, NAII, 2.

79. Letter to the editor, *Arizona Sun,* November 15, 1961, 12.

80. Mrs. Robert Rowe, letter to John F. Kennedy, October 19, 1961, Office of Civil Defense, Central Files, 1961–68, Records of the Defense Preparedness Agency, Shelters and Vulnerability Reduction, September–October 1961, RG397, box 24, NAII, 1.

81. Lawrence G. Weiss, "Moral Dilemma at the Shelter Door," *Denver Post,* October 15, 1961, AA.

82. See Office of Civil Defense, Central Files, 1961–68, Records of the Defense Preparedness Agency, Shelters and Vulnerability Reduction, September–October 1961, RG397, box 24, NAII.

83. Bobby Hightower, letter to the Office of Civil Defense, September 3, 1961, Office of Civil Defense, Central Files, 1961–68, Records of the Defense Preparedness Agency, Shelters and Vulnerability Reduction, September–October 1961, RG397, box 24, NAII, 1.

84. Kenneth Dills, letter to the Office of Civil Defense, November 7, 1961 Office of Civil Defense, Central Files 1961–68, Records of the Defense Preparedness Agency, Shelters and Vulnerability Reduction, November–December 1961, RG397, box 25, NAII, 2.

85. Unknown author, letter to the Office of Civil Defense, July 4, 1961, Office of Civil Defense, Central Files, 1961–68, Records of the Defense Preparedness Agency, Shelters and Vulnerability Reduction, July 1961, RG397, box 24, NAII, 4.

86. Olin J. Farnsworth, letter to the Office of Civil Defense, October 7, 1961, Office of Civil Defense, Central Files, 1961–68, Records of the Defense Preparedness Agency, Shelters and Vulnerability Reduction, September–October 1961, RG397, box 24, NAII, 4.

87. Regional variants detailed in Office of Civil Defense, Central Files, 1961–68, Records of the Defense Preparedness Agency, Shelters and Vulnerability Reduction, NAII.

88. William Lemon, letter to John F. Kennedy, October 1, 1961, Office of Civil Defense, Central Files, 1961–68, Records of the Defense Preparedness Agency, Shelters and Vulnerability Reduction, September–October 1961, RG397, box 3, NAII, 2.

89. Mark Falk, letter to Office of Civil Defense, February 3, 1962, Office of Civil Defense, Central Files, 1961–68, Records of the Defense Preparedness Agency, Shelters and Vulnerability Reduction, February–March 1962, RG397, box 24, NAII, 1.

90. Quoted in Adam Yarmolinsky, memo to Steuart Pittman, October 10, 1961, Office of Civil Defense, Central Files, 1961–68, Records of the Defense Preparedness Agency, Accounting and Finance Files, RG397, box 10, NAII, 6.

91. Ibid., 6.

92. Office of Civil Defense, "Request for Taped Interview," November 10, 1961, Office of Civil Defense, Public Affairs Office, Records of the Defense Preparedness Agency, Subject File: Correspondence Cards, NAII, 2.

93. Alice L. George, *Awaiting Armageddon: How Americans Faces the Cuban Missile Crisis* (Chapel Hill: University of North Carolina Press, 2003), 61.

94. Office of Civil Defense, "Request for Booklet 'Fallout Protection: What to Know and Do about Nuclear Attack,'" November 10, 1962, Office of Civil Defense, Public Affairs Office, Records of the Defense Preparedness Agency, Subject File: Correspondence Cards, NAII, 1.

95. Seymore Melman, *No Place to Hide* (New York: Grove, 1962), 124.

96. Kolko added, "We can only regret that our democratic civilization has absorbed an aspect of barbarism so causally, and without hesitation" (ibid., 128).

97. "North Carolina Council of Civil Defense, Role Progress Report, January 1, 1961–January 1, 1963" (Raleigh, NC: North Carolina Civil Defense Agency, 1963), 256.

98. Melman, *No Place to Hide*, 14.

99. Rose, *One Nation Underground*, 100.

100. *Los Angeles Times*, August 5, 1961, 23; Walter H. Waggoner, "Concern over Civil Defense Increases throughout the Nation," *New York Times*, November 19, 1961, 7.

101. Krugler, *This Is Only a Test*, 170.

102. Karp, "When Shelters in the Backyard Bloom-d," 23.

103. "Ethic at the Shelter Doorway," *Los Angeles Times*, August 1, 1961, 13.

104. "Shelter Access," *Los Angeles Times*, August 5, 1961, 4.

105. Both Adair and Dwyer were reprimanded by their superiors. See "Re: LA Times Article," August 6, 1961, Office of Civil Defense, Public Affairs Office, Records of the Defense Preparedness Agency, Subject File: Correspondence Cards, NAII.

106. Marc Raskin to Adam Yarmolinsky, November 5, 1961, Adam Yarmolinsky Personal Papers, Subject File: Civil Defense, box WH0.9a, JFKL.

107. See Laura McEnaney, *Civil Defense Begins at Home: Militarization Meets Everyday Life in the Fifties* (Princeton, NJ: Princeton University Press, 2000).

108. Memo from Freedom to Information Clearinghouse, November 5, 1962, Subject File: Civil Defense Women Strike for Peace Papers, box 12, SCPC.

109. Arthur M. Schlesinger, Jr., "On Heroic Leadership and the Dilemma of Strong Men and Weak Peoples," *Encounter* 15, no. 6 (1960): 3–11.

110. Cuordileone, *Manhood and American Political Culture*, 206.

111. Schlesinger, *A Thousand Days*, 749.

112. "First Interview with Steuart L. Pittman," September 18, 1970, John F. Kennedy Oral History Collection, JFKL, 6, 5.

113. Schlesinger, *A Thousand Days*, 749.

114. Kerr, *Civil Defense in the United States*, 128–31.

115. David Monteyne, *Designing for Civil Defense in the Cold War* (Minneapolis: University of Minnesota Press, 2011), 36.

116. This argument is also advanced in McEnaney, *Civil Defense Begins at Home*.

117. David Allison, "Fallout Shelters at Once," *Architectural Forum* (February 1961): 127.

118. Cuordileone, *Manhood and American Political Culture*, 234.

CONCLUSION: TAKE TO THE HILLS

1. Lisa Kadane, "Bunker Mentality," *Calgary Herald*, August 7, 2015.

2. For various historians' responses to the question of why civil defense failed (among them, Spencer Weart, Allan Winkler, Margot Henriksen, Guy Oakes, Michael Sherry, and Laura McEnaney), see Kenneth D. Rose, *One Nation Underground: The Fallout Shelter in American Culture* (New York: New York University Press, 2001), 209–13.

3. U.S. House Committee on Government Operations, *Civil Defense*, 97th Cong., 2nd sess. (Washington, DC: Government Printing Office, 1963), 20.

4. John F. Kennedy, "Fireside Chat on Civil Defense," Theodore Sorensen Personal Papers, Subject File: Civil Defense, box 30, JFKL, 1.

5. Federal Bureau of Investigation, *Report on the Minutemen* (October 31, 1966), 5.

6. On the Minutemen, see J. Harry Jones, *The Minutemen* (New York: Doubleday, 1968); and Eric Beckemeier, *Traitors Beware: A History of Robert DePugh's Minutemen* (New York: Hardin, 2007). The group is sometimes mentioned in studies of the New Right during the 1960s: for instance, Maurice Isserman and Michael Kazin, *America Divided: The Civil War of the 1960s* (New York: Oxford University Press, 2000); and Ward Churchill and Jim Vadner, *The COINTELPRO Papers: Documents from the FBI's Secret Wars against Dissent in the United States*

(London: South End, 1990), 227–29. See also Rose, *One Nation Underground*, 112–14; and Margot A. Henriksen Margot, *Dr. Strangelove's America: Society and Culture in the Atomic Age* (Berkeley: University of California Press, 1997), 210–11.

7. Thomas Bishop, "'We Are Now a Nation of Minute-Men': Survivalist Masculinity, Fallout Shelters and Cold War America," in *Imagining the End: Interdisciplinary Perspectives on the Apocalypse*, ed. Thomas E. Bishop and Jeremy R. Strong (Oxford: Inter-Disciplinary Press, 2015), 3–23.

8. "Organization: The Minutemen," *Time*, November 3, 1961, 19.

9. "Join the Minutemen," *On Target*, from the FBI, *Report on the Minutemen*, 5.

10. FBI, *Report on the Minutemen*, 1. Details of the Minutemen's activities can be found in the Mary Ferrell Foundation Collection, Federal Bureau of Investigations, HSCA Subject File, Minutemen Club, Dallas Files, RG105, Memo number 62, 4.

11. Federal Bureau of Investigation, "Dallas Report on the Minutemen," July 13, 1964, 5A, Mary Ferrell Foundation Collection, Federal Bureau of Investigations, HSCA Subject File, Minutemen Club, Dallas Files, RG105, Memo number 56, 3.

12. FBI, *Report on the Minutemen*, 3.

13. "Right-Wing Group Canvases Washington," *Washington Post*, June 3, 1965, 7; Murray Schumachm, "Minutemen Seized Plot Smashed," *Newsweek*, October 31, 1966, 12; "20 Right-Wingers Arrested in State in Weapons Plot," *Time*, October 31, 1966, 32; Gladwin Hill, "Minutemen Guerrilla Unit Found to Be Small and Loosely Knit," *Playboy*, November 12, 1961.

14. Laura Miller, "A Milkman with Plastic Bombs," *Life*, November 10, 1966; Stephen Mahoney, "Zero Hour for the Minutemen," *Life*, November 11, 1966, 51.

15. Peter W. Salschi, "The Minutemen Arrive," *Nation*, November 1962, 41.

16. "Join the Minuteman," 5.

17. Jones, *The Minutemen*, 33.

18. Scholars have yet to consider the local conversations around shelter fatherhood during the 1980s, which, in the Reagan years, often focused on notions of domestic radiation, especially after the Three Mile Island accident in 1979.

INDEX

Abee, William, 133–34
Acheson, Dean, 69–70
Adair, J. Carlton, 155–56
Adenauer, Konrad, 31
Adventures of Ozzie and Harriet, The, 89, 112
Air War and Emotional Stress (Janis), 54–55
Alsop, Stewart, 24
Ambrose, Stephen, 24
Amos 'n Andy, 46–47
anxiety: nuclear, 3, 21–29, 100–101, 125–33, 135, 150, 163–65; parenting, 97–100
Armco Steel, 109
Atomic Energy Commission (AEC), 24

Baldwin, Hanson W., 159
Battle, Phyllis, 68
Battle Creek, Michigan, 33, 86
Beebe, Lucius, 68
Berlin crisis, 1–2, 48–50, 69–78, 79–80, 107–8, 131–33
Berlin Wall, 2
Booker, Jason, 98–99
Boyer, Paul, 5
Brown, Douglas, 45–46
Brundage, Percival, 25
Bulletin of the Atomic Scientists, 28, 74
Bundy, McGeorge: Berlin crisis, 70–72; civil defense, 55–59; congressional funding and shelter loans, 57
Business Weekly, 113

Campaign for Nuclear Disarmament (CND), 28
Carlson, Art, 1–4, 8, 17, 20, 109, 117
Cartwight, Frank, 79
CBS, 37
civil defense: class politics, 6, 12–15, 26–29, 32–35, 40–44, 51–68, 89–98, 123–39, 150, 164; do-it-yourself mishaps, 81, 92; domestication, 9–11, 24–31; evacuation policy, 31; homeownership, 26, 32, 54–55; House Subcommittee for Civil Defense, 29–30; religion, 141–44; tax credits, 36
Chase, Arthur, 78–81
Chicago, 34, 67, 123, 129, 140
Coates, Charlie, 95–96
Colorado: Cheyenne Mountain, 86; civil defense effort, 84–89; Denver, 84, 88–93; Denver Association of Home Builders, 88; Douglas County, 102–4; *Food for Thought,* 87–88; Guffey, 87; Hartsel, 87; housing development, 83–84; Lowry Air Base, 84; Jefferson County, 99–100; nuclear industries, 82–83; Park Hill, 93–94; Pikes Peak, 87–88; Parade of Homes, 88–93; Rocky Flats Nuclear Weapons Factory, 83; Rocky Mountain Arsenal, 83; Toastmasters Club, 91–92
Consumer Reports, 116
Cousins, Norman, 3, 28, 144

Cuban missile crisis, 75–77, 95–96, 120–22, 128–29, 153–55, 161–63
Cuordileone, Kyle A., 16, 32, 43, 133, 156

Dallek, Robert, 156
Davis, Charles, 3, 141
Dean, Robert, 6, 16
Department of Defense, connections to the FHA, 66
DePugh, Robert, 164–66
Deviale, Frank, 147–48
Dills, Kenneth, 152
do-it-yourself: loans, 53; patriotism, 17
Dutton, Fred, 75
Dwyer, Keith, 155–56

Einstein, Albert, 28
Eisenhower, Dwight D.: criticism of civil defense, 35, 47; civil defense policy (1951–57), 22–32; civil defense policy (1958–60), 32–47, 157–58; funding and, 31–32, 36; Gaither committee, 30–32; golf and, 22, 46–47; Luce and, 27; national militarization and, 23–26; Operation Alert, 28–30; private fallout shelter loans, 56
Eldorado County Gold Club, 46–47
Ellis, Franklin B., 20, 53, 134–44
Evans, Linda, 94–95

Face the Nation, 22
Fallout Protection and You, 72–78
Fallout Protection: What to Know and Do about Nuclear Attack, 77
fallout shelter construction companies: Allendale Heights, 90–91; American Shelter Co. (Miami), 111; Atomic Shelter Corporation, 105–7; Chicago Home Furnishing Market, 111; Family Fallout Shelter, Inc. (Pennsylvania), 114; Florida Survival Shelters, 105; Gricar-Anderson (Michigan), 116–17; Mort Kridel Advertising Agency, 114–15; Survive-All Shelters, 114–15; Survival Shelters (Orlando), 126; United Construction Co., 88–89; U.S. Fallout Shelter, Inc., 126–27; Prince George Mall, 125–26; Wonder Building Corporation, 105
fallout shelter loans, newspaper coverage of: *Baytown Sun*, 64; *Beckley Post Herald*, 64; *Chicago Defender*, 65; *Herald Press*, 64–65; *Las Vegas Daily*, 64; *Nashua Telegram*, 64; *Tucson Daily Citizen*, 64–65
fallout shelters: anti-Communism, 98–100; boats, 74; bomb-shelter craze, 13, 47, 67, 73, 122, 127; booklets, 39, 43–44; building permits, 64–69; construction queries, 80, 89–91, 92–93, 98–100, 105; consumerism, 17, 105–30; dual-purpose, 62, 106, 115–16; guns, 3, 18, 47, 90, 128–54, 163; isolation test, 100–102; log cabin, 18, 39; modern-day Noahs, 138–39; modern stockade, 40; numbers sold, 116–17; senator criticisms, 71
fallout shelter salesmen: Ambley, Robert, 115–16; Bartholow, Douglas, 122; Byrne, James, 109, 119–21; Cline, James, 117–18; Edwards, Thomas, 110; Feldman, David, 110; George, Sal, 120–21; Hopkins, Frank, 115–16; Norton, Frank 105–7; Shaw, Howard, 114–15
fallout shelter salesmen, public complaints: Boyd, John, 118; Doolittle, Arthur L., 126–27; Hope, Linda, 118; Laurel, Alice, 118; Pomerleau, Michelle, 118; Wilkins, Charlie, 119
"Family Fallout Shelter, The," 39, 42
fatherhood: Cold War consumerism, 17, 105–30; domesticated, 3, 17–18, 110–13, 117–18; economic incentive, 89, 93–97; heroic artisan, 43; militarized, 3, 17–18, 109–10; new fatherhood of the 1950s, 31–32, 111; parenting, 97–100; pioneer, 40–72; survivalist, 3, 17–18, 99–100, 131–58; white middle-class, 35–36, 38, 101–4
Father Knows Best, 89
Federal Civil Defense Administration (FCDA): do-it-yourself, 26–27;

homeownership, 26–30; internal organization, 26–27; literature, 9; 1954 Annual Report, 26–27
Federal Housing Administration (FHA): African American homeownership, 65; citizen trusts, 63–64; fallout shelter loan applications, 50, 62–66, 93, 127; federal savings banks, 64; Housing and Home Finance Agency (HHFA), 57; home inspectors, 64–65; section 203(k) and 200(h) loans, 62–63; Title 1 home insurance loans, 62–63
Federal Trade Commission (FTC): Dixon, Paul Rand, 124–25; public letters, 114; regulations, 123–26
Fields, Frank, 49
Fox, Sarah Alisabeth, 6, 81
Frank, Henry J., 84–85
Freedman, Lawrence, 70
Fritz, Charles, 158

Gaither committee, 23, 30–33
Galbraith, John Kenneth, 75–76
Gallup poll, 36
Garrison, Dee, 134
George, Alice, 96, 153
Gleason, Eileen, 97
Goodman, Walt, 123
Goodwin, Doris Kearns, 146
Gosden, Freeman F., 46–47
Graham, Billy, 148
Grandma's Pantry, 10
Gruening, Ernest, 71

Hamner, Percy, 66
Hank, Kyle, 139
Hartford, Connecticut, 3
Hayes, James, 98–99
"Hazards of Civil Defense, The," 139–40
Hazel, Edward, 20–22, 47
Heimlich, William, 26, 33, 54, 86–87, 134–36
Hendel, Carl, 98–99
Henriksen, Margot, 141
Hightower, Bobby, 152–53
Hoegh, Leo, 24, 33, 39, 51, 89–91, 102–3

Hoerner, Jack, 90–91
Holifield, Chet, 29–32, 34
Hollings, Ernest Frederick, 41–40
Howard, Katherine, 26–27
Hydron, Rex, 50

Jackson, C. D., 23
Janis, Irving, 54
Jenkins, Mark, 94–95
Johnson, Edwin C., 87
Johnson, Lyndon Baines, 22–25
Jolovitz, Herbert, 51–52, 58
Jones, Mary Florsheim, 46–47

Kadane, Lisa, 159–62
Kahn, Herman, 30–31
Kaplan, Fred, 70, 74
Kaysen, Carl: article in *World Politics*, 58–59; J. F. Kennedy and civil defense, 76; meeting with Sorensen, 59–60
Kelsey Hayes, 1–2, 109, 117–20
Kennedy, John F.: Bay of Pigs, 58–59; Berlin Address, 48–49, 68–78; briefing on civil defense, 51; "Civil Defense Gap," 55; civil defense policy (January to May 1961), 52–62; civil defense policy (May to July 1961), 62–72; civil defense policy (July to December 1961), 72–78; *Fallout Protection and You*, 72; "Fireside Chat on Civil Defense," 163–65; May congressional address, 61–62; private shelter loan policy, 52–55; shelter violence, 143–45; Vienna summit, 69–71
Kennedy, Robert, 70
Kessel, Dmitri, 1
Khrushchev, Nikita, 24, 69
Kirby, John, 33
Knox, Jeremy, 86
Kolko, Gabriel, 154
Korean War, 20, 40, 66, 98
Krock, Arthur, 128

Lapp, Ralph, 28, 54
Leave It to Beaver, 89

Life, fallout shelter special issue, 2–3, 73, 86
Lock, David, 66
Luce, Henry, 27
Lyman, Edward, 26, 33, 37, 134–36
Lynn, Jack, 97–98
LYN, 41–42

masculinity: Cold Warrior, 2, 55–56; hypermasculinity, 15; ideology of masculinity, 6, 8; militancy, 3, 130–58
May, Elaine Tyler, 10–13
McEnaney, Laura, 9, 12–13, 17, 32, 34, 81
McHugh, L. C., "Ethics at the Shelter Doorway," 142–45
McNamara, Robert: Berlin crisis, 70–73; *Fallout Protection and You*, 73
McWilliams, Carey, 139–40
Mead, Margaret, 144
Merchants and Saving Bank, Janesville, 63
Mesta, Perle, 2
Minutemen, the, 164–66
Model Fallout Shelter Display Unit, the, 41–42
Monteyne, David, 157
"Moral Dilemma at the Shelter Door," 151–52
Morse, Wayne, 71
Murphy, Simon, 146–47
Mumford, Lewis, 38

National Academy of Science, 29, 158
"National Pattern of Civil Defense, The," 10
National Security Council (NSC), 22, 26, 46, 58, 154–55; Communist aggression and, 8, 13, 25, 84, 87, 97, 124
National Security Resource Board, 24
National Shelter Policy, 43
Nelson, Otto L., 29
Newhouse, John, 138
New Republic, 28
Newsweek, 4, 18
New York, 34, 66, 68, 101, 123, 127, 150

Nicholson, William, 86
Nitze, Paul, 30–31, 70
North American Aerospace Defense Command (NORAD), 82
nuclear: blast radius, 4, 7–9, 41, 79, 84–85, 102, 140; crisis, 3–4, 11, 18; everyday, 7–8; family, 12–27; *Jupiter* missile, 31; paranoia, 147; policymaking, 4–9; *Thor* missile, 31
nukespeak, 5

Oakes, Guy, 8, 9, 11, 29
O'Brien, Tim, *The Nuclear Age*, 79
Office of Civil and Defense Mobilization (OCMD): African American homeownership, 65, 127–28; *Fallout Protection and You*, 76–78; Frank's "Blast Shelter," 85; homeownership, 33–34; literature, 38–45; Kirt MacBride's fallout shelter test, 100–101; organization, 24; public education, 32–36, 40; reviews, 58–62; standardized replies to public letters, 96–97; trade partners and associations, 108–12
Office of Civil Defense (OCD): Better Business Bureau, 126–27; commercial networks, 113–50; guidelines on shelter selling, 122–23; organization, 53, 134–38; Pittman, Steuart, 120, 154–55; Public Affairs Office, 134–38; religion, 145–50
Office of Emergency Preparedness, 158
Operation Alert, 28–30
On the Beach, 114–15

Parenting, 111–12
Parker, John, 92–93
Parks, Ray, 64–65
Parks, Stewart, 86
Parrot, James H., 148–49
Pauling, Linus, 28
Peterson, Evan, 145
Peterson, Val, 26, 28, 51
"Pioneers of Self Protection in Barnyard and Patio," 112
Pravda, 144

Preparedness Subcommittee, 25
Preston, Andrew, 55
Project Hideaway, 44–45

R-7 intercontinental ballistic missile (ICBM), 22
Rabbinical Council of America, 150
RAND Corporation, 31
Raskin, Marcus: Berlin crisis, 79–80; criticism of civil defense, 58–60; *Essays of a Citizen*, 60; *Fallout Protection and You*, 72, 76; "A Modest Proposal for Civil Defense," 59–60; Stanford Institute of Research, 60
Redbook, 143–45
Reedy, George, 22
Reston, James, 123, 128
Richards, Martin, 89–91
Rockefeller, Nelson, 27, 55, 114
Roosevelt, Franklin D., 24
Rostow, Eugene, 69
Rowan, William, 99–100
Russell, Bertrand, 28

Sanchez, J. R., 40–41
Sane Nuclear Policy (SANE), 3, 28, 127, 154
Sarasota News, 48
Saturday Review, 107–8
Sauer, James, 100–101
Schlesinger, Arthur, Jr.: Berlin crisis, 70; "Reflections on Civil Defense," 76–77, 156–58; *A Thousand Days*, 73
Scott, James, 67
Scott, Robert L., Jr., 67–68
Second City, 129–30
Serling, Rod, 131–33
Shirer, William L., 123
Simonds, William, 93–94
Smith, Charles J., 20
Sorensen, Theodore, 3: Berlin Address, 70–72; on J. F. Kennedy and civil defense, 57; meeting with Raskin, 59; on shelter violence, 140–42
Soviet Union, 22, 106
Sputnik, 13, 22–24, 31–32
Staats, Elmer, 59
Stimson, Henry L., 55
Stone, I. F., 1, 11, 144
suburban home: modern stockade, 3; paramilitary units, 17

Taylor, Harry, 98–99
Taylor, Marvin, 101
Teller, Edward, 22–23, 114
Thompson, Edward K., 73–74
Time, gun-thy-neighbor debate, 3, 141–43
Tuve, Merle, 29
Twilight Zone, The, 131–33

Underhill, John Garrett, 29
U.S. Department of Agriculture, 102–3

Vickers, L. T., 91–92

Weart, Spencer, 131, 146–47
Weinberg, Charles, 150–51
West Germany, 31–32
Whyte, William, *The Organization Man*, 16
Wiesner, Jerome B., 157–58
Wills, Gary, 60
Wilson, Sloan, *The Man in the Grey Flannel Suit*, 16
Wilson, Vincent, Jr., 40
women and civil defense: Davis, Lucie, 150; organizations, 10–13; Rowe, Mrs. Robert, 150–51; shelter violence, 150–53; Shepard, Chloe, 150
Women Strike for Peace, 127–28

Yarmolinsky, Adam, 73–74
Young, Stephen M., 51, 71

www.ingramcontent.com/pod-product-compliance
Lightning Source LLC
Chambersburg PA
CBHW030136240426
43672CB00005B/147